D0909914

SUBLIME PHYSICK

Sublime

Physick

{ESSAYS}

PATRICK MADDEN

University of Nebraska Press
Lincoln and London

© 2016 by Patrick Madden

Acknowledgments for previously
published material appear on
page xvi, which constitutes an
extension of the copyright page.

Library of Congress
Cataloging-in-Publication Data
Madden, Patrick, 1971–
[Essays. Selections]
Sublime Physick: essays /
Patrick Madden.
pages   cm
ISBN 978-0-8032-3984-5
(hardback: alk. paper)
ISBN 978-0-8032-8544-6 (epub)
ISBN 978-0-8032-8545-3 (mobi)
ISBN 978-0-8032-8546-0 (pdf)
I. Title.
PS3613.A28355A6 2016
814'.6 — dc23
2015021064

Set in Arno by M. Scheer.
Designed by N. Putens.

For my children — Patrick, Adriana, Sara, Daniela, Marcos, James — con amor

I study myself more than any other subject. That is my metaphysics; that is my physics.

MONTAIGNE, "Of Experience"

The terrifying immensity of the firmament's abyss is an illusion, an external reflection of *our own* abysses, perceived "in a mirror." We should invert our eyes and practice a sublime astronomy in the infinitude of our hearts.

LÉON BLOY, *Le Mendiant Ingrat*

The essayist's habit of not only giving you his thoughts, but telling you how he came by them, . . . shows you by what alchemy the ruder world becomes transmuted into the finer.

ALEXANDER SMITH, "On the Writing of Essays"

CONTENTS

ILLUSTRATIONS

ACKNOWLEDGMENTS

Books are good enough in their own way, but they are a mighty bloodless substitute for life.

ROBERT LOUIS STEVENSON, "An Apology for Idlers"

I begin by thanking my fellow essayists for their friendship, kindness, and support. The list of deserving friends is much longer than this, but the following people have made particular contributions to this book: Chris Arthur, Robert Atwan, William Bradley, Mary Cappello, Sari Carter, Steven Church, Douglas Crawford-Parker, Mike Danko, Michelle Disler, Brian Doyle, Lina Ferreira, Joshua Foster, Connie May Fowler, Joey Franklin, Ian Frazier, Eric Freeze, Eduardo Galeano, Doug Glover, David Grover, David Hamilton, Robin Hemley, Brian Hoover, Susan Howe, Judith Kitchen, Kim Dana Kupperman, Shannon Lakanen, Amy Leach, Eric LeMay, Phillip Lopate, Michael Martone, Desirae Matherly, Ryan McIlvain, Dinty Moore, Scott Morris, Jacob Paul, John Proctor, Elizabeth Rhondeau, Nick Ripatrazone, Amy Roper, Scott Russell Sanders, Amy Lee Scott, Nicole Sheets, Sue William Silverman, Michael Steinberg, Ned Stuckey-French, Joni Tevis, Mel Thorne, Stephen Tuttle, Robert Vivian, Xu Xi, Cless Young (again, many more!).

I extend a hearty thanks to my long-suffering teachers, John Bennion and David Lazar, who nurtured the writing, and Steve Altenderfer, who nurtured the science, and friends who nudged me along this path, Travis Hubble, Jim Richards, Steve Stewart, plus the friends of my formative years, Vincent Augelli, Chris Petitto, Sona Verma, Mark Walsh, Joe Ziolkowski, and so many others whose friendship has sustained and enriched me through my charmed life.

I also thank my colleagues at Brigham Young University, especially those who've shared my interest in essays and who've contributed to my writing with encouragement or conversations. My college and department have helped me in innumerable ways. And my students! I am truly blessed to have taught so many great people at BYU as well as at Vermont College, where, too, my colleagues and students are delightful.

The University of Nebraska Press staff is stocked with tremendous people, most notably Kristen Elias Rowley, whom I thank profusely for her fine work and patience. I thank again Ladette Randolph for seeing something worthwhile in my writing.

I cannot neglect to thank the fine people behind the Independent Publisher Book Awards, *Foreword Reviews*, PEN Center USA, Utah Humanities Council, AWP, and Association for Mormon Letters, who prized my first book. The J. William Fulbright Commission once again afforded me time to live and write in Uruguay, for which I am grateful, especially to Patricia Vargas. To all the reviewers who noticed and appreciated *Quotidiana*, thank you.

I've integrated the work of many artists, musicians, writers, and creators into my essays, and I am grateful for their contributions, especially Sebastião Salgado, Paul Goresh, Graciela Cabrera, Skoticus, Andrew Fellows, Eduardo Galeano, Brent Rowland, Todd Stilson, and the BIPM. My brother Dan helped a lot with image manipulation and preparation. I consider pages 1–244 to be an extension of these acknowledgments.

Many editors and literary journal staff, too, deserve and receive my gratitude for helping see some of these essays into print for the first time:

"Spit," *Fourth Genre* 18, no. 1 (Spring 2015) [Laura Julier].

"In Media Vita," *Iowa Review* 40, no. 3 (Winter 2010/11) [Russell Valentino].

"Empathy" as "Travels with Eduardo," *Pedestrian* 1 (Summer 2010) [Christopher Spiker].

"Miser's Farthings," *Ninth Letter* online, August 12–27, 2013 [Philip Graham].

"Buying a Bass," *Wabash Magazine*, Fall 2011 [Steve Charles].

"Moment, Momentous, Momentum," *Fourth Genre* 13, no. 2 (Fall 2011) [Marcia Aldrich].

"Fixity," *Southwest Review* 97, no. 2 (Spring 2012) [Willard Spiegelman].

Who was it who said that every child equals a book not written? Certainly I've heard it often, and I feel it to be true, though perhaps that's just an excuse for my plodding (not prolific) literary production. Still, with Joseph Addison, I feel to retort:

> When I see my little troop before me, I rejoice in the additions which I have made to my species, to my country, and to my religion, in having produced such a number of reasonable creatures, citizens, and Christians. I am pleased to see my self thus perpetuated; and as there is no production comparable to that of a human creature, I am more proud of having been the occasion of [six] such glorious productions, than if I had built a hundred pyramids at my own expence, or published as many volumes of the finest wit and learning.
>
> "Defence and Happiness of Married Life"

This book is dedicated to my little troop, and I sing their names again here: Pato, Adi, Sara, Dani, Marcos, and James. They are my greatest source of wonder and joy and much more, not all of it superficially good, yet all, I am confident, beneficial, when I am attentive, at least. I am never happier than when I hold them, and they me, in an embrace. My wider family, too — Uber, Teresa, Pat, Liz, Kathleen, Fernando, Melissa, Ivan, Thiago, Joaquin, David, Graciela, Tiziana, Augusto, Milos, David, Liz, Dan, Ivy, Maverick, Valeria, relatives near and far — all excellent people worthy of my gratitude.

I'm always saying how essays make me a better person, but you know what *really* makes me a better person, more than anything else in this world? Karina. I thank her most of all.

SUBLIME PHYSICK

Spit

These days, as one of my daughters learns to whistle and another learns to snap her fingers while yet another learns to ride a bicycle, I am cast back to a day long ago, walking down a thin path through the thick Maine woods, when I learned how to spit. The sun gleamed off the lake just ahead, through the encroaching leaves of trees and ferns that impinged on the path and scratched the bare arms and legs of roaming boys let loose from our parents for whole days of idle fun, full of the kinds of activities that don't leave an indelible sense of their occasions but which quickly melt into the vague sense of freedom and diversion we retain in our souls long after we're no longer so free (or so diverse). This was me and the Smeraldos, at least Peter and Jeff, whose parents had lived across the street from my parents when I was born, who were older and more world weary than I, at age six, let's say, though who can know now; we'll call it August 4, 1977, on McWain Pond in Waterford, Maine, at 10:40 in the morning, the exact moment when the love of my life, the beautiful mother of my daughters and sons, was born far, far away . . .

Someone was whistling, perhaps, or maybe it was the birds flitting from branch to branch above our heads, and the sun filtered through the leaves high above to cast the forest in a greenish glow. The other kids were spitting along the side of the worn trail into the bushes, and I felt left out or recognized the glamour in their insouciance, so I asked them how did they do that. Peter stopped and explained, "You collect the spit in the front of your mouth, then you tighten your lips, clench your teeth, and push your tongue forward so the spit squeezes through the space between your front teeth."

Armed with this glorious new knowledge, I tried what he told me, and it worked. I spent the rest of the morning sprinkling the plants.

* * *

I eventually learned better ways to spit, not through my teeth (this method works only for thin saliva, prebraces) but through pursed lips and an open O-shaped mouth, the tongue providing the last hammer of propulsion behind pressurized air. I got to where I could spit pretty well, for accuracy and distance, and quantity, and now I spit all the time, from morning until night, in the sink and toilet, the trashcan, the bushes or the grass alongside the path I'm walking. Mostly I seek purging, though I guess there's also a bit of the boyish joy of letting the phlegm fly.

* * *

Living, as I do, in a time and place that frowns on public spitting, I try to be discreet, casting a backward glance before hocking a loogie, always aiming for an unused patch of ground where my offering will lie unnoticed, blended into its surroundings or even appreciated by the bacteria below.

I don't really know whether bacteria have any use for human sputum, whether they find it a pleasantry or a nuisance. Plants, surely, must profit from the water content of spit, no? And as much as I find the stuff repulsive, I know of lots of bugs that put mammalian feces to good use, so perhaps there are even visible invertebrates finding some advantage in spit.

* * *

Humans, it turns out, benefit from spit's antiseptic properties, as the nitrite in saliva reacts with skin to create nitric oxide, a bona fide germ killer. Even more impressive, saliva's histatin, a protein, has recently

2 *Spit*

proven (in Dutch laboratory tests) an effective healing accelerant, and another component, called opiorphin, reduces pain more effectively than morphine. Thus licking one's wounds, an automatic response in certain mammals (dogs especially), seems to be not only emotionally soothing but physiologically curing as well.

* * *

One day, as I was carrying Adriana into church, I turned my head to one side, aimed carefully at the grass, and spit, to clear my system of that last bit of early morning pollution. She did likewise but without careful aiming. Or perhaps she did aim. In any case, she spit right into my face. Karina, following the script, laughed and said, "Serves you right." I made a detour to the bathroom to wash up before entering the chapel.

This is a lesson I didn't learn. If memory serves, the same event has repeated itself with both of Adriana's younger sisters, in roughly the same situation, perhaps because church meetings happen in the morning, when I'm still clearing my esophageal system of the previous night's accumulation, and because nature's urges are more powerful than memory or common sense.

* * *

Nowadays, I spend the whole day spitting, from the moment I wake up to the minutes before I slip into bed again. If I am sick, I leave a disposable plastic cup on my nightstand in case of midnight emergences. If I am exercising, I either run often to the bathroom sink or keep a disposable plastic spittoon nearby. I spit more than most people, as far as I know. In one day, I can spit as much as a liter. This doesn't take into account all the saliva I swallow with food or by itself, and I'm not keen on repeating the experiment to get more accurate average results.

* * *

I've never met anyone else who remembers learning how to spit. I do ask (I am easy enough to find in this Internetted world; please contact me if you do remember). I can also remember how I learned to "gleek," which is a rather silly name to describe the action of propelling a stream of saliva from the submandibular gland by pressing the tongue down and forward, jaw extended, mouth slightly open. As with learning to spit, I found the prospect of gleeking utterly glamorous and desirable and sought to learn how to do it. My friend Greg Rodebush was the only person I knew who could gleek, or the only one who did it habitually in my presence (while we were playing volleyball, mostly, when we had time on our hands and our hands on our knees, waiting for a serve).

One summer day, as we waited at Greg's house for the hamburgers on the grill, I asked him how he did it. He didn't quite know how to explain, but he demonstrated for me, at regular speed and in slow motion. Most helpful, though, was the information that gleeking works best with sour candy or after a yawn.

He had some Sunkist fruit chews in the pantry, as it happened, so he gave me one. As I let the gummy sugar dissolve in my mouth, I could sense the pooling below my tongue, so I turned away from my friend and tried what he had told me. The resultant propulsion barely darkened a few spots on the concrete patio, but now I knew how to do it, so I could practice.

* * *

A subset of the readership has been thinking, *Gleek is also the name of Zan and Jayna's helper space monkey in the 1970s television superhero cartoon* The Wonder Twins. Now those readers can be happy that I've landed on the homonym, but perhaps they will be disappointed by my treatment of it. Like so many childhood memories, this show has melted into vague recollections and image snippets, the most memorable of which being that Zan always got the short end of the deal when the twins transformed. Jayna got to be any animal she liked: an elephant, maybe, a snake, a snapping turtle (I don't know; I refuse to look it up). But Zan had to become some configuration of water, like an ice ladder or a puddle for the bad guys to slip in. When I close my eyes and concentrate, I think I can see a repeating-background travel montage of Jayna-the-eagle carrying Zan-the-bucket-of-water. He'd become a hindrance to the superheroing! When I was a kid, I

thought Zan's power was the ulti-
mate gyp, the kind of decision a
writer ought to be fired for. Now,
I'm not so sure. Maybe, I hope, the
water thing was an inside joke, the
result of a buzzed and rowdy writers' meeting aimed at creating the
most worthless superability ever.
They sure succeeded if that was
their goal. And as for Gleek, well,
I simply don't remember him ever doing much, except getting into
Curious Georgeish trouble or maybe dumping the Zan-bucket on the
evildoers' heads. I do remember that he communicated in a kind of
gleep-de-bloop chatter, which is exactly what I would expect from a
space monkey named Gleek.

* * *

In the midsixties, my father was in the Notre Dame Glee Club, which,
as a show of goodwill, sang a medley of anthems from all the schools
ND would face in football each fall. Decades later, as a show of fatherly
love, he taught me and my siblings those medleys, in parts, as we sat
around the family room after dinner. Probably my favorite is Illinois's
(what glee I get from saying this possessive form of the word, which
sounds just like a mispronounciation of the state name), which declares
blatantly, "We're 'Orange and Blue,' Illinois," then ramps up with

> Our team is the fame protector;
> On, boys, for we expect a
> Victory from you, Illinois!

Given some slight space in the meter, I loved to sing it tongue trip-
pingly as

> we expectorate a victory from you, Illinois!

especially because of the simple wordplay and double meaning available when you separate the multisyllabic into components — "We

expect to rate a victory" — which makes at least a little sense. I hold to this inanity in part because it is my own invention. The Great Arbiter of Uniqueness declares,

```
Your search-"we expectorate a victory from you,
illinois"-did not match any documents.
```

Thus I am satisfied in my originality.

* * *

Another favorite salivary lyrical inanity, one with greater reach and royalties, comes from my favorite band, Rush. Their best-known, most-played song, now three decades old, featured lyrics half-written by Pye Dubois of the band Max Webster, thus Rush's typical clarity and philosophy were muddled by a kind of surreality, and thus "Louis the Lawyer" (Dubois's original title) became "Tom Sawyer," with the exhortation to

Catch the witness, catch the wit.
Catch the spirit, catch the spit.

Nobody I know has any clue about what this "means," so I, having learned restraint in interpreting, attribute it to linguistic punning, the kind of composition that's driven by shapes and sounds before significances. As with so much poetry, there's the rhyme with wit, which is a paring from witness, but I also sense a smidgen of glee in the compression of spirit to spit, which reaches beyond sense to discomfort with the notion of sense. "What does this mean?" seems the wrong question to ask. No question would be appropriate.

* * *

Not everyone is comfortable "being in uncertainties, mysteries, doubts, without any irritable reaching after fact and reason," so the Internet is smattered with interpretations of the "spit" lyric. One commenter believes the song to be about a policeman, and spit is "what they too often receive for their work." Another thinks that "'catch the spit' means that when people spit on you, you're strong enough to just take it." Yet another supposes that "the line simply refers to an incident in the Twain novel where Tom is spitting into his palm and shaking hands to seal a deal. It was meant to show trust and good faith, kind of like sealing in blood, but milder."

I was unable to find this incident, but in searching for it, I found the scene when Tom tries to stay home from school by faking a toe ache and then, when Aunt Polly is skeptical, a toothache, which only convinces her to bring out her thread and yank his loose tooth and send him off to school. Thus thwarted, Tom finds unexpected recompense.

DENTISTRY.

> As Tom wended to school after breakfast, he was the envy of every boy he met because the gap in his upper row of teeth enabled him to expectorate in a new and admirable way. He gathered quite a following of lads interested in the exhibition; and one that had cut his finger and had been a centre of fascination and homage up to this time, now found himself suddenly without an adherent, and shorn of his glory. His heart was heavy, and he said with a disdain which he did not feel that it wasn't anything to spit like Tom Sawyer; but another boy said, "Sour grapes!" and he wandered away a dismantled hero.

* * *

I don't practice revenge, especially not on my children, but the karmic forces sometimes do have a way of balancing the scales (or unbalancing them in our favor when we've been wronged). Remember my oldest daughter, Adriana, the one who spat on me as we entered church one morning? And remember how I spit a lot in the mornings, when I'm just waking up? One morning, I was doing my calisthenics in the den, and I noticed that I hadn't brought with me my customary cup. Already into the routine and unwilling to pause, I scanned the desk and shelves and found an empty Sprite can and began to fill it. It was

Spit 7

an especially fluid morning. When I finished, I stored the weights and other paraphernalia but, in my hurry to leave, left the can sitting next to the computer.

Later that day, Adriana, now ten or so, sidled into the den and noticed the Sprite unattended, beckoning. She cast a glance behind her to make sure she was alone, reached out, shook the can, smiled at the slosh, and . . .

Did you just shiver at that ellipsis? I did. I do every time. Adriana told us this story I don't know when — not immediately, not even soon after — but it has now become for us a shorthand: "the time I drank Dad's spit," the invocation of which never fails to elicit the inevitable groans.

* * *

I gave my back to the smiters, and my cheeks to them that plucked off the hair: I hid not my face from shame and spitting.

Isaiah 50:6

The only time I suffered the ignominy of being spit on happened when I was a missionary in Uruguay nearly half my life ago. Nearly every missionary I knew had caught spit, sometimes at close range and in direct consequence of attempting to preach, other times from a distance and in general. My own experience was of the latter type, perhaps because my calm demeanor and large size convinced interlocutors to keep their venom bottled up. But from aboard a moving bus, passing phantoms twice let loose with their spittle and landed indirect hits, the kind that take a moment to process, so that I didn't realize what had happened until the spitters were too far gone to chase or yell at, which, it seems now, might be my little victory in our anonymous exchanges. Were they watching out the bus window — and I presume they were — they would not have known that they hit their mark, and my distress would not equal their joy. It's a dastard who'll spit at another person and a cowardly dastard who'll spit at a stranger then run/drive away.

8 *Spit*

Now I see the long and short the middle and what's in between I could spit on a stranger

STEPHEN MALKMUS, "Spit on a Stranger"

This from "the band that ruined Lollapalooza" by playing extended, incoherent jams instead of their "hits" (if Pavement can be said to have produced any hits; I am partial to the song "Stereo," which ponders "What about the voice of Geddy Lee? How did it get so high? I wonder if he talks like an ordinary guy"), which provoked the crowd to sling mud and rocks, a gesture equivalent to spitting, but at a greater distance and with the possibility of injury. Attacking in the other direction, Pink Floyd's Roger Waters once grew so flustered at a group of rowdy, inattentive fans (who were yelling and even setting off firecrackers) that he goaded one of them to approach the stage, then spit in his face. This incident at Montreal's Olympic Stadium, July 1977, is considered the low point that gave rise to the band's best-known, most-philosophical album, *The Wall*. In a graffito on the wall exhibit at the Rock and Roll Hall of Fame, Waters recalled,

In the old days, pre–*Dark Side of the Moon*, Pink Floyd played to audiences which, by virtue of their size, allowed an intimacy of connection that was magical. Success overtook us and by 1977 we were playing in football stadiums. The magic was crushed beneath the weight of numbers. We were becoming addicted to the trappings of popularity. I found myself increasingly alienated in that atmosphere of avarice and ego until one night in the Olympic Stadium, Montreal, the boil of my frustrations burst. Some crazed teenage fan was clawing his way up the storm netting that separated us from the human cattle pen in front of the stage screaming his devotion to the demi-gods beyond his reach. Incensed by his misunderstanding and my own connivance, I spat my frustration in his face. Later that night, back at the hotel, shocked by my behavior, I was faced with a choice. To deny my addiction and embrace that comfortably numb but magic-less existence or accept the burden of insight, take the road less traveled, and embark on the often painful journey to discover who I was and where I fit. The wall was the picture I drew for myself to help me make that choice.

Nice save, Roger! turning that shameful event into an inspiration for resurgent art and healing.

* * *

Usually when I think of biblical spitting, my mind goes not to the Old but to the New Testament, to the fulfillment of Isaiah's prophecy, in the Christian tradition:

> Then the soldiers of the governor took Jesus into the common hall, and gathered unto him the whole band of soldiers. And they stripped him, and put on him a scarlet robe. And when they had plaited a

crown of thorns, they put it upon his head, and a reed in his right hand: and they bowed the knee before him, and mocked him, saying, Hail, King of the Jews! And they spit upon him, and took the reed, and smote him on the head. And after that they had mocked him, they took the robe off from him, and put his own raiment on him, and led him away to crucify him.

Matthew 27:27–31

I have known this story from the time I was a child, so that it feels to me originless, with me always; I cannot recall having ever learned it. When I read it now, I admire the paucity of the prose as much as the stoic hero's resolve. I know, of course, what comes next, and after that, so that I, too, can bear the agony and ignominy without fainting. It is a triumph story, its ultimate resolution never in doubt. For me, and for you, too, whether you believe it or not, it happens only in the context of having already happened, which is to say that we cannot feel the drama, we cannot go back to unknowing, we can never even remotely occupy the place of those scared and scattered disciples who skulked in the shadows afraid for their master, protecting their own lives. As we chanted each Sunday, "Christ has died. Christ is risen. Christ will come again." This means for us an atonement, a reparation, a type and a figure of hope of return.

* * *

And he cometh to Bethsaida; and they bring a blind man unto him, and besought him to touch him. And he took the blind man by the hand, and led him out of the town; and when he had spit on his eyes, and put his hands upon him, he asked him if he saw ought. And he looked up, and said, I see men as trees, walking.

Mark 8:22

In a Bible whose references to spitting mostly point to it as negative — spitting to revile, to mock, to scorn — the story of Jesus healing the blind man at Bethsaida stands out as redemptive. A very similar story appears in the gospel of John, though in that version, Jesus spits on the ground to make mud, which he then rubs in the blind man's eyes. I prefer the story as told by Mark because of its shuddering shift in verb tense, its ambiguously referenced pronouns, its concision in getting to the point, but mainly because I figure that most people would have difficulty spitting on someone's eyes — they'd get saliva all over the place. But Jesus would have perfect aim, so no problem. And just when I'm getting carried away in this frivolous imagining, the healed man looks up and offers this achingly beautiful bit of poetry: "I see men as trees, walking."

Spit 11

I like to think that Jesus was okay with this, recognizing the beauty in strangeness or understanding that the man's vocabulary had yet to catch up with his vision, like the formerly blind healed by cataract surgeons (mentioned in *Pilgrim at Tinker Creek* by Annie Dillard, who borrowed it from Marius von Senden's *Space and Sight*), who had no concept of space or solidity or shading to indicate shape. They had no context, no categories; they had not yet learned to interpret what they saw. Emblematic of the miracles is the little girl standing amazed in a garden before "the tree with the lights in it," because she cannot comprehend the sun shining through the spaces between the leaves. This becomes a guiding metaphor for Dillard, but not a metaphor only; before the book is finished, she has sought for and experienced her own vision of the tree unclouded by preconceptions and familiarities.

Another newly sighted girl insisted that "men do not really look like trees at all," so one assumes that she had gained perspective enough to compartmentalize, like the blind man after Jesus placed his hands on his eyes and shook him out of his metaphorical view, so that he saw clearly, "clearly" perhaps serving as euphemism for categorically or correctly, fit within preconceptions, familiar and redundant, just like everyone else.

Meanwhile, so many of us, the artists and writers and musicians, spend so much effort to see things unclearly again.

* * *

In the course of writing this essay, I discovered the old card game called Spit, which I learned and taught to my daughters. I invented a modified version for three players, and we laughed through a pleasant afternoon of shuffling and battling our cards. The basic game reminds me of War, the simplest of card entertainments and probably the shortest lived, as its novelty wears off quickly, especially as the players mature and their brains desire more sophisticated entertainments.

12 *Spit*

Spit can serve to heal the wounds of War, as it gives players more to think about by complicating the card interactions, but not too much. Also, it works in the opposite direction: instead of gathering cards to win, you want to get rid of them. Its basic form involves two players with half a deck each. They lay before them five piles of one, two, three, four, and five cards and draw from the remaining "spit" cards to begin two additional piles. It's a game of chance and speed, as players try to empty their five stockpiles by forming runs, up or down, back and forth, without regard for suit. When a stockpile empties, a player may fill its space on the table with a card from another pile, so that she always has five face-up cards to draw from. When play freezes because no one can play a card, the players "spit" a new card from their face-down piles and begin stacking anew. Once one player has exhausted her five stockpiles, both players slap at one of the face-up piles, hoping to claim the smaller of the two. Then they gather all remaining cards, reset their five staircase piles, and begin spitting again. Eventually, one player will not have enough cards to fill all five initial piles; she fills them as much as she can, and then both begin to play their cards on only one spit pile. If the player with fewer cards clears out her draw piles before the other, she will win; as there is only one spit pile, it goes to the slower player.

* * *

Over the years, my friend John Anderson and I kept in touch, visited each other at college, and attended concerts together, but I learned something unsavory about myself one night in the parking lot outside Brendan Byrne Arena. Hurting for home, eager to escape the riot of drinking that kept me holed up in my dorm room soberly studying every night, I'd made a surprise visit home from Notre Dame just in time to catch Friday's Rush show. So I found myself wandering to section B-23, where you'd always find the kids from Whippany, not quite tailgating, but hanging out, listening to music, smoking, and drinking. I was always ancillary, a member of the group by geography but not by sympathy. Still, the other kids knew me and never pestered me to participate, never passed me the joint or poured me a cup. I'd established my ground already, and I was generally okay with their herd behavior, as I saw it, doing themselves damage because it was cool. But that night, in the autumn dusk, surrounded by the buzz of vapor lights and a haze of smoke, I saw my friend John suddenly on the other side, left ear newly pierced, joint in hand, and I felt betrayed. He smiled and smoothtalked, "Hey, man, [something about the show]." We'd been great friends the past couple of years. He had been as unsure and nerdy as I was then, but now I saw him moving away, leaving me without an ally. Who knows what I said or how he responded, but I made clear my disappointment; he responded with a how-dare-you; me: "You're not cool like them"; he: "Who are you to tell me what to do"; escalating in whispered shouts under the din of boom boxes; and then, in disgust and feeble frustration, I spat at him, right in his face.

He glared a moment, wiped his face with his hand, then walked back to the others.

* * *

I take great care not only to write myself noble, kindhearted, longsuffering but to be those adjectives, in public and in private, to overcome my baser motivations, vanquish my impulse toward vainglory. So it's difficult to publish these sad tidings, to confess such a sin. I might say that it changed me. That would be true. Or that I've never done such a thing again, also true. I am sure I apologized to John the next day or next week, maybe even that very night, after our emotions had cooled, but I can't remember doing so, so I'm stuck with the image of my weakness, how I judged my brother despite my many imperfections, how underneath my imperturbable exterior I craved friendship and belonging yet spat my rage at a true friend. Writing the story now brings tears to my eyes, not because John never forgave me — he did; we still talked and listened to music whenever we were in the same place; I stayed with him in his dorm a couple of times once he started attending Michigan State the next year; and we kept up a kind of slowly distancing friendship that, yes, faded, though mostly due to our diverging geographies — but because it's been ten

14 *Spit*

years (ten years!) since John died of a heart attack while surfing, so there's no chance now to reconnect and laugh about our youthful misadventures.

And it's difficult, near impossible, for me now to reinhabit that ✳ ✳ ✳ who stood, full of disappointment and loneliness, raging and spitting. I'm not sure I know who he is, "that 'other me,' there, in the background." I don't want to claim him.

I was me but now he's gone.

JAMES HETFIELD, "Fade to Black"

Yet it was me, and as much as I regret what I did, I did it. As much as John forgave me, I do not forget.

✳ ✳ ✳

Which is exactly what you'd expect me to say, given the tired cliché and because I'm the one telling you this story, which is another way of saying that I cannot entirely escape the system of myself to see me from the outside. Yet I have changed. When I was young, I was deathly afraid of talking to store clerks or of singing in public. I refused to join the school choir, though I loved singing at home with my father, who encouraged, cajoled, even obligated me to approach cashiers to ask after the new KISS album or *Star Wars* action figures. Little by little and in a giant leap when I walked the streets of Uruguay wiping the sweat from my brow and the spit from my shirt, I became comfortable both asking and singing, so that now when I have a question in a store, I gather all the uniformed workers I can find and serenade them.

Perhaps I've swung too far in the opposite direction, now that I write essays about myself and share them with the world. But I hope not. I'm not sure I agree with E. B. White, or I hope he was hyperbolizing when he said,

Only a person who is congenitally self-centered has the effrontery and the stamina to write essays.

I feel a greater resonance with Alexander Smith:

The essayist who feeds his thoughts upon the segment of the world which surrounds him cannot avoid being an egotist; but then his egotism is not unpleasing. If he be without taint of boastfulness, of self-sufficiency, of hungry vanity, the world will not press the charge home.

"On the Writing of Essays"

I reflect often on that dreadful night before the Rush concert and on the person I think I am now. Although Hazlitt assures us that

The spirit of malevolence survives the practical exertion of it. . . . We give up the external demonstration, the brute violence, but cannot part with the essence or principle of hostility.

I'm not so sure. I search and find in me no trace of that decades-old hostility. In its place, I find only shame. Given to metaphorical self-understanding, I sing equally with John Newton and Kerry Livgren:

I once . . . was blind, but now I see.
Though my eyes could see, I still was a blind man.

I am cheered to believe myself less self-righteously judgmental, less inclined to shield myself from smoking and drinking and drugs by believing that those who partake of them do so out of weakness, more likely to locate weaknesses in myself, less likely to place myself above others in deed or in thought, more, I think, compassionate, fellow feeling, sincerely interested in the stories of others.

* * *

But first, a bit of background:

I thought, as I wrote this essay, that I might use spit the way the television crime-drama forensics experts do: to determine DNA connections, to seal a wrongdoer's fate or as exculpatory evidence to free the wrongly accused. My brother Dave, the biology and chemistry teacher, quickly disabused me of the simplistic notion that spit itself contains genetic markers but pointed out that skin cells in our mouths, which might be present in spit, do. Undaunted (even by the price tag), I eagerly swabbed my cheeks and sent my cells to be analyzed at a laboratory. Weeks later, I got the basic report, including the details of folks who share a common ancestor with me. There weren't many — details or folks — and the closest relatives I found share a common male ancestor within twenty-three generations (there were thousands within one hundred generations, which gets us back at least to the time of Jesus). I suspect that the scarcity of impressive results has much to do with a science still in its infancy and a diversity of services all promising the same vague things, meaning that any one of them has in its database only a small group of others one might be related to. So I was disappointed, yes, but I'm an essayist, dammit, not a pessimist. I write with what I got. And what I got was a short email from my distant cousin Kevin:

> hi there got a message saying you and i have a common ances-
> tor 23 generations or so ago 8). which is a hell of along time
> ago. i am adopted so for me you are the closest person that has
> similar dna that i have ever talked with. i didnt realize it was
> only ancient ancestors they were able to tell you about. guess i
> jumped the gun a bit 8(guess ya gotta take what you can get 8)
> take care cuzz 8) kevin

Always willing to let my subject find me, I gladly responded, explaining my essay project and asking for more information. Kevin replied quickly, summarizing his youthful misadventures ("i was kinda a rebel without a clue. got in trouble at a young age and was put in reform school til i was 16. got my * * * together by the time i was 20. somewhat.") and expanding on his adoption. He had essentially put the whole issue out of his mind, he said, until he was contacted by the Canadian government, telling him that the laws had just changed and they'd located his birth mother . . . and she didn't want any contact with him. "I asked the guy if he wanted to set an appointment to come kick me in the nuts while he's at it," he said, and I understood what he was saying.

Kevin and I have kept in touch sporadically, even talking on the phone one day, which meant that we could hear each other's voices, which let me believe that I knew him more than when he was only his emails. He spoke with a gruff voice that made me smile and an easy calm that let me believe he was comfortable with me, or perhaps with life in general. I felt like here is a decent guy who, despite our superficially different lives, could be a friend. The kind of guy I'd like to have a beer with, if I drank beer. I also thought about how if we were younger and living in the same town, though, circumstance and interests would likely have kept us apart and, hell, I'll admit it, I'd have likely kept my distance intentionally, judging him unkindly. But here we were, both in our early forties, in Utah and Ontario, married, with and without children, with and without nearby blood relatives, and with a scant knowledge of ancestry, chatting on the phone and becoming friends because we share a great-great-great-great . . . grandfather, some lowly peasant subsisting in fifteenth-century Ireland (I presume).

As it turned out, between our first contact and our phone conversation, nearly a year had passed, and in that time, Kevin's life had turned upside down. One moment, we were talking about how discovering your birth mother isn't always the solution you'd hoped for (he had friends who'd experienced this), and the next, he was telling me, carefully, a bit guardedly,

> I have recently been going through some mad change. I was pretty stable for the last twenty years, and then, basically, worlds have collided, so now I've got myself in a bit of a situation. The person I've been for the last twenty long years . . . I am now in a state of complete change. Everything I've been working for for the last fifteen years is now in a state of . . . it's just in a state that it wasn't in before. It was a much more sturdy structure situation, and now it doesn't seem to be built on as strong a foundation as I thought I'd laid down. But, you know, you get knocked down seven, you get up eight.

I didn't feel like I should press for details, but after a while, Kevin explained just a little bit more, noting the ironic coincidence of the day his woes began:

I came home to my house on Mother's Day this year to a ladder up against my house and went running in thinking all kinds of nasty things, that someone was in there with my wife, and all sorts . . . Didn't turn out to be any of that, but someone had definitely been in there, and in the process there were old guns that I had inherited from my father, who passed away, old hunting guns — there was a .22 and a shotgun and a little revolver — but, yeah, it's a bad mess, man.

That's really all he said by way of narrative details, though he suggested that I might look online for more information, which led me to several Toronto news sites telling the same story about a man who'd arrived at the hospital with a bullet wound in the leg claiming to have been shot in a drive-by. Police who questioned him doubted his story and searched his house, where they found "a mini-arsenal" and enough marijuana to charge him with trafficking. They claim that he shot himself in the leg, but nobody had a theory on how or why. Weeks later, when I mentioned what I'd found, Kevin said that he wasn't sure where they got their information from but that it wasn't even close to what happened.

Although he hadn't realized it at the time, looking back now he sees that conversation with the government worker as a turning point, the jostle that set his life lurching in expanding staggers toward the chaos he currently finds himself in. "Bro, you have no idea. That was like so . . . earth . . . shattering," he said. "When I look back at the devastating impact, and when things started to sort of . . . at first you get angry and you get mad and all that, but when you start really thinking about it (which I'm pretty good at not doing until much later, if at all) . . ." He trailed off, but the suggestion was clear. His life had been routine, smooth sailing, and he hadn't been overly concerned about who he was or where he came from, until one day when the phone rang, unexpected, unsolicited, to quash the hidden hope he'd kept about a mother who'd loved him but who, because of circumstance, couldn't keep him. This was the first crack that grew to crumble the sturdy foundation he'd built his life on. When I reminded him of his earlier statement about being a rebel without a clue, he agonized, "I thought I turned that all around. I really did, brother. It really wasn't b.s.ing. I really had turned it around. I was really living like a stand-up guy. It was unbelievable . . . almost like your picture story of a reformed guy. But I wasn't even all that corrupt in the beginning. I just wanted to smoke pot." He laughed, and I laughed, and he added, "I've lived my life by trying to hurt no one and help people when I can."

After nearly half an hour, Kevin explained, "I kinda gotta go. I got my mom looking at me, staring about dinner being ready," but we kept talking for several more minutes, mostly about my plans for the essay (I really didn't know what I'd do with it, I said; I'd figure that out in the writing) and about Kevin's current limbic state. "I'm really in the search mode," he said. "I'm just trying to figure my * * * out, to be honest. I just want to be good with * * *. That's all I'm looking for. I just want to be content." And I thought, as I often do, about how we all want the same things and how "every man contains within himself the entire human condition."

When we were finally really ready to hang up, he said, "We got the same blood running through our veins; we can stay in touch by email. That's the coolest thing ever," and I agreed, but only intellectually, really, because things are so much different for me. "You don't understand, man," and I didn't, not in the way he meant. "I don't know anybody . . . nobody I know looks like . . . all I do know is Christmas after Christmas looking around the table and knowing I wasn't from here."

* * *

Having grown up in an atmosphere that whispered forgiveness as the greatest good of God and man, having absorbed the idea of repentance as central to identity, and having always believed in the possibility of change, I find Kevin's story disconcerting, a challenge to notions I hold dear. Maybe what unsettles me is that Kevin had changed but then, like a tragic hero or fool, seems to have lost all the ground he gained, certainly without intending it and almost without agency. Just a year ago, he was the embodiment of the returned prodigal son — minus the squandered wealth, I suppose — making good on a difficult and somewhat wayward life. And now? Who knows what happens next? To me, he presented a stoic figure — "knocked down seven times, got up eight," as he is fond of saying — a guy who'd figure a way through all this and come out stronger because of it. I sincerely hope he does, but sometimes people don't. And where does that leave me, except feeling distantly empathetic? But in reality, I can't feel anywhere near the anguish that Kevin himself feels over this. He may wind up in jail, or even in the best-case scenario, he'll spend his life's savings mounting a defense. I can say this: as I read the knee-jerk comments below the "stupid criminal" story on the news sites, my stomach churns at the schadenfreude exhibited there, and I cannot summon that kind of vitriol or even censure, and not only because now I know Kevin and we are distant kin. I think, really, that I distrust all such simplification, and I know that there is always more to the story than what I'm reading and that there is always a complex human being behind every seemingly boneheaded act. And this: my primary goal for Toronto has always been to visit Rush sites, but now, if I ever make it there, I'll first look up Kevin, and we'll go to Alex Lifeson's Orbit Room together, where he'll have his pint of Guinness and I'll sip my A&W.

* * *

Whereas Kevin has begun to trace his current misfortunes to that tragic external shock and will soon tell his story to a jury of his peers and whereas Roger Waters has had many years to revisit and reconfigure his very public spitting incident, I have had no one to answer to for the past decade. And while Waters has successfully accepted/ deflected the blame, nobly admitting his culpability while simultaneously indicting the soul-destroying system of fame and adulation, I have maintained a quiet, unnoticed life, and I blame nobody but myself for my spitting incident. I believe that Waters believes his account and his explanation for the repercussions, yet I suspect that — like Kevin, who sees only now the destabilizing force of that phone call — nothing so profound consciously drove Waters's actions that night. Is this not the very definition of creative nonfiction? We do not write (if we write well) only what happened; we explore our memory, grasping at meaning, to explain ourselves to ourselves. No doubt Waters's spit was driven by a "spontaneous overflow of powerful feelings," yet his rationalization arrived only as he recollected his actions in tranquility. As I recollect that night in the parking lot, everything happened at a distance from our gathered friends, during a pause in time, a kind of slow-motion irreversible error in judgment and, given John's death, an ultimately irremediable expression of a disdain I felt for the briefest of moments. Thinking on it, I feel the drama is transformed — not what I felt then but a heightened, parallel drama: I know what comes next, and though I would, I am unable to get to any other ending. That outpouring made an indelible mark, not just on John, who is no longer here to remember it, but on me. What I'm trying to say is that there's nobody on this earth today who recalls my great shame but me — that if I wished, I might obliterate the happening, seal it tight in mind or spit it out, perhaps — but I find I cannot do this, and that even writing it here seems no expiation at all.

Fisica Sublime

I've got some explaining to do.

This is the part where I give some background, explain the book's title, characterize my writing within the long tradition of the essay, apologize and instruct a bit about essays in general (*aren't you always doing that?* my friends are thinking), and generally introduce you to *Sublime Physick*. I'd have done it in the first chapter, as a proper introduction, but for a few important factors. First, I'm wary of titling any piece "Introduction," which, they tell me, frightens readers into skipping ahead to the first "real" chapter. Second, I have learned the hard way that in the twenty-first century, online booksellers provide free access to a book's first chapter by default and will not skip it to, say, the second, which might be a more interesting and appealing teaser (this is why, for my first book, at Amazon or Google Books, you can read "The Infinite Suggestiveness of Common Things," which is really an undercover introduction, instead of "Laughter," which, they tell me, would have been a better lead). And third, Alexander Smith did it in *Dreamthorp*, which opens by introducing place and people and then steps back in chapter 2 to meditate "On the Writing of Essays."

I might mention, also, that I have a gift for choosing obscure, off-putting titles. This book was to be called *Fisica Sublime*, but I have yet to find one person who's not scared away by the Latin or Italian or Spanish or whatever it is. Unwilling to give up the metaphor completely, I

have translated and archaicized it to *Sublime Physick*, in order to retain some of the allusiveness and instruction inherent in the term and to give a two-word title to book number two (book number one had a one-word title; I hope to call book number three *In Medias Pensées*, which, I recognize, is more egregious than *Fisica Sublime* for its unconscionable mixture of Latin and French). Like most writers, I like challenging titles that evoke some curiosity and mystery in readers (assuming readers who enjoy essays). What's more, I want titles that are partially synonymous with or definitions of the essay form. Thus *Quotidiana*, a coinage meaning, crudely, "collection of everyday things," describes not only my own essays but essays in general. Likewise, *Sublime Physick* seems to me to tell us something about the dual nature of the essay.

Allow me to unpack the meanings I am aiming for. There are plenty.

Most basically, there's the oxymoron of a sublime (metaphysical, perhaps spiritual, certainly idea-airy and abstract) physics (physical, natural, tangible, etc.). This juxtaposition is at the heart of the way I first heard the term used. I was researching Amedeo Avogadro, for an essay about vastness, and learned that he was appointed chair of Fisica Sublime, a department at the University of Turin, which is something akin to our modern-day theoretical physics ("the outpost of science closest to philosophy, and religion" — Alan Lightman). That makes sense. But before "sense," I was attracted simply to the music of those words together — *fisica sublime* (I'm pronouncing it in my best Spanish-inflected Italian accent, where each of those words has three syllables) — and to the way they made me stretch. Poetic language both confirms and challenges meaning, causing us to question the very apparatus whereby linguistic meaning is conveyed. This may be done in a single word (perhaps as we encounter a new definition or can piece together a meaning because we know the component parts from Latin), but really the smallest unit of poetic meaning is a pair, often an oxymoron. I knew what *fisica* meant; I knew the adjective *sublime*; but I'd never considered how the latter might modify the former into so many new possibilities.

And that's what got me thinking about essays: how they, too, are oxymoronic characters, rooted in the natural world, derived from real experience (personal, historical), traceable to nonfictional events, even often concerned directly with the environment, Nature with a capital N. But they're also always reaching toward ideas, trying to transcend mere description or depiction. Thus, essays perform a kind of sublimation of the solid; from the concrete, they attain abstraction.

But that's not all I mean, not the only way the metaphor works for me.

I mean *sublime* in its colloquial sense of beautiful, inspiring, because that's the way the best essays make me feel.

I mean *physick* in its medicinal sense, especially the imprecise premodern version suggested by the spelling, because essays can often be palliative, though they are never a sure or quick fix.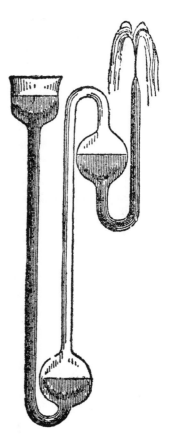

I mean *sublime* in its attitudinal sense of sanguine and cheerful, because even with essayists' melancholy and pensiveness, I believe this is our goal, which we often achieve.

I mean *physick* in its scientific sense, "the studie of naturall things"; as we used to chant in Mr. Altenderfer's class, "physics is everywhere" and "everything is physics."

Sublime as seeming linguistic oxymoron in itself, as *sub* in any other word I know means "below" and yet when paired with *lime* means "above."

Physick as relating to the human body, as essays have long and consistently been.

Sublime as suggesting the highest sphere of thought, intellectual or spiritual elevation.

I even mean *physick* in the laxative sense, as cathartic, though I'll admit that this is primarily "because it's there" in the dictionary. I wouldn't have thought to call essays laxative on my own. But then, given the logorrhea evident in the coming pages . . .

And putting these two words together creates significances unavailable in either of them individually.

When I hear *sublime physick*, I think alchemy, mysterious transformations, common into uncommon, gold from dross, "the ruder world transmuted into the finer," as Alexander Smith says of the essay's work to make art from reality.

When I hear *sublime physick*, I think transubstantiation. I think Jesus returned from his fasting and temptation, predicting his detractors: "Physician, heal thyself!" because the best essays look inward to find fault and sometimes, almost by mistake, find insight that the rest of us can use to improve ourselves.

When I hear *sublime physick*, I think lack of stability, a "languid rocking to and fro," approximating direction, aiming at but always missing the target, until the target disappears.

I think transcendentalism, the philosophy of everything connected, nonconformism, individualism, an essential sage idealism that doesn't hide from hard reality; I think of the ideas that spurred the development of the essay in America.

I think, with Longinus, an elevation of literary style rooted in simplicity; I think noble (my name, Patrick, means "noble") yet lowly (Madden, "little hound"); I think essayists "noble enough to win the world but weak enough to lose it." Whenever all the exalted adjective meanings of *sublime* start to worry me or carry me away to boasting about the essay form or essayists or even myself, there's the *physickal* grounding attached, a mud stain on the tuxedo.

I also return to (theoretical) physics, as we think of it today: the scientific study of matter and energy, which, as we know, are one and the same, despite appearances to the contrary. This may be another way of exemplifying that glorious phrase *sublime physick*: the energy and matter of existence. I think quantum mechanics and the governance of probabilities. I also think — sideways — time and space, another equivalence that we experience separately but whose components open up to bewildering understanding when merged. I recall how physics was my first love — how when I met her in high school, I was smitten by the comprehensibility of Newton's laws and by mind-stretching engagements with experiments. I think back fondly on my days as a young man studying physics in college, driven by a desire to understand the ways the world works . . .

This is still my motivation, though I no longer seek it via equations. For my temperament, I've found essaying to be a much richer, more fetching avenue. And so, in this collection, I will try to grapple with some of the fundamental principles and questions, not quite seeking any grand unified theory (I don't really believe one exists, nor would I want one), but always dimly aware of it just out of the periphery. Though the essays are personal, there will be plenty of externalities. There may be some mathematics. But there won't be any equations. In one or two instances, there may not be much of a consideration of what we normally term "physics," but "some word of it will always be found, off in a corner." The essays all derive, in some way, from the physical world, and all reach, always insufficiently, toward the sublime.

Perhaps, I'm beginning to think, everything we think we know is a kind of sublime physick, an abstraction derived from concretion and a double-aspected entity that we think we know in two distinct forms, yet which is really a unity: matter-energy, space-time, mind-body, emotion-intellect, self-others, inside-outside, nonfiction-fiction; you could go on and on listing apparently opposed binaries and find, again and again, that where they meet, there is beauty.

Entering and Breaking

I had just walked through my office door and sat down at my desk, hours later than I'd hoped, and was clearing away the weekend's accumulation of hassling emails, when the phone rang, breaking my concentration. It was Karina, in a tizzy; the boys were missing. She'd been in the bathroom only a few minutes, and when she came out, the back door was ajar, Marcos and James nowhere to be found.

Understanding my role in situations such as this, and having lost and found children numerous times before, and worrying that I'd made the half-hour commute only a few minutes ago, and staring down the pile of petty tasks I'd wanted to finish, and wishing for some quality writing time before an on-time departure, and realizing that on this Halloween night I'd get no work done at home, I spoke calmly, reassuring Karina that the boys were certainly nearby, maybe in the head-high weeds in the empty lot just across the backyard, maybe in the garage, maybe at the Andersons' — had she checked the playroom upstairs?

"Of course I checked the playroom!"

Ditto on the other places. She wanted me home right away. I wanted to avoid driving halfway there only to get the relieved phone call. I wanted peace and systematic thinking, a plan, but I also wanted to not get worked up, to solve the problem by paying it no heed. The statistics on such disappearances were overwhelmingly in our favor.

Most kids were found after a few minutes, innocently playing, unaware that they were causing their parents consternation. Marcos and James, barely three and not yet two, were overwhelmingly more likely to have wandered off than to have been taken, more likely to be safely ensconced than in any sort of danger. The fact that I was making up these statistics based on guesses and wishes did not dissuade me from believing them. I offered to call friends and neighbors to enlist their help, which I did, and then went back to work dispatching emails.

When Karina called again a few minutes later, I expected good news, but she was growing more distraught. I explained that the neighbors were already searching, which she knew, and suggested that she stay close to home so the boys would find her there when they returned. She had called the police, and she wanted me home now. So I quickly packed up and began the drive.

By then the boys had been missing for thirty minutes. I was not worried, I told myself as I waited at a stoplight. They'd show up, and we'd release our tension with a good laugh. I'd not even allow myself to get cross about all the undone work left waiting for me.

At each highway mile marker, my thigh felt a phantom buzz from my cell phone, but Karina never called. When I hit the exit for Pioneer Crossing, I called her, half-expecting that in her jubilation she'd forgotten to notify me. But there was still no sign of them. The police were there. The neighborhood was filled with neighbors. The elementary school had been alerted. It had now been forty-five minutes.

I strained to guess where they might have gone, to get inside their heads or to hear the whisperings of the Spirit, to be guided to my sons. I took a right on 1100 West instead of 1700. I drove as slowly as I dared, scanning the tall grass and trees along the roadside. Nothing.

Knowing that these words will fail to convey even the remotest measure of the lived experience, I will cut the tension here to let you know the outcome. The boys were found. (I'll tell you how in a minute.) I ask you not to sympathize or to enter the mind space I inhabited then but to think with me now, at a distance. For instance, let us take for a moment one sideways path that I have considered in the aftermath:

There was a time, only four years ago, when I thought four children were plenty. Karina and I had matched our parents' output, had reached a reasonable return on our marital investment. Our car, a minivan, allowed us to travel together to Yellowstone or to the grocery store. Our house was comfortable, with the three girls sharing a large bedroom and with their older brother occupying his own room across the hall.

But the births of Marcos and James were the most irreversible of irreversible processes. Though they've existed for only a fraction of my life, they've so inserted themselves into my consciousness that they seem to have existed always; their lives are so entangled with my own that I feel as if without them I am not. Though I'd been content with a quartet, there was no going back to four children without destroying me.

After I'd been home for over an hour — comforting Karina; talking with police and friends and school aides; running and driving everywhere within a half-mile radius; checking and rechecking the drainage ditches, the donkey farm, the empty lot, the house under construction, the cars along the street, the elementary school hallways, the city ball fields, the Bushmans' farm, the church parking lot, the entrance to the mink farm, the highway crossing the length of road as far as I could imagine they might have walked; praying frantically against the encroaching dread with each creeping minute with no news — I returned home broken. With my mind racing with a thousand scenarios, I trudged across the yard to the back deck, where Karina was weeping and two officers were explaining that they'd called police from nearby towns, and firemen were parading their trucks noisily through the streets in hopes of calling the boys' attention. They were serious now, somber, willing to discuss the possibilities we'd dared not voice. They would set up a base at our home, resystematize their search, go door-to-door and enter the homes they could. The Amber alert was active. It was now nearing two o'clock. The boys had been missing for two hours.

Let us break away once more on another path, even as our story heads toward its already determined resolution:

30 *Entering and Breaking*

I have traveled for conferences and for work, have visited family, have stayed home teaching while Karina took the kids to Uruguay for a month before I joined them there. I have spent weeks without seeing my children, days without speaking to them. I have learned, on the phone, of their injuries and emergency room visits, the discovery that the littlest has a peanut allergy. But in those lacunae I have always felt peace, have never suffered from the slightest suggestion that they were unsafe. Yet that day, across the protracted expanse of just two hours, I entered a place in my mind I had never visited or imagined was there. As I stepped up onto the deck, slumping my shoulders, breathing slowly, holding my gaze fixed on the middle distance between our house and the street behind, I was bereft. I had abandoned hope.

As I listened to the officers' tentative plans, I no longer believed that Marcos and James were nearby just playing; I'd personally checked all the places they might have been hurt or worse, and so had a hundred other people. The only option left was that they had been taken. I asked, "Are there any traffic cameras close to here? At the light on Pioneer Crossing? At the school?"

My mind conjured a grainy black-and-white still image of a dark sedan. The camera angle was just low enough to allow a glimpse of a small boy (I thought) in the passenger seat under the hovering dark figure of an adult.

They weren't sure, but they would find out. It was unlikely. Meanwhile, they were doing everything —

My lethargic stare narrowed and locked on the slightest blur of movement across our backyard, the Rosses' backyard, the street, the Rasmussens' driveway.

"Who is that kid!?" I yelled. My body sprang off the deck and began sprinting.

"Who is that kid!?" With each shout, I expelled all the air from my lungs; with each stride, the form came closer into focus. It was Marcos. When he saw me, his eyes went wide and he sat down on the driveway. Anita Burroughs, who'd been walking along the sidewalk, got there with me and scooped him up while I ran past, bounded up the front stairs, and barged into the Rasmussens' house. James was standing surprised in the front entryway, his mouth ringed by a chocolate goatee. I sobbed as I gathered him up and ran back outside, where his mother and the officers and a small group of neighbors were smiling and sighing, perhaps crying as well.

The ensuing hours involved lots of research and explaining. Marcos and James, unable to comprehend our questions or communicate any answers, were no help. The police entered the home, found no one there, and determined that the boys had let themselves in and had plundered the bananas and Halloween candy. They'd been watching cartoons. They'd broken a vase. In all, their crimes were misdemeanors, easily remedied. We called our friends to call off the search, and the word spread quickly that everyone could go home and return to their usual level of vigilance. Several gathered instead in our yard, to offer what compassion they could. The threat was over, and our minds could settle on the real results, not the excruciating possibilities that had haunted us for the past pair of hours. Karina's friends, especially, hugged her and shared their own lost-child stories, all agreeing that none had suffered as long or as dreadfully. I called my neighbor Lonnie, whom I barely knew, to tell him that my sons had ransacked his home. He laughed a little, told me not to sweat it. I promised to replace the vase and the candy. He said, "If you want, but get the vase from the dollar store." Later, he pieced together that one of his kids had left for school by the front door, leaving it unlocked, while everyone else went out the garage. Later, Karina and I mused on the improbability that the boys had gone so far so quickly to a house they'd never visited on just the day that the front door was unlocked and the cupboards were stocked with enough candy to keep them occupied for a long while. Later, Trevor Smith explained that he'd been checking all the basement back doors on the street but hadn't thought to do more than ring doorbells at the front.

Our friends in our front yard made what small talk you'd expect, verbal sighs of relief and offers to help in any way at all. Karina expressed her thanks that, given what we'd recently learned about James's peanut allergy, the Rasmussens had no Reese's Peanut Butter Cups in their cupboards. People nodded. They commented on how God had watched over the boys.

32 *Entering and Breaking*

But I, with my young sons returned, could still not quite leave the dark place my thoughts had settled, could not heave off the feeling of despair that had overcome me. Then and for the next several days, I was on edge, jittery. I had no appetite. My head ached. I thought, as I do too often, of the parents whose children weren't protected, who really were lost forever. Even recently, even nearby: a toddler who was stolen and raped and killed by her neighbor; an adolescent refugee who was persuaded and raped and killed by her neighbor; a teenager who didn't come home from school one afternoon, whose mother reported her missing to unbelieving police who refused to investigate, citing statistics that most young adults that age were not abductees but runaways. But she had been abducted, by a jealous rival and the boy they both liked, and then beaten with a baseball bat and left dead in the desert. Not thirty miles away, not a decade earlier, fourteen-year-old Elizabeth Smart was taken from her home in the middle of the night and held captive for nine months by a mad preacher rapist until an *America's Most Wanted* episode led to her recovery. Thus she was one of the "lucky few" who ever get home again. After the first forty-eight hours, the statistics say, the probability of finding a kidnapped child reduces to near zero.

That night, once the sun had set and the ghosts and goblins began their spooky actions, our trick-or-treating took twice as long as usual (or netted half the candy), because we paused at nearly every home to retell the story and to laugh nervously about how little Peter Pan and Captain Hook had already eaten their fill of the holiday booty. Everywhere we went, everybody knew. The feeling in the air was a big exhalation.

The next day, after classes, I showed up a few minutes late to a faculty seminar. David Allred was explaining to some of the others the principles of quantum entanglement, the double-slit experiment, and the indeterminacy of photons. I listened intently, fascinated, to his description of single quanta beamed through one or another slit and the resultant disappearance/omnipresence of the photon from/on both paths until it strikes a target in an interference pattern, having acted as a wave, interfering with itself. Until the energy resolves at the absorptive screen, it cannot be said to exist in either space definitively, or it "samples reality" along both paths, and not simply because our senses and instruments are too crude to find it. To put it another way, a particle exists in a range of possible locations until it is observed, and the observation fixes it in a particular place. Stranger yet, a photon or an electron can be split in two, with one part carried far away, and any observation or action on one half results in an immediate and predictable effect on the other. In this way, either information travels faster than the speed of light or the very notion of location in space loses meaning. The nature of the quantum universe is this very simultaneity and nonentity, untraceable and unknowable, affected by our observations and fundamentally beyond our ken, yes, but also fundamentally unknowable in moments of irresolution or inattention. With all we have learned, we have finally arrived at Sophocles: we confront our unbreachable ignorance.

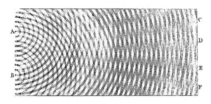

This, I sensed vaguely — I still sense only vaguely — was a metaphor, a gift, an unsought connection sent to nudge me: everywhere and nowhere, indeterminacy, separation and reunion. Before my sons had appeared in one particular place, I had felt viscerally that they were both everywhere and nowhere. In a way, the time of their disappearance and the fact that I could not observe them produced in my mind a superposition of possible locations, until by observing them, I fixed them in only one place, one of the only acceptable places they might have been.

It was also a familiarity, in an off-center way, reminding me of the hours and days I'd spent studying such counterintuitives as a physics major in college. Lately I'd been thinking that when the philosophers noted that our senses are untrustworthy, they did not mean that we are so fully deceived as to think a coin is a duck but that the metaphors we build our understanding on are flawed, easily dismantled when scrutinized. The orbital model of the atom, for example, is an explanation for certain behaviors, not a photograph of an atom.

34 *Entering and Breaking*

Thinking of light as a particle helps us understand reflection but not diffraction, for which we posit light as a wave. Experimenting to test our hypotheses, we learn that what we intuit about the way the world works is often wrong. We are born Aristotelians, certain that the heavy ball falls faster than the light ball. Though we observe falling objects all the time, only when we read of Galileo atop the Tower of Pisa do we rend the veil of our ignorance and pass through the rift into deeper understanding. We gather information on the scale of our senses; our imagination creates the stories that tie our observations together. Sometimes new knowledge can overpower our equivocal certainties, but not always. Exit exams of college students with one semester of physics reveal that we hew to our old notions long after they're disproved. We retain what feels comfortable even beyond the arrival of contradictory evidence.

More and more I am coming to believe (and to be comfortable with) the notion that everything is probabilities, only probabilities. But this did not occur to me when I was in the thick of things, sitting in lectures and studying for exams. Nor did it comfort us when I could not locate our sons.

A couple of weeks later, I was shuffling down concourse C in the Salt Lake City airport, when I saw the stately blonde figure of Elizabeth Smart, now grown, recently returned from a mission to France. She was walking toward me, sharply dressed in pressed gray skirt and red blouse under a wool overcoat. Nobody bothered her, though a few heads, like mine, quickly turned in her direction as she glided past. I was leaving my family for a few days, about to catch a flight to Spokane, where I would give a reading and meet with students at Whitworth College. She was coming home.

In Media Vita

In media vita. — No, life has not disappointed me! On the contrary, I find it truer, more desirable and mysterious every year, — ever since the day when the great liberator came to me, the idea that life could be an experiment of the seeker for knowledge — and not a duty, not a calamity, not a trickery! — And knowledge itself: let it be something else for others, for example, a bed to rest on, or the way to such a bed, or a diversion, or a form of leisure, — for me it is a world of dangers and victories in which heroic feelings, too, find places to dance and play. "Life as a means to knowledge" — with this principle in one's heart one can live not only boldly but even gaily and laugh gaily, too!

FRIEDRICH NIETZSCHE, The Gay Science

MARCH 26, 2006

Today is my birthday. We're gonna have a good time. Happy birthday to me!

My plan for the past long while has been to begin an essay today, my thirty-fifth birthday, because Dante did semilikewise — began the *Divine Comedy* on his thirty-fifth birthday — in the year 1300. Here is how he begins, according to Longfellow:

Midway upon the journey of our life
  I found myself within a forest dark,
  For the straightforward pathway had been lost.
Ah me! how hard a thing it is to say
  What was this forest savage, rough, and stern,
  Which in the very thought renews the fear.
So bitter is it, death is little more;
  But of the good to treat, which there I found,
  Speak will I of the other things I saw there.

Where Nietzsche seems utterly joyous in his revelation, Dante is rather gloomy, but each edge of feeling is at least authentic, if I may judge by my own experience. At more or less the midpoint of my own life, I find myself gainfully employed as a university professor, happily married to the girl of my dreams, contentedly harried by my brood of small children, meaningfully challenged by deep considerations sparked by confrontations with a wildly varied world that escapes my best efforts at apprehension. Most days, I awake refreshed and chipper, ready to sate my curiosity on the bits of experience and knowledge that come floating into my purview, glad to dance and play and laugh whether the path be straightforward or lost. But I'd be lying if I claimed that my life is always sun and giggles. Certainly there are times, too, when I edge close to despair and fear nigh unto death at the suffocatingly savage forest that seems to close in and close off the world of possibilities. Then I comprehend the Psalmist, whose poem gave us the notion of thirty-five as "midway upon the journey of our life":

We spend our years as a tale that is told. The days of our years are threescore years and ten; and if by reason of strength they be fourscore years, yet is their strength labour and sorrow; for it is soon cut off, and we fly away.

90:9–10

Solon, the Greek reformer, in counseling and reprimanding Croesus, sets the outer limit likewise:

In Media Vita 37

A long life gives one to witness much, and experience much oneself, that one would not choose. Seventy years I regard as the limit of the life of man. In these seventy years are contained ... twenty-six thousand two hundred and fifty [days], whereof not one but will produce events unlike the rest. Hence man is wholly accident.

HERODOTUS, *Histories* I

I am aware, of course, that current actuarial research gives me and my kin a bit longer on the earth, simply by virtue of our diet, environment, economic status, medical coverage, etc., so that the outer limit, according to the Guinness Book and confirmed by local and global authorities on such things, may be 122 years, which is how long Jeanne Calment lived in her native Arles, France, until her death in 1997. As you might expect, she was healthy and active long into her long life, learning fencing at 85, riding her bicycle until she was 100, living unassisted until 110. She smoked, too, until only two years before she died, ate a lot of chocolate, drank port wine regularly. But beyond those variables, says her biographer Jean-Marie Robine, was her seeming immunity to stress. Moreover, it seems to me that she had the soul of an essayist: "I dream, I think, I go over my life," she said. "I never get bored."

By way of contrast:

There is a sort of dead-alive, hackneyed people about, who are scarcely conscious of living. . . . They have no curiosity; they cannot give themselves over to random provocations; they do not take pleasure in the exercise of their faculties for its own sake; . . . they cannot be idle, their nature is not generous enough; and they pass those hours in a sort of coma, which are not dedicated to furious moiling in the gold-mill. . . . As if a man's soul were not too small to begin with, they have dwarfed and narrowed theirs by a life of all work and no play; until here they are at forty, with a listless attention, a mind vacant of all material of amusement, and not one thought to rub against another.

ROBERT LOUIS STEVENSON, "An Apology for Idlers"

Who can doubt that Stevenson's straw man is the antiessayist? It's certain from his rhetoric that he, and now I, and surely you, dear reader, want nothing to do with these living dead. We want vibrant, meditative, internal lives, the ability to find pleasure, even joy, no matter our circumstances. Boredom, thus considered, may be a cardinal sin or a shortcut to the grave.

But enough about generalities and strangers across the sea and centuries ago. I am thinking about my life, my prospects for sticking around, my character and my temperament, my successes and failures, my quest to find peace and contentment, which, I suspect, lie somewhere not only in the midst of life but in its middle. Dropping any inclination toward a saccharine nostalgia for my untroubled youth, when the future was bright and limitless before me, I am disposed to take it from here, to take stock, to take it to the streets, take it easy, take flight. (Just now, as I attempted to utilize the zeitgeist to supplement my brain to discover more idiomatic uses of "take," I found that the only work known by the Internet to contain the clichés "take stock," "take flight," and "take it from here" is *New Moon* by Stephenie Meyer.) But where was I? Ah, the middle.

It's an old notion: the golden mean, inspiration for Aristotle and Confucius and their followers, as well as for Montaigne, who gave us the essay, which may suggest, along with his many nods to the principle, that this form of writing is always and inherently interested in middles. Even so. Let me reveal my title:

One begins with the notion to write an essay from the middle of life, per Dante, per the Psalmist, with a yen for the exotic or the archaic lent by Latin, with a vague idea — the idea a curious Catholic would arrive at after listening to hymns and remnants in the Mass (supplemented by two years' study of Russian in college) — of Latin's grammatical declensions, a knowledge that *life* is *vita* and *middle* is *media*. From here it is only a few finger strokes to the originless Middle Ages say-ing, survived in hymns and a Mass, "media vita in morte sumus":

In the midst of life, we are amidst death

Or as Montaigne frames it,

Death mingles and fuses with our life throughout.

"Of Experience"

This, though it was not originally part of my unwritten essay as it germinated in my mind, is my theme.

WHAT LIFE EXPECTANCY CALCULATORS SAY ABOUT ME

While the Psalms are inaccurate for modern lifespans among citi-zens of the first world, they're not *too* inaccurate, especially if we take *limit* to mean *mean*. Nevertheless, given that I've already made it to thirty-five, I increase my life expectancy beyond the typical 75.29 for American males. All those people dying in their cribs or in children's hospitals or on city streets and highways have brought the averages down. Thirty-five is a good vantage point from which to see the world or to see what the world sees in me.

To get the most accurate estimate on my mortal duration, I must use the latest technology, which is to say that I sit idly in my chair, facing a screen, typing in answers to health and "lifestyle" questions, to find out that according to _____, I've got _____:

MoneyCentral.msn.com: eighty-one years
BBC: eighty-two years
Northwestern Mutual Life: eighty-four years
LivingTo100.com: eighty-five years
gosset.wharton.upenn.edu: eighty-seven years

Despite Jeanne Calment's example, I'm staying away from tobacco and alcohol, which seems to please these computers. Not only that, but I always wear a seatbelt, I exercise and play sports regularly, I eat fairly well, and I'm married, which can keep you alive longer, I assume, not only because you have companionship and a reason to live but because you have someone to find you soon after your heart attack or stroke. My wife, Karina, learns that she should live well into her nineties (between ninety-two and ninety-eight), a fact that troubles her greatly, she says, precisely because she doesn't want to live without me. Perhaps my favorite question, from nearly all the quizzes, is "Do you have a bowel movement at least once every 2 days?" I wish I could get extra credit, but that was not an option. In any case, I'm keeping it in mind. When one's bathroom routine involves a good book, one moves one's bowels as often as possible. Sometimes it's the only way to get a break from it all.

In any case, my frequent and regular forays may stave off or ameliorate the effect of genetics: my grandmother died of colon cancer when she was only fifty. Keeping things moving seems to reduce the probabilities of such cancer by decreasing contact and stagnation time. It makes sense.

Of course, nothing is certain. While you're guarding your back door, you may not see the frontal attacks. Montaigne, whose kidney stones led to his death at age fifty-nine, kept a regular schedule.

Both kings and philosophers go to stool, and ladies too; public lives are bound to ceremony; mine, that is obscure and private, enjoys all natural dispensation; . . . wherefore I shall say of this act of relieving nature, that it is desirable to refer it to certain prescribed and nocturnal hours, and compel one's self to this by custom, as I have done; but not to subject one's self, as I have done in my declining years, to a particular convenience of place and seat for that purpose, and make it troublesome by long sitting: and yet, in the fouler offices, is it not in some measure excusable to require more care and cleanliness? . . . Of all the actions of nature, I am the most impatient of being interrupted in that. I have seen many soldiers troubled with the unruliness of their bellies; whereas mine and I never fail of our punctual assignation, which is at leaping out of bed.

"Of Experience"

Me, too!

As for the life-expectancy calculators, I'm partial to my academic colleagues at the University of Pennsylvania, who give me until age eighty-seven. I'm hoping their experiment outmatches their web design. Or better yet, that their calculations are inspired by or mired in the present moment's medical technology. Decades of research before my demise may yet overcome our most common killers and extend my life even longer.

THINGS I'VE ONLY RECENTLY DISCOVERED

The way this has been going, you might think that my interest lies only in morbidity. Not true. I want to think of middles. I want, what's more, to perform this "experiment of the seeker for knowledge." Yes, I am somewhere in the middle of life. Yes, the years seem to fly past ever more speedily with each revolution about the sun. Yet there is more for me to learn to live gaily. Here are some of the things I've only recently discovered (usually through some mental effort or epiphany, though sometimes through questions and research):

That our months are named numerically: September (seventh), October (eighth), November (ninth), December (tenth); my daughter, age eight, has also realized this, beginning with "octo" for eight. I looked up the discrepancy (that October is our tenth month now) and found that the Roman (pre-Julian) calendar included also the months Quintilus and Sextus and that about sixty-one winter days were not assigned any month, which feels to me like an escape from the order imposed by systematizing men. I consider this a good thing.

That "wish[ing] they all could be California Girls" is not necessarily a slight to girls elsewhere but a desire that they could all be closer at hand.

That "play[ing] it cool by making [one's] world a little colder" is the action of "a fool."

42 *In Media Vita*

That "with a name like Smucker's" a company would have died out long ago if its products weren't so "good."

That "Twinkle, Twinkle, Little Star" has the same melody as the Alphabet song, which has the same melody as "Baa Baa Black Sheep."

The same can be said of "For He's a Jolly Good Fellow" and "The Bear Went over the Mountain" and of "Frere Jacques" and "Where Is Thumbkin?"

What's more, I've only recently verified by observation the origins of the clichés "like water off a duck's back" and "the blind leading the blind." The latter I witnessed one night while awaiting a bus on the corner of Minas and La Paz in Montevideo. Just across the street, near Palacio Peñarol, a sports arena, I saw two intrepid men, both in dark sunglasses, the first with an outstretched stick, the other with a hand on the first one's shoulder. They shuffled deliberately to the other side of La Paz, then into the imperceptible shadows.

ZENO'S PARADOX OF MOTION

I think the two blind men have stayed with me not only because their appearance gave an image to a linguistic expression but because I admired their pluck. They seemed to challenge the challenge of Jesus' parable:

> Can the blind lead the blind? shall they not both fall into the ditch?

Maybe not, I thought. Or *not yet.*

This may or may not speak to the strength of the human spirit, which may or may not take the time to analyze its moves and motivations but may at times become overwhelmed by the seeming impossibility of even the simplest tasks, but usually not. For Zeno, at least in theory, even motion was impossible, given that for an arrow to arrive at its target, it must first traverse half the distance to the bull's-eye, and before that, half the distance to halfway, and before that, half the distance to a quarter way, and so on, infinitely dividing distances in half, with no half too small to be again divided. Once you've divvied up your distance into infinite subdistances (while sitting in your chair,

In Media Vita 43

thinking), you get lost in the dark wood of thought, and it gets rather daunting to pull back that bowstring or to take that first step toward getting somewhere else.

When I was young, my father told me a kind of logical riddle, which now resides in the same brain file as Zeno's paradoxes. It went something like this: A prisoner is brought before the king. The king tells him, "You will be executed within one week's time, but you will not know the day." The prisoner, fretful, sent once more to his cell, sets his mind racing to discover a way to live. He realizes, soon enough, that if he can know the day of his execution, the king's word will be nullified, and he will be set free (for this king inhabits the puzzle world; his actions advance the plot). He keeps himself awake at all hours, straining to hear the conversations of his guards. He sends for the doctor, hoping the man will take pity on him. He promises the slop boy riches he doesn't have to give. Nothing works. The guards, the medic, the slop boy seem to know nothing, in any case. But he has made it to the end of Saturday, and he is still alive. Suddenly he has this revelation:

The king cannot kill him on Friday, because then all the other days will have passed and he will know the day of his execution. He cannot kill him on Thursday, either, because, excepting Friday, he would know that Thursday is the only option. Moving backward through the week, then, Wednesday is out because both Friday and Thursday must be. Tuesday is exempt for the same reason. Monday, too. And Sunday, well, you don't execute people on the Sabbath, do you? Plus, once you've discounted all the subsequent days, it's too obvious that the execution would have to happen on Sunday, so then he'd know.

The prisoner convinces his guards to bring him once more before the king, who, confusedly impressed by the prisoner's logic, sets him free, sending him along his way with riches more than the prisoner had promised to the slop boy. The end. Oh, also, the prisoner was a nice guy, wrongly imprisoned, and so on.

The fun thing about this logic puzzle is that it *seems* to work about as much as it *seems* not to. The no-Friday realization is acceptable enough and maybe even Thursday, too, which makes me believe that the regression through the week makes sense, but once I arrive at Saturday night again and look forward, I'm no longer convinced that I *know* the day of execution must be today. In fact, wouldn't it be kind of funny if the king said, "That's very clever," and then winked at the executioner standing just behind the prisoner, and the executioner took a running sidearm swing with his ax and took the prisoner's head right off? "Betcha didn't know that was gonna happen today!"

Obviously, the riddle depends on the time frame. Had the king said that he'd execute the prisoner "sometime," there'd be no last day from which to discard days based on the promise that the prisoner wouldn't know the day. So does knowing that I've got an outer limit of eighty-seven years affect my existence of today? Of course, I have no promise (from God?) that I won't know the day, nor, if I had such a promise, could I rightly expect to escape death. How many of us know the day of our demise? There's a certain comfort in sensing the approach of death: one can set one's affairs in order, say one's goodbyes, make peace with God and with fellows. Still, the acceptable death I envision happens only late in life, far beyond where I am now.

> And those who keep themselves going with the thought that some span of life or other which they call "natural" promises them a few years more could only do so provided that there was some ordinance exempting them personally from those innumerable accidents (which each one of us comes up against and is subject to by nature) which can rupture the course of life.
>
> MONTAIGNE, "Of the Length of Life"

There are days when the perils of life rise up in my imagination to give me pause before I step out my door in the morning. I could be in a car accident. I could be struck by falling construction debris. I could have a heart attack, an aneurism. I could be shot or stabbed. I could fall down the long flight of stairs I take to my weight lifting and basketball. I could contract a fatal disease. The belligerent, unrepentant plagiarist I nudged on his way to expulsion could show up at my office door with rage in his heart. I could be sliced in two by a detached helicopter blade. I could be conked on the head by a turtle dropped from high above by an eagle. For me, "natural" death is a long way off, down a path strewn with obstacles and traps. The newspaper and television bring me stories of other kinds of death, at other times, as do the obituaries, which my wife peruses religiously and leaves open on the kitchen table, reminding me that there is no age that is safe, no mile marker along this highway that does not afford an exit. So I finish my cereal, slip on the shoes I left last night at the front door, pull on my coat, and go outside.

WHAT THE HOROSCOPE SAYS ABOUT ME

The fact is I cannot know, at this point, with relative good health and no ominous sense or bad dreams, what might befall me. I don't put much stock in mystical prognostications, especially the kind published daily in the newspaper by strangers for everyone born in a certain range of dates, no matter the year. That first logical step trips me up: how could my birth date determine my fate? (Immediately, I begin to think of ways in which my birth *year*, at least, in general or relative ways, has determined my clothing, my haircut, my musical taste, etc.) I appreciate the sometimes uncanny coincidences people find within the horoscope, and I can believe that some folks find direction or cosmic comfort in the advice. If the advice is good, it's good no matter when you were born, so that's fine. But I've never believed that such things held a power beyond what any sensible human being could muster. You will forgive me this skepticism, I pray. The beliefs I do hold must certainly seem untenable to certain others.

> The easy confidence with which I know another man's religion is folly teaches me to suspect that my own is also.
>
> MARK TWAIN, note in Conway's *Sacred Anthology*

When I was younger, I had a maroon-and-gold bookmark with an Aries poem below a golden ram. Though I've forgotten most of it now, I remember the last lines: "The first to begin, the last to succeed." I may have believed, for a time, that this ditty described me, but it doesn't. Not at all. I'm also curious about this recent bit of advice I found, which tells Aries, "Your usual modus operandi is 'get things done. NOW.'" While this is not a direct contradiction (one could intend to get things done quickly, begin immediately, and fail), it damages the credibility of the enterprise.

I'm much more inclined to trust the rhetoric of a seasoned essayist, whose approach is less finger-pointing and more personal. Alexander Smith says,

> You have lived for more than half your natural term; and you know the road which lies before you is very different from that which lies behind.

"An Essay on an Old Subject"

"Very different," while linguistically noncommittal (it could mean that you've now got the money to buy that boat), obviously equals "much worse." And this from a man who had lived half his life by age eighteen. Despite the evidence, I'm inclined to protest: not necessarily, friend! But the sages gather to chant a similar message from before and beyond in different tones:

> After thirty, a man wakes up sad every morning excepting perhaps five or six until the day of his death.

RALPH WALDO EMERSON, journal, August 1, 1835

> Once I used to mark the burdensome and gloomy days as extraordinary. Those are now my ordinary ones; the extraordinary are the fine serene ones.

MONTAIGNE, "On Some Verses of Virgil"

My own life experience is that when I thought I had things sorted and I was in control, something happened that completely undid everything I had wanted to do. And so it goes on. The illusion that I had some control over my life went up to about my thirty-fifth birthday. Then it stopped. Now I'm out of control.

W. G. SEBALD, "Interview with Joseph Cuomo"

I've arranged these quotes in order of increasing appeal, partly by their rhetorical flavor (Smith directs himself to me personally, and I say, *not I*; Emerson makes a general statement applicable to all; Montaigne and Sebald both focus on themselves), partly by the palatability of their claims (Emerson moves the hump back five years and allows a maximum of six happy awakenings thenceforth; Montaigne doesn't delimit the fine, serene days, though they're still extraordinary; Sebald sees his later lack of control as revelation or resignation). I'm most sympathetic with Sebald, probably because the others scare me, though that doesn't stop me from trying to control my life, and nothing in what he said indicates that he had either. Part of my resistance to the seeming pessimism evident in the others is my belief that essays can make people happy and that they're perpetrated by optimists. On the balance, this is probably yet true for individual essayists and for essayists as a group. And perhaps that phrase I've carelessly tossed in is significant: "on the balance." An essayist seeks the golden mean.

Solon, who belongs to those old days, nevertheless limits the extreme duration of life to seventy years. Shall I, who in all matters have so worshiped that *golden mean* of the past, and have taken the moderate measure as the most perfect, aspire to an immoderate and prodigious old age?

MONTAIGNE, "Of Experience"

Montaigne made it to fifty-nine, felled by kidney stones, as we've discussed, in the middle of a Mass performed in his room. He seems to have seen it coming. Emerson held on until seventy-eight, through years of memory loss, then compounded a cold with a walk in the rain, contracted pneumonia, and died. Sebald was only fifty-seven when he had a heart attack while driving, lost control of his car, and parted from this life. Alexander Smith spent his last years in deep melancholy. Unable to rest his weary mind and body, he eventually succumbed to typhoid fever on January 5, 1867, five days after his thirty-sixth birthday.

We've made it back to a consideration of longevity, with barely a mention of the horoscope. I'll remedy that now. With all the possibilities, I decided to consult the newspaper for March 26, 2006, the day I began this essay, the day I turned thirty-five. I sought the "If You Were Born on This Date" horoscope, on the premise that it would be more specific, although I notice that several phrases are stock. No matter, let's see what's in store:

> You'll express your ideas with confidence as you come to value your personal views above all else. Your determined efforts to build financial stability will pay off over the next three months, and by the end of the year, you'll be able to splurge on a trip or purchase that has always seemed beyond your reach. Insist on more balance between work and play, as you have a tendency to overdo one or the other. . . . You can increase your capabilities at work by gathering information on the internet or in relevant publications. . . . Your lucky months are May and January.

Not bad, I suppose. As an essayist, I do value my personal views, though I try to express my ideas with lively trepidation, as befits a seeker for knowledge. I've not yet established any kind of financial stability, nor are my efforts determined. Yet I did purchase a Fender Geddy Lee–model jazz bass at a Black Friday sale, so perhaps that's my splurge. I think my work and play are actually in a decent balance. I do tend to use the Internet for work (as evidenced). I'm more interested in my lackey moths than in my lucky months (though I did wed my true love long ago in the merry, merry month of May). Ultimately, I find the advice listed here generic and undaring, which may be the salient feature of newspaper articles in general.

Economically speaking, if you've got your airfare and hotel covered, you would do well to get your palm read in Mexico City — over Redondo Beach, California, for instance. So I am content that the young woman I awoke one Saturday morning on Airline Highway was

unwilling to let me record our conversation. It would interfere with the cosmic vibrations, she said. Okay, lady, I'll keep my twenty bucks. A month or so later, I avoided the question of permission altogether by having my friend Steve hunch nearby with a digital recorder in his shirt pocket.

This is what Briston, sitting under a blue tarp on a diagonal path through the middle of Mexico City's Parque Alameda, told me for about two bucks:

> The life you have is a long one, but any kind of strange symptom in your organism, or pain, you should get checked with a doctor. There's a small operation they can do for you, but you can avoid it. Here we have the line of success or triumph. It tells us of an economic stability, but right now there's a situation; you'll have to wait for your plans to improve to achieve everything you want. On this side, we see that sometimes differences could present themselves between you and your family, because there have been problems in the past that have caused you to leave for a while. Here, the lines represent that you'll speak to a person or have business transaction, something that will mark your destiny or give you a new work opportunity.

> Now ... you were born to speak of God, to belong to a congregation that speaks of God, because that's your destiny. And in your hands you carry a gift of healing ...

While encouraged by the promise of a long life, I get mired in the easy generalities of avoidable health problems and delayed economic stability. I do belong to the Church of Jesus Christ of Latter-day Saints, as does Steve. And we had both served missions to Spanish-speaking countries; our facility with the language and interest in literature led to our reason for being in Mexico: to meet Eduardo Milán, a poet we'd been translating into English.

The reading gets more interesting from there, with a person who's trying to hurt me but can't because of a "block" on my palm; there's news of a family sickness, a reencounter with a long-lost friend, the possibility of a stable romance with my wife as long as we talk about it, a threat of solitude if not. All of these seem unspecific, not all true, but otherwise easy to place in the inevitable events of any life. Briston seems to have been using context clues: that I take a lot of trips; that I will take a trip to a place with water; again with business plans that can be "favorable." Sure. Not long after this, Karina and I went to Iguazú Falls to celebrate our ten-year anniversary. I remember no business conversations there, though we did discuss our marriage, and things seemed stable and romantic. Playing the odds, Briston predicted for me one . . . no, *two* children, or maybe two sons (the Spanish *hijos* leaves ambiguous the question of gender, ultimately, because the masculine noun is grammatically dominant), but only after some "block." Because I already had four children, I took this prediction with a knowing smile. But later I revisited it: this was soon after Karina had miscarried. What's more, I can tell you through the telescope of time that eventually two more sons *would* come, in relatively close succession.

Perhaps more bizarre was the palm reader's revelation that I have a "mental energy" manifest in strange dreams and visions, as if my imaginings were real. This I should "try to decipher," and I have: my sleeping dreams slip almost always and almost entirely into oblivion, but here I am writing, mediating imagination and reality, or reality through imagination to a textual reality, deciphering experience. Briston also found palmic evidence that it was raining when I was born, cold and thundering (my mother says she can't remember), so I should wield the "lightning stone" for "good luck" and "positive vibes" in my destiny. This revisitation passed right through my mind when it was spoken, but now, listening to the recording, I am ineluctably brought to César Vallejo:

Me moriré en París con aguacero,
un día del cual tengo ya el recuerdo.
Me moriré en París — y no me corro —
tal vez un jueves, como es hoy, de otoño.

I will die in Paris, under clouds and rain,
on a distant day I've already seen.
I will die in Paris — I won't run away —
in autumn, a Thursday, like today.

Briston's final words, before small talk and fixing a price, were "Also, there could be a situation of conflict . . ." Exactly here, the only loud truck of the afternoon passes, smothering the last warning under a blue tarp of grumbling reverberation.

MEDIA VIA

I can imagine that a reader will see my incessant returns to the subject of mortality and decide that this is trickery or artifice: the writer constructing a subcutaneous theme to trump his stated objectives. But as I write, I am repeatedly surprised. I laugh. Where did that Vallejo poem come from? Only from the poetic notion that it was raining when I was born, just as Vallejo predicted rain when he died (my research tells me that he died at age forty-six on Good Friday in early spring, just as the Fascists conquered the Republicans in his beloved Spain; he did die in Paris; I've not discovered a weather report). So, another recalibration: an exhortation to avoid extremes, to find contentment in contemplation of the middles of life, within my consideration of the middle of life, a consideration of the middle itself?

Popular opinion is wrong: it is much easier to go along the sides, where the outer edge serves as a limit and a guide, than by the middle way, wide and open, and to go by art than by nature; but it is also much less noble and less commendable.

MONTAIGNE, "Of Experience"

52 *In Media Vita*

Montaigne assumes a hallway, it seems, rather than a mountainside path, but even in the latter case, there is one solid edge to hold to, even if the other edge may crumble beneath the weight of a wayward step and send you tumbling to a painful death or if, metaphorically, the fall may lead to despair or madness. His writing, and by extension *essay writing* in general (What Would Michel Do?), is ever a quest for the middle, a constitutional aversion to the extremes of opinion and living, some utopic wending through life failing at finding the ideal contentment of excellence through mediocrity. My friend has said it better than I am able:

> One of an essayist's aims is self-analysis sometimes, but *via* writing — that is, through *relatively* limited but continuous discursive forays, inquiries into areas of one's existence, unified by style. Style? By the discovery of a form, *via* discipline, *this* particular discipline of *the essay*, toward a kind of "middle" position, ground, stance, voice, attitude, state of being and consciousness and awareness. This middle isn't a persona, front, or façade — it's genuine and hard earned and the truth.
>
> I periodically swelter and welter (perhaps abjectly, with all lines-of-differentiation between self and external world dissolved, un-differentiated?), burn for, again, the middle, not *a* middle. I'm moderately flexible, adaptable, but *a* middle would be too relative. If I am only an assortment of specific centers, or enthusiasms — and perhaps I am — or loves, or interests, or curiosities, occasional angers, passions, intensities both bad and good, perhaps, but *the* middle that is appropriate for me, personally — then I am lost beyond hope.
>
> michael danko, "Whistling in the Dark"

When I grade my undergraduate students' essays, I find myself again and again controverting their assumptions, arguing with them, writing in the margins the exceptions to their assertions. When I review the copies of my own early essays with my professor's comments, I find the same quarrel happening, in questions and exclamations: "Really?" "Are you sure?" "Not necessarily!" I think what we're doing is humbling one another, cutting short unfounded bold pronouncements, tempering hawkish or mawkish judgments, reminding each other of the inherent splendor in this complex world, recognizing that although each individual has an important story and a right to opine, we are all simply middling, middlebrow, muddling meddlers meandering through a world sometimes beautiful, sometimes hostile, usually better with companionship and contemplation.

WHAT THE HANDWRITING ANALYST SAYS ABOUT ME

Which is essentially the motivation behind not only essaying but behind all this otherworldly analysis in the search for self: something to think about and someone to share it with. I had heard of the wonders of handwriting analysis, both the comparative, forensic kind and the mystical, prognosticative. I have handwriting that I would describe, insensitively, as schizophrenic (not the writing *of* a schizophrenic but writing that is itself Jeckyll-and-Hydden). At times, it seems to me quite elegant or handsome or interesting, in a sloppy kind of way. At other times, it becomes verifiably ugly. Always it is small. But what might this reveal about my character? Like A. A. Milne, I thought I'd give it a whirl.

A woman, who had studied what she called the science of calligraphy, once offered to tell my character from my handwriting. I prepared a special sample for her; it was full of sentences like "To be good is to be happy," "Faith is the lode-star of life," "We should always be kind to animals," and so on. I wanted her to do her best. She gave the morning to it,

54 *In Media Vita*

and told me at lunch that I was "synthetic." . . . I begged her to tell me more, for I had thought that every letter would reveal a secret, but all she would add was "and not analytic." . . . I had no idea what it meant.

And how do you think she had deduced my syntheticness? Simply from the fact that, to save time, I join some of my words together. That isn't being synthetic, it is being in a hurry. What she should have said was, "You are a busy man; your life is one constant whirl; and probably you are of excellent moral character and kind to animals." Then one would feel that one did not write in vain.

A. A. MILNE, "The Pleasure of Writing"

After a failed (or interminably delayed) attempt that revealed only that I was "intelligent and organized," a friend referred me to her friend, who struggled a bit with my customary print (cursive is easier, she said) but ultimately discerned that I am evasive and deceptive, private ("though outwardly he presents himself as a personality who gets attention easily"), practical and methodical, self-sufficient, emotionally restrained, self-motivated and ambitious, aggressively firm in my resolve, and averse to change.

Any alteration, on this earth of mine, in diet or in lodging, puzzles and discomposes me.

CHARLES LAMB, "New Year's Eve"

Overall, I'm pleased with the accuracy of the interpretation, though of course I deny the charges of evasion and deception. It's true that I am generally firmly resolved, outwardly unemotional, ambitiously methodical, and so on. What's worse, I often feel that this is the only way to be, and others' sloppiness or impracticality distress me more than change does. (I am thinking of you, children of mine!) More deeply than I know my foolish consistencies, I know "changes aren't permanent, but change is." At some level, all is change.

WHAT MY COWORKERS AT THE ALFRED DUNNER WAREHOUSE IN PARSIPPANY, NEW JERSEY, SAY ABOUT ME

During my wandering time, after I served a mission and before I entered graduate school, I worked for a season at a warehouse, shuffling women's clothes from one end to the other, losing at dominoes to my Puerto Rican coworkers during breaks as the Jamaicans slipped melodiously into their pidgin, which beat my ability to comprehend. When I explained that I would be returning to school soon to study English, one of the foremen let out a long, three-syllable "No-o-ohhh" and a lecture: "You have the brains, man! You have to become a doctor and help people!" He was stuck at Alfred Dunner, but I had a chance. If he had half the brains I had, he'd learn the medical arts and save people's lives.

I did become a doctor, of course. (Insert here your favorite joke about the [f]utility of a PhD.) But like Roland Barthes, "I must admit that I have produced only essays." Or with William Hazlitt, I feel to cry out,

> What have I been doing all my life? Have I been idle, or have I nothing to show for all my labour and pains? Or have I passed my time in pouring words like water into empty sieves, rolling a stone up a hill and then down again, . . . What abortions are these Essays! What errors, what ill-pieced transitions, what crooked reasons, what lame conclusions! How little is made out, and that little how ill! Yet they are the best I can do. I endeavour to recollect all I have ever observed or thought upon a subject, and to express it as nearly as I can.
>
> "The Indian Jugglers"

The thing is, I'm not quite convinced that essays "are the best I can do." Maybe they're not even "the best I do." I love my wife and children; I try to support her and to raise them well; I teach young people (my children and yours) not to be so self-centered and knuckleheaded; I give my time, money, and efforts in small ways

56 *In Media Vita*

to serve my fellow beings. I do all of this insufficiently, sometimes halfheartedly, rarely boldly. And if Hazlitt was serious here, lamenting that he'd never learned to juggle or perhaps that painting was only a hobby for him or that his biography of Napoleon had bankrupted his publisher, then there is a part of me that thinks, "I probably *could* have become a doctor, the kind who heals people with his hands." I think I have the brains for it, and probably the self-discipline. (I could also, I believe, be a better thief than the thieves you hear about, but that is a subject for another essay.) And as much as I love essays and believe them to be salubrious for writer and reader alike, I cannot, in my more reflexive moments, believe them to be more important than the proverbial cure for cancer. I've lost people I love to that festering crab.

> If I could be sure of doing with my books as much as my father did for the sick.
>
> MARCEL PROUST, comment to his maid, Celeste

Still, whether or not it's truly too late, I don't intend to change my life so drastically. I'm mostly happy where I am, a place I believe to be somewhere in the middle of it all, looking out, contemplating the world of dangers and victories. Even on my bad days, when I can't find a purpose or when I feel I've wasted my time, I can recall the great teaching of Montaigne:

> We are great fools. "He has spent his life in idleness," we say; "I have done nothing today." What, have you not lived? That is not only the fundamental but the most illustrious of your occupations.... Have you been able to think out and manage your own life? You have done the greatest task of all.... To compose our character is our duty, not to compose books, and to win, not battles and provinces, but order and tranquillity in our conduct. Our great and glorious masterpiece is to live appropriately.
>
> "Of Experience"

In Media Vita 57

Which This argument sounds suspiciously like the platitudinal consolations your friends offer when you're down on yourself, wondering what your purpose is and where the time has gone. But maybe this is literature: to say what has already been said, or will be said long after, in words (even translated words) that sing.

WHAT THE MYERS BRIGGS PERSONALITY TEST SAYS ABOUT ME

When I dance, I dance.

MONTAIGNE, "Of Experience"

I shall keep dancing. When I seek insight from the Myers-Briggs Type Indicator, answering personal questions about my punctuality, my objectivity, and my perception of humankind's destiny, I find that I fit in the "rationals" quadrant (the other three are "guardians," "idealists," and "artisans") under the one-in-sixteen title of "mastermind." Because I have always enjoyed that secret-code guessing game (enough to create a Fortran version in my numerical methods class in college), this appellation is appealing to me. In acronymic terms, this means that I am an INTJ, which means that my preferences are for

Introversion (over Extroversion)
iNtuition (over Sensing)
Thinking (over Feeling)
Judging (over Perceiving)

From Dr. David Keirsey's website, I learn that masterminds are the least common personality type, accounting for only about one in one hundred people, which makes the sexadecant doubly pleasing. If we're all torn between a desire for belonging and a desire for uniqueness, introverts like myself lean harder on the uniqueness side, even while recognizing the value of the middle road. I am not surprised to see the humorously bushy mustache of Friedrich Nietzsche gracing the gallery of famous masterminds from history at the top of the page, along with other folks I respect and have wanted to emulate: Isaac

Newton, Niels Bohr, Stephen Hawking, all of whom are physicists. This recognition, too, massages my ego: I thought I was a physicist once, but I left that behind to become an essayist. I consider this a kind of moral evolution, or a sort of living transmigration from a slightly lower form to a higher. Given my nearly balanced "thinking/feeling" score and my barely dominant judging over perceiving, I fantasize that I am built to be an essayist and that (leaving behind my recent doubts for a moment) "essayist" is the highest calling one can attain.

Yet I also find — in answering so many questions about my leisure habits, my imagination, and my mind and heart preferences — that my natural inclination, or at least my regular practice, may be at odds with the ideals of the essay, which, since Montaigne and especially since the British periodical essayists in the eighteenth and nineteenth centuries, has privileged leisure, idleness, fancy, speculation, etc. So maybe I'm catching up to the bewildered people who, upon first meeting me, find an inherent contradiction in my path from physicist to essayist, bachelor's degree in the former, doctorate in the latter. What I mean is, Who has the time to be so damned leisurely nowadays? I do my best (with no Blackberry, no cyborg earpiece, a cell phone that functions only as a walkie-talkie between Karina and me), but with five children, a dog, a mortgage, a job, two cars, a half acre, deadlines, expectations, inefficiencies, pressures . . . The test asks, "Is it worse to have your head in the clouds or to be in a rut?" Well, *du-u-uh!* And yet I am more often in a rut.

We are all in the gutter, but some of us are looking at the stars.

OSCAR WILDE, *Lady Windermere's Fan*

It's no wonder that masterminds are often found in jobs requiring technical proficiency and intellectual problem solving. They are scientists and engineers, geneticists and medical researchers, business analysts and strategic planners, according to Dr. Keirsey. Also, university professors, which is where I fit in. Masterminds may also be artists, which I'm going to take as confirmation of my unpaid profession. Why not? There have never been enough essayists in the world to constitute a "representative sample." Representative of what? Each essayist is his own star in a galaxy far, far away. In any case, I might discover more about myself and my quest within the broader descriptors scattered here and there across the vast Internet:

☑ Do I understand complex operations involving many steps?
☑ Do I prefer not to lead, though I am able?
☑ Am I a "thoroughgoing pragmatist"?
☑ Does inefficiency (human and material) drive me nuts?
☑ Do I resist traditional rules and authority?
☑ Am I allergic to slogans and catchwords?
☑ Do I trust my own mind above other sources?
☑ Do I work fanatically in pursuit of my goals?
☑ Am I stimulated by this work?
☐ Do I focus my criticism on the positive instead of the negative?
☑ Do I make decisions firmly, after sufficient research?
☑ Am I strong willed and self-confident?

Like everything else in this essay, personality theories abound and conflict, filling library shelves and days' worth of web surfing, potentially. And the grain of salt I take with the largely validating and praiseworthy character traits I find here is, yeah, but couldn't this describe anybody? What say ye, dear reader? Where do you find yourself in the list above? Or what do the other types say? Maybe I can fit my personality into any or many of the sixteen. At random, I chose "champion" and found that maybe that's not me: Great passion for novelty? Enthusiasm for telling everyone about experiences? Nah. But keen observation and writing toward understanding? Okay, that's me. How about the "inspector"? High sociability? Nope. Ignorance of latest fashions? Yep. Zealousness for rules and institutions? Here I am torn: I *used* to feel this way, but not anymore. This evidence that one can change one's inclinations would seem to undermine the notion of fixed types, yet I'm not certain that any of these descriptors claims to *determine* thoughts, feelings, actions.

In any case, underneath all this seeking for belonging or affirmation (a kind of "test for echo," a shout out into the void), I think that what I really believe is that no personality test, no reading of my physiology

60 *In Media Vita*

or graphology or astrology can contain me, because I am unique, mi generis, neverbeforeseen in this world.

You, too!

Right?

I mean, these indicators and prognosticators can only be marginally useful, or they're as useful as we allow them to be. We find comfort or irritation; we conform or resist; we choose to define ourselves by the definable characteristics, or we defy the characteristic definables. The same might be said of the activities we engage in or the television shows we watch, the websites we browse or the essays we read. If at a party I am happier to talk with a small group of friends rather than meet new people, if I am rarely late for appointments unless I'm traveling with my wife and children, if I do not relish adventure yet enjoy reading and camping and walking unknown streets and woods — these facts can only approximate a life that is not all adventures and appointments and parties. And perhaps I might determine that my punctuality is less important than my peace of mind, or I might skydive or bungee jump one of these days (I won't).

I double back again, to see these tests more compassionately: they are like essays, or *we* are like essays, making stabs at understanding a self or a world that is inherently inscrutable, yet this is the best we can do. And when we relinquish the need for completeness or objectivity, we find ourselves awash in the joy of bewildered discoveries, which may sum to some knowledge but never to omniscience. So let's try one more.

WHAT THE TAROT CARD READER SAYS ABOUT ME

Economically speaking, if you've got your airfare covered and you're staying with relatives, you would do well to get your tarot card reading done in Montevideo, in the extra bedroom of a divorcée with high school–aged daughters who does, in addition to her tarot, Reiki, deep massage, color therapy, and anything else currently popular among "New Age" folks, as she told me candidly after she'd gotten to know me a bit. She confines her tarot ads to the *Util Publicidad* weekly, while her Reiki and so forth go in *Colón Hoy*, which, she presumes, is read by more respectable people who want nothing to do with questionable occult practices (her words in my translation).

As with Briston in Mexico, I planned to record my reading on an old iPod hooked into an aftermarket microphone. As I stood outside Jacqueline's apartment building, I hit Record Now on the device and then slipped it into my voluminous cargo pocket before I knocked on the door. During the interview, as she shuffled two worn decks — one large, one small — and laid out trios of cards in rapid succession, with or without comment, I sometimes fiddled with the bunching of my shorts and the location of the iPod to keep it open to the air. Jacqueline was talkative, running through a brief life history and explanation of her color theory books, so I ended up staying for over an hour. By the time I left, my brain was a bit frazzled, and I didn't quite remember everything she'd said, only that she repeated herself often, as if trying to home in on some vague recognizable correct prediction based on my responses to her questions or my expressions to her statements. Relieved, I walked away briskly, and once I was out of sight, I pulled out the iPod, intending to stop the recording. This was when I realized that the thing hadn't recorded at all.

When I got back to my in-laws' home, my brother-in-law Fernando, who knew Jacqueline because her apartment is near his best friend Willy's, said that this was proof of the power of Jacqueline's voodoo. So I quickly sat down with Karina and told her everything I remembered, in condensed form, without redundancies. This is yet another condensation of what I remembered:

I was headed for a falling out, perhaps with my wife, but we could overcome our difficulties.

I was about to embark on a big journey, which might be the cause of my problems because Karina didn't want to go. Did she? Eh? Right?

The baby's whole life would be blessed; we wouldn't have to worry about him. But his sister Sara would give us trouble.

It takes two to tango. If she wants to argue, just keep your mouth shut. Don't fight back; let her vent.

I was on the verge of a great change, perhaps good, perhaps bad; it depends on how I take it.

I was headed for economic improvement, likely because my
   book would do well. *El Mago* meant that I had put my magic
   into it. *El Diablo* meant that it would find material success. *El
   Mundo* meant that it would find its way into many hands.
I would soon sign a contract with an older person, and this
   would bring great benefit.
I should listen to the advice of an older man who loves me
   (perhaps my father).

I never explained to Jacqueline that I was doing skeptical research
for an essay, and she kept fishing for the source of my anguish. I was
forthright in all my answers, but not expansive, so she knew I was up
to something, but she couldn't ferret it out. Like Briston, she gathered
from my accent that I was a traveler, so her revelations often pitted
my rambling against the stability I must be seeking. I'm guessing she's
used to seeing people only when they're troubled, so she returned
often to my reasons for consulting the tarot. How could I tell her
that my principal interest came from Rush's "Peaceable Kingdom,"
an intelligent and veiled 9/11 song that plays tarotic metaphor against
Quaker Edward Hicks's postapocalyptic paintings? The kicker was
when I asked her to tell me when I'd die.

"Why are you so worried?" she asked, nearly taking my hands in hers.

"I'm not worried," I countered.

She threw the big cards, which were primed to reveal
events close at hand. The first card was *La Muerte*.

I laughed. When she said, "No, no, no, *La Muerte*
doesn't always mean *death*," I laughed again. When she
said, "You will live well past your seventies," I breathed
a sigh of relief, just to humor her. When I returned
home to find Karina and Graciela chatting, Fernando
upstairs playing video games, my mother- and father-
in-law preparing a stew for the evening's supper, my
children and niece and nephews lying on the floor or
bouncing toy cars off the walls, I was witnessing a rare

In Media Vita 63

and beautiful convergence: the Cabreras and their progeny congregated from far away not only for exceptional events but for the mundanities of coexistence, even if briefly. This was the fulfillment of their desire: to gather their children and grandchildren in their home, to pass the days without adventure or fanfare, in tranquility and order. There were conversations and arguments, deep questions and petty grievances, gentle shouts over the voluminous children's movie playing on the west wall, an abundance of herbs emanating from the kitchen to the north; and as I stood amid the hubbub, I thought, as I have often thought when in Uruguay, nestled among silent streets under swaying trees, that I had found contentment.

I did not consider, then, that the family was incomplete, that Bernardo was gone forever.

PLENA VITA

On the way home on the 174, as we passed the Cementerio del Norte's southeast corner, where the Army Pantheon stands shining dully in the mist, my father-in-law said softly, "There's my son," half to me, half to himself, or to the air, or to God. Sometime later, the next minute or next year, I imagined it translated instead, "Behold my son." I knew. I had been there before. I said, "I know." Then we traveled on in silence until he said, "Just imagine the millions of dead." The bus stopped, people got off, people got on, a woman embraced a bouquet of flowers, children played in the fields, an old man sat against the cemetery wall holding his maté, we traveled on in silence.

My father-in-law is home today, I imagine, or chatting with his friends at the central market, haggling over vegetable prices, loading up his bags of garlic, counting out worn pesos with worn hands, buying a ticket north; and I am sitting, thinking, remembering . . . But aren't we also still on that bus, because I have written it?

> Children their kites a-flying,
> Grandsires that nod by the wall,
> Mothers soft lullabies sighing,
> And the dead, under all!

WILLA CATHER, "In Media Vita"

When I have the chance to write, most of my time is not spent writing, because I am collecting and piecing together, not drawing entirely from my previous experience. This is a serendipitous quest, moving from one thing to another in a pattern reminiscent of thought, wanting to come together to become something meaningful. It is a joy to sit down to write when the children are off to bed and my wife is away at work or in the early hours before even the dog has the energy or motivation to follow me downstairs. Then I can concentrate enough to string words and ideas together.

In the course of these explorations, I believe I have found the answer to a question I had forgotten almost entirely, a question a friend asked me one-third of my lifetime ago. We were eating at the only Chinese restaurant in Uruguay, his treat, discussing the deep things that friends discuss, things that seem new, neverbeforethoughtof, to the parties at the table, though they seem drivel and dreck to an eavesdropper (there were none, I assume, that day in Montevideo, since we were speaking English; everyone else, Spanish). All of this is lost or hidden from my mind but the one question he asked that I couldn't answer: *What would you have written on your headstone?* I told him instead what Robert Baden Powell had engraved on his: the circle with the dot in the middle, the Scout trail sign for "I have gone home." I was worried then about originality, so I wouldn't copy Powell, but I wanted a similar punch of meaning in so little. Perhaps I wanted a bit of an enigma, a riddle for the living to puzzle out. Now I am not so much obsessed with originality. Perhaps I don't believe in it anymore. After all, my father proposed to my mother singing the Beatles' "When I'm Sixty-Four." When Sir Paul reached that stately age, Linda had died years before; he was divorcing from his second wife. I had expected some festivities, a television special or some such. But there was nothing. When my father reached the milestone, his children and grandchildren gathered at my home from far away and, playing piano, guitar, bass, and drums along with a clarinet recording, sang him a slight variation of the Beatles song. By sixty-four his own father had lost his mind to Alzheimer's. So I don't mind borrowing a clever inversion, a phrase used by composer Robert Simpson or poet Steven Curtis Lance, a phrase that has already adorned the death notices of theologian Heiko Augustinos Oberman, who in turn borrowed from Martin Luther:

> If you listen to the Law, it will tell you: "In the midst of life we are surrounded by death," as we have sung for ages. But the Gospel and our faith have changed this song and now we sing: "In the midst of death we are surrounded by life!"
>
> MEDIA MORTE IN VITA SUMUS

MARCH 25, 2007

As I sat atop a hill overlooking Utah Lake and the sprawl between, my children tumbled down wrapped in a blanket. Below me stood my son, arisen from his roll, enshrouded in the quilt with its pale squares, and I thought: he is a jawa or a shaman or a ghost or, better still, Father Time himself, hobbling toward me. But look: the quilt is long, and he has stepped on the hem of his robe; he trips, falls flat to the rising earth, and I laugh; Karina at my side laughs; my children laugh. What is Time to us?

66 *In Media Vita*

Empathy

In memoriam: Eduardo Galeano (1940–2015)

This essay posits travels literal and literary with Eduardo Galeano. The dual journey is probably the oldest story in the book, or *before* the book, when stories of the hunt or of war were told to family and painted on walls with blood and ashes of plants to dance in the flickering of twilight fires. Storytelling was then, is now, and ever shall be the way we share our lives, bring loved ones along with us on our travels, or bring the world back to them, to share in imperfect yet viable ways our minds; it is the way we make ourselves *understood*. So perhaps this essay is nothing new: I read Eduardo Galeano's stories; I walk with Eduardo Galeano in the mountains near Provo, Utah. In both ways, he teaches me, and I begin to know others. Later, I reconfigure my own experience, think on it, share it with you.

But first, who is Eduardo Galeano? I'd love to live in a world that knows him or at least knows him more widely than it does. It may help to recall President Barack Obama's April 2009 trip to Trinidad for the Summit of the Americas. There Hugo Chavez, president of Venezuela, mugged for the cameras as he handed Obama a book: *The Open Veins of Latin America*, by Eduardo Galeano. The book's subtitle is *Five Centuries of the Pillage of a Continent*. It was a political move, of course. The book criticizes the economic imperialism of Spain and, later, the United States. It views continental history through socialism's lens. Or it wonders why things are the way they are; where did all this misery come from? Or it whispers possibilities. Still it rages, four decades after it first shouted out across the Western Hemisphere. People continue to read it and be moved by it.

But that is not how I came to know Eduardo Galeano, who sat up nights smoking, guzzling coffee, scribbling furiously while I slept soundly in my crib two seasons away. My Galeano is the author of *The Book of Embraces*, a fragmentary celebration of humanity's foibles and glories, brief insights into the unknown of the world: real people writ large in small paragraphs, not reduced to the few words he gives them, but brought seemingly whole into others' consciousnesses, across time and space. I got the book as a gift from my brother- and sister-in-law, sent from Uruguay for my birthday. I loved its Frankensteined pictures: a fish with an umbrella, a gun firing a bird with a man on its back, a tentacle-headed boy, a boot-headed woman. But I loved more its words. I read it every chance I got, and then I read his other books, all outward looking, all bravely poetical, all celebratory, reveling in the complexities of our fellows, all written in unassuming prose that makes me forget I'm reading, so I can almost believe in a direct transfer of thinkingfeeling.

As the literal travels go, there were my several visits to Montevideo, our chats in Café Brasilero in the Ciudad Vieja, a walk through a street market, interviews formal and informal, but let me focus on the most recent and most vivid in my memory. So it was that Eduardo Galeano came to Utah: I wished it to happen and asked him about it one day at Bar Los Olímpicos in Malvin. He said he'd be doing a quick U.S. book tour the following spring, so I contacted his agent, Susan Bergholz. She told me yes but then called to cancel — the schedule was too tight, she's sorry. Then, only a few weeks beforehand, she called again to say, yes, plan on it, can you make arrangements? So I gathered up funding from all corners of Brigham Young University and various Utah government agencies, paid airfare and hotel, touted the coming of Uruguay's finest living writer, and cleaned up the kitchen. Then there he was, smiling in a green sweater with a bag at his side, anonymous amid the throng of passengers but for the faded halo above his head, so dim you might not even notice it if you hadn't read some of his books.

Of course, one doesn't simply begin by picking up a famous author from the airport. Before this point, there must be years of intense admiration and study, porings over and livings through books the author has wrought, perhaps a few visits and chats in spirited cafés, an interview or two, but mostly it's the books. Those books had taken me around the world to almost every clime and circumstance. They'd offered small glimpses of Oliver Law, a black Chicagoan killed fighting for the Spanish Republic; Phoolan Devi, a young Indian woman seeking revenge on her torturers; Ana Fellini, an orphan of the Argentine dictatorship, herself a casualty of the knowledge that her parents were murdered; Diego Kovaldoff's first, dumbstruck visit to the vast sea; Helena Villagra's bold, colorful, poetic dreams; José Manuel Castañon's conversion to poetry and to democracy through César Vallejo's words; Julio Ama's inability to photograph a soldier caressing his dead twin against a bullet-riddled wall; Nelson Valdés's long bus ride after the driver got off to give flowers to a pretty woman; Eleutorio Fernández Huidobro and Mauricio Rosencof's finger-tapping conversations between dungeon cells during the decade they were held as hostages by the Uruguayan military.

Galeano celebrates victories over tribulations but also simplicities and commonalities. Every person has a story, he seems to say, something to be shared, sometimes celebrated, sometimes condemned. Always, though, we are better off to understand one another. "If you don't want to be mute, you should begin by not being deaf," he told the audience at BYU. "That's why God gave us two ears and one mouth, in order to hear twice before speaking once." Sometimes he tells the stories of people we already know: Jackie Robinson, Billie Holiday, Galileo. Sometimes his protagonists aren't heroes: Francisco Franco, Adolf Hitler, Nero. A history book would give you more information, certainly, but Galeano gives you a deeper access, a connection.

Reading Galeano — or hearing him read, haltingly, in a thick accent — was an experience quite like what Galeano envisions centuries ago —

He was in prison in Genoa when he dictated the book of his travels. His fellow inmates believed every word. While they listened to the adventures of Marco Polo, twenty-seven years wandering on the roads of the Orient, each and every prisoner escaped and traveled with him.

"Marco Polo"

—a deep sharing, a vibrant transformation, "an attempt to communicate a soul" (Woolf), or, more correctly and impressively, to communicate *souls*. How many people's stories live in Galeano's books? Thousands, I would guess. And thousands among billions may seem like very few, but the great expansive power of the focus on individual stories in individual lives is that now all souls seem important, worth our compassion and understanding.

His stories are sometimes bitterly ironic, revealing the hypocrisies, laying bare the rank evils of the outwardly pious, but underlying this apparent cynicism is a man seeking to honor humanity, to grant a fleeting insight into another's soul. The insights are also, at times, personal:

> I would tell you stories about when I was small and you would see them happen in the window. You saw me as a child wandering about the fields and you saw the horses and the light and everything moved softly.
>
> Then you would pick up a shiny green pebble from the window and squeeze it in your fist. From that moment on it was you who were playing and running in the window of my memory, and you would gallop across the fields of my childhood and of your dream, with my wind in your face.

"Dreams"

Most affecting, perhaps, are the stories of children. Here is one, from Fernando Silva, about to leave the children's hospital in Managua one Christmas Eve:

70 *Empathy*

He took one last look around, checking to see that everything was in order, when he heard cottony footsteps behind him. He turned to find one of the sick children walking after him. In the half light he recognized the lonely, doomed child. Fernando recognized that face already lined with death and those eyes asking for forgiveness, or perhaps permission.

Fernando walked over to him and the boy gave him his hand. *Tell someone, . . .* the child whispered. *Tell someone I'm here.*

"Christmas Eve"

And so he has: from Fernando Silva to Eduardo Galeano to Cedric Belfrage, his translator, to me and now to you. We don't know this boy's name. We don't know his age. Beyond Managua, we don't know his location. We don't know whether he plays soccer, listens to music, likes a girl; whether he yet lives or has long ago died. But we feel a sorrow and want a different life for him; and with that feeling, we know a life we have never known. Perhaps we are changed. Perhaps we act differently. Or perhaps we should.

Of course, this is what all good literature should do: make visceral the pains and joys of others, stir in us, as we sit in our chairs, our eyes glancing across lines of letters, some grand emotion beyond what we might find even in living.

Who knows if it's doctrine, but I've certainly heard the lament at the impotence of mere words. A father tells his son, "Words can never express . . ." A wife tells a newspaper reporter, "It's impossible to describe . . ." "You had to be there," we tell absent friends to explain our laughter. A daughter buys a ready-made card, adds a date, and signs, "Love, Sally," before licking the envelope, applying the stamp, leaving the perfunctory offering in the outgoing mailbox around the corner from her desk. It's true, then, that sometimes words fail us. They're only noise amid silence or black shapes against the vastness of everything. So I went along with it, figuring that because I'd experienced the incompatibility, the grasping at expressions, sounding the bugle to marshal words only to discover that none heed the call . . . that the failing went only one way.

But sometimes, maybe, words can do more than signify or convey. Put together in never-before-seen orders, with musical rhythms and branching connotations, words can beat reality. Who has not seen and ignored, or worse, brushed away as a nuisance, a grain of sand? Yet see how William Blake sees more and, because of his seeing, spurs us to look more closely, to recognize possibility:

> To see a world in a grain of sand,
> And a heaven in a wild flower,
> Hold infinity in the palm of your hand,
> And eternity in an hour.

"Auguries of Innocence"

When they're arranged in just the right way, connecting things and ideas, making metaphors of both concrete and abstract stuff, words create their own reality, as affective as any slug in the jaw or sliced onion oozing juices. And despite my humility when faced with the daunting task of translating the marvels I receive through my senses and process through my gray matter, I also must recognize the profound power potential in words. So when I say that I have gone outside myself, beyond myself, that I have bettered myself by reading Eduardo Galeano's books, it is not hyperbole or metaphor — it is magic at the edge of comprehension. I have come to understand others and to change my stance toward them, which has changed my actions in ways no news report or lecture or sermon ever has.

Of course Galeano's visit to Utah was exceptional. We spent hours walking around Provo, comparing Utah to Uruguay, recalling the pleasures of that small country, looking for calm adventure. We ate with university administrators, who required Eduardo to pay for his beer because school funds could not be used for such things. We bought a twelve-pack of Heineken at the Smith's on 200 North and 200 West, and I introduced Eduardo to the self-checkout, a concept that fascinated him. That night we ate at my house a typical Uruguayan

72 *Empathy*

meal prepared by Karina, who was born and lived there for her first nineteen years. My children draped themselves from patient Eduardo, who was a good sport about it, mugging with them, singing songs, transforming himself into a "tickle monster," to their delight. Another night, at Robert Redford's Tree Room restaurant in Sundance, Karina, Eduardo, and I waited forty-five minutes past our reservation time, then waited another forty-five minutes for our dinners. During the wait, we got to talking about the ridiculously small portions of nouvelle cuisine. When our entrées finally arrived, the waiter first placed dishes in front of both me and Karina and then dropped a gigantic bowl in front of Eduardo. Inside was a bed of greens sprigged with onion and dashed with spices; in the middle, a single lobster raviolo. We laughed heartily. This was the height of laughter, we thought, until the waiter, promising to fix the oversight, brought a replacement with another lone raviolo cowering in the middle of another vast bowl.

At his reading, people filled the auditorium past capacity, sitting in the aisles and standing against the back wall. After his reading, people lined up and waited up to an hour to buy his books and chat for a brief moment as he signed their fly pages. He had read of fossilized footprints in Tanzania, taking us back to that prehistoric time, to ancestors too distant to even know. He had taught us, once more, the importance of the human touch in medicine or the touch of words in a love letter. He placed us in a Spanish theater following the performance of García Lorca's *The Shoemaker's Prodigious Wife*: afterward the audience erupted into thunderous stomps, "applause for the playwright. For the playwright executed for being a pinko, a fag, a weirdo. Maybe it was a way of saying, 'Listen, Federico. Hear how alive you are'" ("That Applause").

Afterward, when the commotion had died down and he could escape, we took a short drive up American Fork Canyon to Mount Timpanogos Cave National Monument. Eduardo had warned me that he suffered vertigo when confronted with sheer drop-offs. I decided to risk it. We paid for our spot on the 2:40 tour, then began the slow ascent to the cave entrance. Eduardo hugged the inside wall to keep his eyes off the steep slope only a few feet away. Whenever a group

Empathy 73

of hikers came barreling down beside us, he'd stop to admire the mountain face at close range. We talked about all sorts of subjects, from the close at hand (I had to admit my utter ignorance of the local flora) to the long ago and far away. I wished I had brought a tape recorder.

An hour and a half later, we'd reached our goal. The cave greeted us coolly; the ranger gathered us in and explained the forms growing from all sides. We saw strips of stone bacon and overflowing cauldrons of thick stone sauce. There were long stalactites dripping incrementally downward and stubby stalagmites gathering what impetus they could from the water splashing from above. There were straws and popcorn and frazzled bolts of rock grown in every direction. Beside us, handrails. Below us, asphalt. Tucked generally out of sight, electric lights to show us the path and demonstrate the beauties inside the earth. Among these was the "heart of Timpanogos," a hanging bit of meaning, lending credence to the legend of the princess turned to stone to rest for eternity without her true love.

Judging by the glimmer in his eyes, Eduardo had found the menacing hike worthwhile.

As we neared the exit of the cave, just after our guide shut off the lights for the darkest ten seconds I'd ever known, we watched as the ranger shone his torch on a rumpled formation of rock. No stalactites, no stalagmites, no popcorn, no bacon — just globs of stone poured like globs of mashed potatoes over painfully vast stretches of time, added to just this morning with the slow trickle of melting frost seeping through yards of earth above. This feature, he explained, was animal rock, in which visitors often found the forms of their favorite fauna. See? An elephant. A shift in his beam: an alligator. A gorilla, shouts a kid. A flamingo. A flamingo? Yeah, see the curved beak? You, sir? (I had raised my hand.) A camel. Yes, I see it: a camel (the light tracking over a single hump behind a distorted head — a dromedary). These are the stories the cave itself tells across eons: slow drips piling slivers on vertical rods, undulating sheets of moist curtains, raucous explosions of straws and puffs, a smooth heart that beats only diastolically, with all the time in the world: dizzying variations in mineral and water slowly growing in invisible colors, waiting to be seen, interpreted, understood. I imagined Eduardo contentedly noting that we see different things in the same view, that it's all a matter of perspective.

Next to me, he whispers, "I don't see it."

As we make our way to the exit, he whispers again, "I wish I had seen an animal of my own."

But it is too late; we're herded out one last dim tunnel into a blinding burst of afternoon light.

From there, it was another circumspect wending along the meandering trail, Eduardo holding to the mountainside, pausing to observe and to think now and then, trying out variations of the word *awe*, which he'd known previously only from military propaganda — "Shock and Awe" (which gave him a generally negative impression of it) — but which he'd recently found in a book given him by a fellow writer, who dedicated it, "To Eduardo, in awe of your words . . ." It was an appropriate sentiment, one that I easily shared. For me, our experience here in nature, with a writer I admired, invoked the psalm:

I meditate on all thy works; I muse on the work of thy hands.

Psalms 143:5

Empathy 75

For Eduardo, I assume, not so much. But no matter. I kept pace with my friend, stopped when he stopped, rested when he rested, admired the alum's root and firecracker penstemon growing amid the rocky slopes, looked out across the canyon and into the valley to the west, to all those houses and roadways, teeming with people too distant to discern.

Then, as we rounded a corner, Eduardo drew a sharp breath. "There it is," he said. I followed his eyes to the rock outcropping just ahead. "An eagle, about to take flight." His words were tinged with reverence. Immediately I saw what he saw, but he traced it with his finger anyway: "There's the head, outstretched, and its wings are extending."

Of course.

Eduardo smiled, nodded his head slowly. Did he take a tiny notebook from his pocket and scribble a note? I can't recall. Did we cover the discovery in words, or did we absorb the shared experience in silence? Unless Eduardo recorded them, the succeeding moments are lost now. Was it just then or half an hour later, once the great stone bird was out of sight, long behind us, that we saw an eagle soaring softly above and then land on a naked branch, and we thought (both of us, I am sure, though we gave it no utterance),

There it is.

The eagle glided with the currents, then, pausing to observe, thinking beyond itself, wondered out at the valley below, oblivious to the two men watching its flight, wondering through its mind, smiling.

That was it: Eduardo found his eagle. I thought, I have to write about this. And for three years, I couldn't figure out how, what meaning to make, what context to bring out, what connections to explore: the air-port, the restaurant, the supermarket, the kitchen table, the auditorium, the valley, the cave, the conversations (fading rapidly from memory), the rocks, the forms, the cool air, the pitch dark, the animals . . .

Only a year later, among the first pages of *Mirrors: Stories of Almost Everyone*, Eduardo wrote,

> Stalactites hang from the ceiling. Stalagmites grow from the floor.
>
> All are fragile crystals, born from the sweat of rocks in the depths of caves etched into the mountains by water and time.
>
> Stalactites and stalagmites spend thousands of years reaching down or reaching up, drop by drop, searching for each other in the darkness.
>
> It takes some of them a million years to touch.
>
> They are in no hurry.
>
> "Caves"

Of course.

Miser's Farthings

On Friday, March 7, 2007, in the elevator on the first floor of the Joseph F. Smith Building at Brigham Young University around noontime, two young women, in spritely health to all views, jumped on just as the doors were closing, with an "oh, good!" and followed by something like "I can't believe we made it" or "good timing," then pressed the button for the second floor. I begrudged the lost seconds that the door took to close again and the seconds waiting on the second floor for the second of them to get out as I made my way, fully justified I thought, from the basement below to the fourth and top floor of the building. *This is time*, I thought, *that was robbed from me and is gone entirely.*

At that moment, there came to me the recognizable spiritual tingle that indicates an essay in embryo. Anymore, I feel that essays preexist me, that I have the charge of transcribing them, as amanuensis, a word I had learned only recently in the context of essay writing, from Alexander Smith: "The world is everywhere whispering essays, and one need only be the world's amanuensis." It's one of the few non-rock-and-roll-lyrical quotes I have committed to memory. In any case, it helps my theory (of myself as scribe, not creator), too, that no matter what novel idea I think I have, I inevitably find it, writ better, in an essay by one of the Great Dead.

Indebted, then, I borrow all the more. Before I take us further, I ought to direct our attention to the source of my allusive title, which I would hope to be common knowledge but which I know not to be. It is Charles Lamb talking about mortality, under the spell of the New Year:

> I begin to count the probabilities of my duration, and to grudge at the expenditure of moments and shortest periods, like miser's farthings.

Ah. Lamb was then forty-five years on this green earth, and I am now forty. But the feeling has been with me for some time, too. It derives from a tenuous balance between the blithe change of early years and the besieged melancholy of latter. Perhaps I, with all my children, more than Lamb, who never wed, am confronted by the paradox of stability in mutability. The middle-aged essayist, especially, finds it impossible to "take no thought for the morrow." He is irretrievably metacognizant, existing doubly, *within* the begrudgedly passing moments and *about* them, thinking on the events as well as living them. (When I hear of that ghostly sensation in dreams and near-death experiences of floating above oneself, looking down and seeing the body as some externally extant character, I sometimes think, *This is how the essayist lives always.*)

What we know, or think we know, is always surrounded by mystery, which makes an essay both necessary and indeterminate, both essential and futile. This is why we're almost obligated to damn the obstacles, capture those moments and specimens, hold them still for examination and meditation.

I once heard Sebastião Salgado, the brilliant Brazilian photographer, humbly submit that an entire book including hundreds of images represented only a few seconds of accumulated time, given that each picture captured only fractioned seconds of reflected light. Of course, just outside those images were hundreds and hundreds of hours spent studying and practicing and traveling and waiting and developing and selecting. And inside those images were enduring souls with whole lives of sleeping and waking and working and playing . . . Each picture was an inconceivably small intersection, a pinpoint of time suggesting the briefly crossed paths of photographer and photographed. I thought, *Perhaps this is the scale we work at.* A collection of a few thousand words, easily read in half an hour, represents the labor of a hundred hours. In order to create something worth sharing, we must toil away our lives.

This is what concerns me: that the vast part of life is absorbed into the unremembered whole; that so much is routine and forgotten; and that, going forward into what time we have left, so much of our life is a pointless spinning of wheels converting experience into sand through a glass or a sweeping hand around a clock face. And worse, we consent to live this way, only partially present, sleepwalking through life, as the poet says.

STOPWATCH RESULTS

So I determined to live deliberately, or at least to clock the expenditures, to time my moments and give me some record of what I do all day, to rescue by remembering at least a few days of drudgery (and perhaps to find that it's not drudgery at all). Often I spout to unsuspecting bystanders my kinetic theory of tasks, designed in parallel with Boyle's discovery about gases: our chores expand to fill the volume of the temporal container we have available. I feel as busy during my summer vacation as during a full semester of teaching. Until I am pressed to finish something, I dillydally, telling myself that I'm working on it. But in reality, I'm fiddling and idling. So with stopwatch dangling fashionably about my neck (Karina says I look like "an absolute weirdo"), I set out to time my life.

Those elevator doors that bounced open to admit the young women, stood still a while before closing, then opened just one floor up, a floor they could have easily walked to on the stairs — they take 8.9 seconds to close again. An entire trip up from the basement to my floor takes 27.2 seconds. That trip with two stops (say on the first and second floors, where those energetic girls got on and off) takes at least 55.6 seconds, and that's if nobody actually gets on or off. Add in time for dawdling at the doors, and you're close to a minute and a half. Pushing the Close Door button gives you such a small advantage over not pushing it that I am unconvinced it really does anything. I know these approximate-accurate numbers despite the dozens of unwitting coworkers and students attempting to foil my measurements. Although I performed my experiment during the summer, when no classes were in session, and in the late afternoon, when most people should have gone home, nearly every time I tried to get a clean run or to test the doors, somebody was waiting to get on (and then, soon after, off). They gave me a variety of quizzical looks as they noticed the stopwatch and whenever we'd reached top or bottom and I refused to exit.

Like most people, I remain quiet in elevators, staring at the door, shifting from foot to foot, avoiding eye contact, mostly keeping to myself. Sometimes I think — rather, always I think, but rarely do I think about anything profound or beautiful. But the time I've spent in elevators, as representative of all the moments I've spent simply getting from here to there, sums to a significant segment of my life, almost entirely forgotten. I cannot tell you a narrative of any elevator ride, except the above mentioned and the time Karina and I rode to the top of the Empire State Building to share a first kiss, after *An Affair to Remember*, which I know only from *Sleepless in Seattle*, which revises that central plot point, succeeding where the other tragically fails. So I guess, really, we were reenacting Tom Hanks and Meg Ryan's rendezvous, as well as the cliché perpetuated by countless other hopeless romantics.

But wait a minute, you cry. Foul! Nobody kisses atop the Empire State Building, either in *An Affair to Remember* (Deborah Kerr, struck by a car, misses the appointment with Carey Grant)

I'm sorry that I doubted you; I was so unfair.
You were in a car crash, and you lost your hair.

RINGO STARR, "Don't Pass Me By"

Miser's Farthings 81

or in *Sleepless in Seattle* (the hapless characters finally meet, against all odds — except for movie-formula odds — and hold hands while gazing amazed into each other's eyes). You're right, I suppose, but I didn't quite know that then, it being the very earliest days of the Internet, before I could rewatch the final five minutes of a film for confirmation, and me being much more interested in brushing my beloved's lips than in renting old movies to verify their plots. And even if I had known that each represents the building as *unattainable* bliss, I think I'd still have taken Karina there, so untroubled was I by the stain of cliché.

Nor was I then so troubled by time's irrepressible flight. The fleeting moments that made up my life seemed to stretch before me to a point so distant it may as well have been the edge of the universe. I was giddy with memories of Karina's stunning beauty (we'd met in Montevideo, when I was a missionary, and relationships were off-limits) and afloat in the touch of her hand, the lilt in her laugh. I'd dreamed of her for torturously long months, and now here she was, as present as any being had ever been.

> There are few moments in life when you are idly dreaming about a book, a place, a meal, a girl, and you look up and there is your dream before you.
>
> BRIAN DOYLE, "The Meteorites"

In that long-ago elevator, I was rapt, understanding dully that time was passing but experiencing the string of moments as a caesura, a suspension of life. Her gaze spellbinding, our fingers intertwining, I held infinity in the palm of my hand, felt eternity in a tower.

Yet the kiss a few moments later, on the observation deck, lasted all of three seconds, I would estimate. Subsequent kisses in quick

82 *Miser's Farthings*

succession, attempts to fit our lips in all configurations, moving noses this way and that, might have lasted two minutes more before we rejoined our sisters (they'd discreetly wandered to look out over New Jersey) and eventually descended, still hand in hand.

Since then, I have kissed Karina and she has kissed me thousands of times, perhaps hundreds of thousands of times, sometimes quickly as one of us takes leave, sometimes in prolonged passionate pecks, oscillating osculations (thank you, thesaurus!). I wish now that I had timed our smooches, the better to aggregate them here, but suffice it to suspect that across our seventeen years, I have been locked to her lips, and she to mine, for weeks and weeks (and sleepless weeks, at that). And of course, a kiss does not happen only in the moments of contact.

> The close, luscious, devouring, viscid melting kisses of youthful ardour in my wanton age left a sweetness upon my lips for several hours after.
>
> MONTAIGNE, "Of Smells"

And for years after, in memory. Not a bad way to spend time, to build a life beyond that distant afternoon on top of the world when our lips first met.

Of course, life is not all kisses and hand-holding. Days are utterly filled with menial tasks, the kinds of things we'd rather avoid, hire someone else to do, automate. My routine is far from routine, but lately, at least, I tend to wake up early, around five thirty; roll out of bed; shuffle into the bathroom; brush my teeth; urinate; wash my hands; put on shorts, socks, sneakers, and T-shirt; and then make my way downstairs to exercise. I'm usually down there within eight minutes, because I move a bit slowly in the mornings. I would guess that I also daydream a bit, because those tasks don't seem like they should add up to eight minutes. It's difficult to get an accurate read. For one thing, I always forget to grab the stopwatch as I shut off my alarm and emerge from the bedcovers. For another thing, who knows when to click the stopwatch button? When I brush my teeth, do I time the walk from my side of the bed into the bathroom? Do I begin timing once I cross the bathroom threshold? Once I stand in front of the mirror? Pick up the toothpaste? Certainly once the brush contacts teeth, "tooth brushing" has commenced. But then when does it end? Once brushes no longer touch teeth? Just after I rinse the brush and finish flicking the bristles with my thumb? To complicate matters more, and in accordance with twentieth-century physics and old wives from centuries past (who knew that a watched pot never boils), I learn that when I am timing my brushing for posterity, I tend to keep at it longer, just as when I share a bathroom at a campsite, I like to shuffle the bristles round and round until my neighbor has finished. It's as if we're both slow-racing, trying to be the most hygienic. What I'm trying to say is that I never brush my teeth for the full recommended two minutes, unless someone is watching me. Most mornings, I get the toothpaste on, in, dispersed, lathered, rinsed, etc., in fifty-seven seconds. That's an average. I might also average the time I take on my other tasks, but let's just say that before I leave the house for work, I've spent almost two hours mostly on basic personal maintenance. When my children wake up around seven, my interactions with them are quick and perfunctory: "Get up." "Get ready." "Did you brush your teeth?" "Make sure you eat breakfast." And so on. None of it is what we call "quality time."

One day recently, when I stayed home to play with the kids and relax a bit and build an IKEA wardrobe thing for our master closet, my major events went something like this:

0:17:23 — conversing with my brother Dave about the Vitamix blender, music, health, old photographs, etc.
1:39:37 — first stint building the IKEA furniture before going to get Dani from kindergarten
0:16:26 — walking to get Dani from school
1:22:58 — second stint building IKEA closet
0:14:03 — driving to Kohler's food store to get bread crumbs for milanesas for dinner.

Plus, I apparently did some other stuff. Notice that those numbers don't add up to anything remotely like a whole working day. They're barely half of one. Once all the kids were home from school, we told

84 *Miser's Farthings*

each other how our day was going so far and . . . frankly, I don't quite know what else we did. I forgot to time it. We likely did some kind of cleaning. Maybe I showed them the new wardrobe. We did not joke about escaping through it to Narnia, though for the sake of this essay, I wish we had. I'm certain that we ate dinner, but only because we do that every day. We might have watched an episode of *Phineas and Ferb* on Netflix (we do this often). But the fact is that the day's events did not imprint on me any particular memories, and when I reflect on this fact, I become melancholy. No wonder we hope for a heaven of restoration and continuation, angels recording our every deed and every thought, eternity to increase in knowledge and empathy with our most loved ones.

But isn't this life?

Another day, Karina came to campus with our three youngest children to share a lunch with me. We sat just south of the art museum, on a stone bench along a stout wall of greenery. The kids raced to the museum stairs and back while I timed them on the stopwatch. Daniela's record was a dad-assisted seventeen seconds, though sometimes she hung back and encouraged her two- and three-year-old brothers, bringing her, and them, back in around twenty-five, sometimes thirty, seconds. We sat for almost an hour, munching and laughing, Karina and I chatting, the boys exploring among the plants, sneaking away as far as they dared before turning back to the safety of their parents. Daniela kept running, her hair fluttering, arms flailing, skinny legs leaping ever forward. When we finally called the children to go, it took 10:08 just to get them to the car. That was the price of patience in this instance. We did not cajole, did not bribe or threaten, did not pick them up and carry them where we wanted them to go. We simply meandered toward the parking lot, pausing often as the children found a new rock or an alcove in the bushes to investigate. I had things to do waiting for me at my desk, but I spent the moments extravagantly on my family.

The boys will not remember the day at all, and even reading about it, as I hope they will do in the future, will not jog anything more than the vague recollection of that terrace surrounded by buildings,

Miser's Farthings 85

a place we'll have visited often. Daniela, though, if we talk about the races soon enough, may fix in her mind some recapturable sense of that wind through hair, that jostling through grass, that dappled light through leaves. Already she has surprised me by recalling events I'd nearly forgotten, sometimes from years ago, when I thought she wasn't paying attention, like the long, apocalyptic conversation we had on her abuelos' front porch when she was three; she told me the trees would catch fire and the birds would fall in flame. She's such a strange child, always leading with non sequiturs, speaking in future tense for things that have already happened, seemingly processing life at a different speed from the rest of us.

They say that our first years imprint us indelibly, shape our selves in unalterable ways. So I take care to get my children out of the house, turn off the television, limit their video game playing, stock the shelves with good books, and encourage them to read. We have a large backyard and a small, undeveloped city park behind that. There are kids to play with all over the neighborhood. But those first few years of childhood experience produce no definable memories, only general impressions that we cannot trace. So maybe one reason I'm so obsessed with moments is that I'm surrounded by little people who can barely conceive of time's passage, who cannot form the merest thought of their own mortality, who have no access to notions of events because they do not yet form memories. I worry, too, that they are losing me minute by minute, yet they see me as a static creature, fundamentally extant in their lives, preexisting them and always to be. I am Dad, a decent fellow who works a lot and lets them get away with things, who tickles and wrestles and reads stories. They have not noticed my steadily graying hair or my deepening wrinkles. If I am forty today, then perhaps I was always forty, or perhaps forty is essentially the same as twenty-six, my age when the first of them was born. It might as well be. Yet I see them change like garden plants, each day a little closer to ripeness, transforming from wrinkled gophers curled in the space between my elbow and hand into long-boned, long-haired antelopes just in the time it's taken me to write this essay.

Maybe another reason is that I'm yoked with another person who disparages time's passage. Karina is habitually late (church, meetings, parties, dinner) yet never seems to care. Perhaps this is her Uruguayanness showing, but it's a source of stress for me. My daughters exhibit some of the same tendencies, finding a way nearly every morning, no matter when they wake up, to be gulping down a last spoonful of cereal and ripping a brush through their hair as they stumble to slip on sneakers and sling an unzipped backpack over one shoulder when the neighbor kids ring the doorbell so they can walk to school together. Because I'm often the one in charge of getting them safely started, I am again subject to stress. No matter what I do, they never seem to care. And it's not just not caring. With Karina, it's a kind of perpetual self-delusion about what can be done in a certain number of minutes. Ten minutes before our Sunday services start, she'll get into the shower. Fifteen minutes before our guests are to arrive, she'll head to the store to buy another bag of cheese curls. On the rare occasion that she asks me whether there's enough time to do such and such, I always answer "no," and I'm always right. Yet she is always right, too, that it simply doesn't matter. So we sit in the back of the church, or I entertain our friends and explain that Karina will be home shortly. Who cares? They're used to it. In a big way, I wish I could be more like her; I try to turn off my anxiety and lay back. I've done some amateur studies of the longest-lived people to have graced the earth, and the most common factor among them is "immunity to stress." This is far from my natural state.

During the Madden family trip to Europe last spring, we ran for every single train we took. Literally ran. Two haggard parents and six energetic children, two in strollers pushed by their siblings, everybody wearing a backpack, big kids rolling wheeled suitcases, Karina and me wheeling and carting two large suitcases each, one with a duffel bag perched precariously on top. In a twilit cavern, we dashed alongside the train, huffing with anxiety, shouting instructions and encouragement to one another, finally arriving at the nearest door, then tossing bag after bag after bag into the vestibule after unbuckling and tossing child after child after child into the train so-close-to-departure-it-seemed-to-be-rolling-its-eyes-and-tapping-its-foot-with-impatience. The first time this happened was from London to Liverpool. After settling into the surprisingly unoccupied car, then breaking out the snacks, then sitting still for ten minutes, I began to suspect that something was up. Out the window, I saw a conductor walking past, so I ran out to ask him why we weren't moving. Looking at his wrist, he said, "We're not scheduled to depart for another forty-five minutes." He clarified that there had been another train on another track that had left promptly at 9:10; sheepishly, I returned to tell my family what we'd done. We had a good laugh about it and simply cut short our visit to the Beatles sites by an hour (and wound up running along Menlove Avenue to catch our city bus back downtown later that afternoon). So, technically, this first run for the train was a mistake, maybe a lesson. But I failed to learn it. And from London to Paris and from Paris to Kaiserslautern and from Kaiserslautern to Frankfurt, the trains really did begin to roll only seconds after we'd boarded, all flustered and giggling.

Of course, I know that laughing is the only way to meet such frustrations once they're on me; but during the uncertain times, I've been unable to overcome my nature, which quickens my pulse as I worry myself into a rage. And I suppose, thinking on it now, that I should be glad to have made a little adventure of the journey, instead of arriving at a sensible time in order to spend long moments idle in the train station. Chesterton has somewhat to say on this count, scolding me for my wrongheadedness:

An inconvenience is only an adventure wrongly considered.

"On Running after One's Hat"

The point being that a great deal of our pleasure or misery is determined by our attitudes. So I revise the fusspot I was, experiencing those tense moments, into the father I am, telling the story of our many nearly missed trains, reenvisioning our ragtag band rumbling through the stations never knowing whether we'd make it until we'd made it. We sit at the dinner table of late, smiling in conversation, my wife and children rightly making fun of my anxiety, as we recall our

88 *Miser's Farthings*

day in Liverpool walking fast from Strawberry Field to St. Peter's to Mendips, a kind of pilgrimage to be in those places that shaped the man who wrote the music we love so much.

JOHN LENNON

How much time and effort our species has spent trying to freeze time, revisit and reimagine the past, translate it into other, more durable forms. We tell stories, we draw pictures, we write letters and essays and books. We snap photographs, film videos, record speeches and songs. We want to share our lives with others, including our future selves. We want to leave a trace. We want to matter. Our feelings reach out beyond us.

I, as one specimen of *Homo sapiens*, inhabit the early twenty-first century, a time of immense technological good fortune (I hear the pre-echoes of the future's laughter: "You have no idea what technologies await!"). For me, the most salient method for holding the past is sound recording, particularly produced music, not live events, but songs put together piecemeal by layering controlled performances into a new thing that never was, that never existed as such until it was engineered. Thus, the song on the record becomes sui generis (though it be reproduced thousands of times, pressed into vinyl, magnetized into tape, coded into a disc or an ethereal file), a kind of melding of parts into the ideal representative example. But each note was at some point performed, and I get caught up in the notion of hearing, now, sometimes decades after that one perfect take in the recording booth, replicated vibrations that transport my imagination to the moment of their creation. Especially because vocal tracks are so utterly human, I allow myself to be convinced that with each listen I am reconstituting some vanished conjunction of time and space and human performance and electronic sensors scribing on magnetic tape, the briefly crossed paths of lungs and tongue, shaped exhalations made sensible through language and melody. I can't help but move my thinking beyond the waves of sound created by a needle in groove and think of them as created by another human being. And in the ever-more-common case of a singer who's passed on, I sometimes believe I am resurrecting a soul from oblivion.

You could say this about almost any song recorded after the mid-twentieth century, and some of this you could say about any extant sound recording (some of them egregiously bad, unlistenable). But as my example, I want to talk about John Lennon's penitent "Jealous Guy."

Having been raised singing Beatles songs in the family room with my father, I'm predisposed to like Lennon's solo work, but "Jealous Guy" isn't quite a favorite. I much prefer "Nobody Told Me" or "Watching the Wheels" or any number of his straightforward rock songs. So I'm not entirely sure why I'm drawn to it as epitomal of the kind of song that generates that spooky feeling in me. A few thoughts come to mind, though: (1) Lennon was assassinated at age forty, my age now. I remember hearing the news of his death quite clearly. Though I was sad at the time, I was also irreverent. At my friend Vin's kitchen table, I drew a cartoon of John crying out, "I'm shooted!" This drew a lot of laughs. Though I was only nine at the time, I still feel bad about doing that. (2) I have seen filmed footage of Lennon in the recording studio singing, as far as I can tell, the actual vocal part that Phil Spector kept for the final version of the song. Seeing him with his eyes closed behind those yellow-tinged granny glasses, his hands on his earphones, his head bobbing in and out, toward and away from the microphone to match his engagement, lilting up and down to match the notes' rising and falling, I can feel more fully the emotion of the lyrics even as I hear the small waverings and imperfections in his voice, so that, no, they're not imperfections — they're improvements, marks of their creator's presence. (3) I love to sing along with Beatles (and former Beatles') songs, but Paul McCartney sometimes hits notes just out of my vocal range. Aside from the throat-shredding one-take "Twist and Shout," Lennon's voice always stays where I can reach it, so I especially appreciate him. (4) But in "Jealous Guy," he also whistles — a plaintive touch I think — hitting notes I cannot match no matter how tightly I purse. This amuses and confounds me, both.

(5) Though the timing is all wrong, I cannot help thinking of this song's lyrical message ("I didn't mean to hurt you. I'm sorry that I made you cry," etc.) as a response to his rocky relationship with Yoko Ono, from whom he split in 1972, after cheating on her. His fourteen-month bender in Los Angeles convinced him to beg her to take him back, which she did. And though I have a typical slight-dislike of Yoko, I'm glad she did. (6) I know, nonetheless, that the music was written in 1968 after an inspiring lecture by the Maharishi Mahesh Yogi and that it was in the mix of potential songs for the White Album as "Child of Nature" (different lyrics). (7) And that Paul McCartney once said that the song was about him, that John's jealousy was sparked by "everyone [getting] on the McCartney bandwagon," and that the song was his apology to his friend. (8) Of course, one can't help hoping that John was also apologizing to Cynthia, whom he treated so poorly so often. (9) And to Julian. (10) And, of course, one important reason the song is so resonant, even forty years later, is that it speaks for so many of us, at least in part. Forget Yoko, Paul, Cynthia, Julian; this song expresses something universal. Sometimes it is me singing my regrets to Karina, to my children, to my friends.

I'm not sure all those facts and speculations are relevant to my reasons for returning so often to that song as resurrected moment, but the fact is I do. When I hear it (the whistle especially), I both see and hear something beyond remnants or evidence. I think, *This was once an event and is now again an event, of a different sort*. I think, *Here are four minutes from May 24, 1971, at Tittenhurst, west of London*. I think, *There once was a man named John Lennon, who changed the world with his music; he is now gone, but here he remains alive*. I grow a bit sad at the loss, but also confused. I open my mind to the incomprehensible motivations of some of my fellow beings. I cannot follow the twisted course of logic that brought Mark Chapman to think of himself as Catcher in the Rye (I have felt the pull of that book, too), to fantasize beyond record burnings when Lennon claimed that the Beatles were bigger than Jesus Christ, to rail against the hypocrisy of singing "no possessions" while maintaining so many, to want so badly to link his name and destiny to the great Beatle. In that briefest of moments on

December 8, 1980, at the Dakota Building off Central Park in Manhattan, the paths of musician and murderer crossed inextricably, to far more devastating and permanent effect than any of Lennon's previous encounters with others, or even with Chapman himself. Earlier that day, John had graciously signed the cover of *Double Fantasy* for a then-placid Chapman. Paul Goresh was on hand to capture the scene's split second of reflected light.

> Life is what happens to you while you're busy making other plans.
>
> JOHN LENNON, "Beautiful Boy"

He's gone, and that's why I hold so tenaciously to the idea of all those recorded moments, all the photographs, films, music. But not just for John, for all of us, even those who're still here, counting out the moments. It is, in part, why I write.

There's a part of me that sympathizes with Zeno, who thought himself into the quandary about whether anything can happen at all. Such are the porous boundaries between moments and the limits to possibility when one action is chosen over another. This manifests itself sometimes in my paralysis confronting tasks, especially around the home (and perhaps it explains my sympathy for Edward Thomas, the indecisive friend who inspired Robert Frost's "The Road Not Taken"). Thus several sprinklers remain broken, leaving large swaths of the lawn brown and dying. Thus the weeds in the garden grow more vibrantly than the tomatoes and the peppers. Thus our framed pictures, which would make a nice and welcoming addition to the upstairs hallway, remain unhung years after we moved into this house. Thus the hole I accidentally knocked in the drywall on the stairs remains only partially repaired, a gaping temptation for my children, who have already filled it with toys, clothing, and diapers (unused, thankfully) once before. It's partly why I'm sitting here typing while so much needs to be done today (a Saturday, when we're expecting friends to visit).

And even though recorded music is almost never the record of any single event, but a cobbling together of various performances, maybe so much of what we perceive as a unity was never a unity until it was brought together by an engineer, or a perceiving consciousness. So what is "Jealous Guy" if what we hear never quite *happened*? I begin to conceive of the song (or all songs, all events) as a probability, one result of many, a new happening each time it's listened to, created and existing in the perception of a listener, each agent effecting the reality of the thing we call "Jealous Guy."

So I remember those lazy afternoons when I was young, when my father pulled out his Beatles records and placed them on the turntable so we could listen together and sing along. Those, too, were events, singular and sacred, the meeting of lives across distance and time. We added our voices to the waves reverberating and slackening, interfering and deadening, ripples of temporary vibrations converted — before they fell silent — into electric impulses in my brain and stored as memories.

A LIFE OF SINGULAR EVENTS

But this essay is not only about memories. It's about the ways small moments accumulate into a life, make a person, in ways identifiable and, even more, ways unconscious and imperceptible. Maybe it's about the partially false sense we have that events can be distinct, separate from one another, or about the qualitative judgment we apply to what happens and what we do. Certainly there's *something* real about the feeling that only sometimes are we "really living," while other times we're stuck in ruts, making other plans, watching the wheels go round and round, even slipping backward, wasting time. But I'm not sure the distinction bears scrutiny. Any container we make for experience is porous, easily breached by the thought that *I'm still here.* You can tell just by looking at me that I'm no longer that gap-toothed goofball in

a stunningly fashionable shirt. But on the other hand, I feel like I've always been me. Mostly without intending to, I've strung together a seamless life full of change and influence, recognizably mine, easily broken into stages, full of minutiae to which I can bear only general record.

I am the product of long corridors, empty sunlit rooms, upstairs indoor silences, attics explored in solitude, distant noises of gurgling cisterns and pipes, and the noise of wind under the tiles. Also of endless books.

C. S. LEWIS, *Surprised by Joy*

I, too, could catalog and condense the whole, tell the generalities that made up my early life, but let's not. Instead, let's remember here things that happened only once and yet struck with such force that they shaped me. For instance, because it arrived first, one summer afternoon (or was it spring? fall?) when I was in college (or earlier?), my family gathered for a picnic with a large group from church at Malapardis Park in Cedar Knolls. The purpose was recreational/celebratory, with grilled meats and potato salads, five-gallon jugs of "bug juice," and intermittent games of softball and horseshoes. Bored, my brothers and I began our own competition, vaulting the softball field's back fence to see who could clear it the most times within a minute. David won, as usual. Then we spied the backstop.

It was a straight-up twenty footer, not one of those bent-over specters. As I remember, we each had the idea simultaneously: let's race over *that*. As the oldest, I went first, while David kept the stopwatch. On "go," I jumped high, grabbing into chain-link diamonds, inserting my sneaker tips, then scrambling at a respectable speed up and gingerly over the pokey top, and, after a step or two down, fairly jumping the rest of the way to the ground. My brothers cried foul about both jumps, up and down, but were calmed soon enough when they realized the impossibility of judging what was "too high." The goal here was to

94 *Miser's Farthings*

get over the top and to the ground on the other side. They each took their turns, like me avoiding the pain of the top by moving cautiously and like me earning a time somewhere in the low twenty seconds. As you'd expect if you knew me and my brothers, things quickly got more competitive. Dave was the first to pioneer a new method of scrambling up the front side and diving headfirst over the top, barbs be darned, so that his arms were a good four feet down the fence and he could simply kick his legs over, twist sideways, and drop to the ground. Sixteen seconds. Dan, undaunted, used the same style, to even better effect: fourteen seconds. I failed at the fence flop and essentially bowed out of the competition, but Dave and Dan kept at it a few more times, eventually getting down to twelve seconds and change, with Dave crowned this summer's (or spring's? fall's?) World's Strongest Madden.

I'll never get through the flood of moments that's come upon me these days, as I've trained my mind on recalling these singular events. (And with what joy do I welcome them, having long believed my memory so poor.) Yet I'll revisit a few and fix them in language:

There was that one time we neighborhood kids entered the abandoned Whippany Paper Board Company property not across the Whippany River dam but through an underground tunnel that opened across the railroad tracks, hopping from dry patch to dry patch across the fetid puddles, our flashlights illuminating the cracks and insects, and that other time we hung and shimmied across a pipe over the river. Once, we found a string of train cars sitting still on the tracks, so we uncoupled them and loosed their brakes, setting them rolling slowly toward the buildings in the distance. Two men shouted angrily and gave chase; and though I tripped on a railroad tie, falling quickly behind the older kids, we all had enough of a head start that we escaped unrecognized and uncaptured.

One winter night not long after that, I was snooping through Notre Dame's underground steam tunnels with my volleyball teammate Bill "Super Primetime" Raney (the area was off limits, the tunnels were dangerous and spooky, and the entrance doors in the dorms were nearly always locked), when we happened on an unlocked door into a dimly lit computer lab. There were all those machines, available for the taking (they certainly weren't locked to the tables, though there may have been security cameras in the dark corners), but we surreptitiously closed the door and kept on our way through the university's underground. For nearly two hours we explored, sometimes walking upright, sometimes crouching, sometimes crawling on hands and knees, sometimes slithering between boiling-hot pipes on the pizza boxes we'd brought along for the purpose. Eventually we made our way into a dirt-floored, cobwebbed section that seemed to narrow to the point of impassability. Smudged with dirt and grime, sweaty with the heat of the steam, we climbed a wooden ladder resting against some pipes, up through a trapdoor, and into a chemistry professor's office, right under his desk. We decided that despite our filthy tank tops and shorts, it would be too uncomfortable and would take too long to wend our way back to our dorm underground, so we unlocked the office door and walked out into the hallway, past the students moiling in the computer lab, and out into the bitter cold.

One afternoon, playing two-person water-balloon hide-and-seek at John Lenox's house, I had the tremendous idea to sneak inside, climb the stairs, fill a bucket with water, scramble through the bathroom window onto a small roof overlooking the backyard, and wait patiently for him to happen by, which he did, slinking slowly, looking everywhere but up, making a very easy target. I intuited enough physics to time the drop just right, utterly soaking John. It was a moment of pure joy. John knew I had bested him, so we laughed and laughed and recounted the brilliant strategy with amazement for years after.

Many years ago, when I was flying from Utah to Uruguay to begin my two-year mission, having been primed to talk amiably with whoever crossed my path, I struck up a conversation with a large fellow seated next to me on the plane between Miami and Rio de Janeiro. This was a big mistake. Instead of opening an opportunity for me to share a message about my church, it gave him a chance to tell me about his exploits. For eight hours, when I should have been sleeping, he chewed my ear off. He had been everywhere, done everything, known everyone, he claimed. Early in the flight, I quickly shifted into "nod and keep quiet" mode, hoping he'd sense my disinterest or notice my obtrusive yawns. At the very least, I'd add no more fuel to the conversational fire. But he had his own fuel, some deep-seated need to be admired, I suppose. Ultimately, the only specific detail I recall is that he claimed to be one of David Byrne's close friends, and as proof of this, he offered the lyrics to the Talking Heads' song "Life during Wartime," specifically "This ain't no Mudd Club or CBGB's," two music clubs in New York that this fellow used to frequent. (With Byrne? I can't remember. Probably.) *He* was (somehow) the inspiration for that cryptic song. I'm sure he explained to me exactly how.

But what's interesting is how those several hours of forced insomnia, which in their initial happening were so full of unbelievable stories and extravagant details, are now reduced to a cautionary tale in which the young missionary intent on proselytizing gets his comeuppance. All I can muster from memory is a minute's worth of summary.

By simply choosing to focus hazily on these singular events, I'm avalanched by them, far too many to write. So let me leave behind the listing for a moment, to shift to the things that become "things," family inside jokes, one-time events that we convert into stories, always poised to spring forth from the conversation, like the time I voiced my misunderstanding of a national jeweler's slogan, "Every kiss begins with Kay." Vexed by rampant commercialism and exaggerated claims, I said to the room, "What a stupid commercial. You don't need one of their rings to get kissed." My children, incredulous, waited for the punch line but, when none appeared, started laughing. Karina soon explained that it was a pun, that the word *kiss* begins with the letter *k*. And I call myself a writer! So now not only when that commercial comes on, but whenever someone feels the urge to poke fun at Dad, you'll hear from the end of the dinner table or the back seat of the car that jingle, "Every kiss begins with Kay," followed breathlessly by their best Dad imitation: "What a stupid commercial." It's always good for a laugh.

I'm not always the slow one, not getting what's obvious to others. Before Karina and I married, during the few months she lived nearby and ate with my family often, this scene played out at the dinner table:

Dad sat at the head, Mom next to him, I on his other side, Karina next to me, my youngest brother, Dan, at the other end of the table. Plate piled high with hamburgers and hot dogs hot from the grill, bag of buns, jar of pickles, sliced tomatoes and onions oozing juices into the cutting board, bottles of mayonnaise and mustard and ketchup scattered here and there, a pile of junk mail and napkins, all acted as centerpiece.

DAD: Please pass the ketchup.
Silence
DAD: Pass the ketchup, please.
Stares
DAD, *getting impatient*: Pass the ketchup.
Confused, shifting looks
DAD, *fully angered*: Dan! Why don't you pass the ketchup!?
DAN, *cowering*: The ketchup's right in front of you . . .
DAD: Oh. I mean the mustard.

This is how Karina began to understand what she was in for if she married me, and my father began to understand that he was in for a lot of (new) ragging from then on. Nowadays we skip straight to threat-level orange, and we no longer bother with condimental fidelity to the original (indeed, nobody seems quite sure whether he was asking for ketchup or mustard, just that he'd switched the two). So it's "Dad, pass the pepper!" when we want salt, or "Dad, pass the juice!" when there's only milk on the table.

FAREWELL

What have I done here, dear reader, if not engage in the same disgrace as my neighbor on the plane to Rio? The difference, I guess, is that you have been free to close the book, to cut off my rambling, to stop listening to my listing. Also, that I have not dropped any names (none that you'd know or be impressed by, anyway), nor have I claimed to be the inspiration behind any quirky pop songs. But if you must know, one detail I neglected to mention about the elevator ride to the top of the Empire State Building, where Karina and I shared our first kiss, is this: as we got off at the observation deck, Bryan Adams, the singer, got on, going down. I don't think our brief, anonymous encounter inspired his 1998 hit "Cloud Nine," with its "Well, it's a long way up and we won't come down tonight," but you never know. What I do know is that one time, playing basketball with faculty and graduate students at Ohio University, I jumped to take a shot with elbow cocked, then crashed on the head of internationally renowned poet Mark Halliday, sending him bleeding to the emergency room. I like Mark, and the game that day was very tame, so you can trust me that my attack wasn't intentional. But I still felt kind of bad, not only for him, but for all of us, because without him and the fellow who drove him to the hospital, we no longer had enough guys to play. But the reason I'm telling you this is that unknown to me, that exact day he had achieved the exact age his mother had reached when she died, so he wrote a poem called "Head Wound," in which one "big Patrick" figures prominently. This ain't no "Life during Wartime," but my story's more easily confirmed.

And maybe that's what this all comes down to: questions of worth: time as container or time as elevator, or time as atmosphere, an inescapable measure of duration as well as value. As long as we still live, we are held in its sway; it runs on interminably, ignorant of our progress or regress, our wishes to linger or pass over. The things we do to fill it may bring us joy or sorrow, may leave an imprint on memory or meld into our general perceptions or flow off into oblivion. Some efforts may be worth the while; many, in our flawed judgment, will not. We have a measure of control over the what and the when, but we are not entirely free, certainly not to determine significance or to decide what we will remember or how. Even the most seemingly important or most narratively appealing event (I appreciate every kiss with Karina as much as I did when our kisses were new) may fade into background, and does, more often than not.

I wish there were some small moral to give us hope, but I'm allergic to simplifications, so I'll avoid the bromides about seizing days or living each moment as if it were your last.

Miser's Farthings 99

Suppose this moment, or let us say the next five minutes, is really my last — what shall I do? Bless me, I can't think! I really cannot hit upon anything important enough to do at such a time.

ELISABETH WOODBRIDGE MORRIS, "The Embarrassment of Finality"

Of course, I am well aware of the irony that while I am writing and while you are reading, envious time is fleeing,

Life consists in what a man is thinking of all day.

RALPH WALDO EMERSON, *Journals*

but perhaps I am never more alive than when I am essaying.

Buying a Bass

I have an aping and imitative nature. . . . Anyone I regard with
attention easily imprints on me something of himself.

MONTAIGNE, "On Some Verses of Virgil"

Not long ago I spent nearly two hours on the phone buying a Fender
Geddy Lee model jazz bass at a post-Thanksgiving 20 percent discount
off the already artificially and universally reduced price of $799.99.
It was a torturous morning for me. When I couldn't get a line ("All
circuits are busy; please try your call again at another time"), I waited
half an hour on queue for a live Internet chat with a Guitar Center
representative. I watched my spot in line slowly count down from thirty
to one, then groaned at the pop-up message — "No representative is
available" — and shot an annoyed email into the void.

Then I trained my left-hand middle finger to alternate between
the Redial and the Flash buttons on my phone, and I settled into a
deep boredom, warm in bed, except for my left hand, left holding the
handset. After thirty-seven minutes of this nonsense, I failed to hear
the signal ascending trio of beeps, I stayed my practiced finger, and I
settled in for another twenty minutes of holding (after selecting my
desired menu options), barraged by a stream of commercial messages
and song snippets.

All of this is well and good, but I am writing not to tell you about my frustrating morning of Black Friday shopping, nor to wring out the suspense I felt not knowing whether I'd ever get a chance to lay down my credit card to shell out $681 of my hard-earned money, nor even to argue about how hard earned that money really is. Instead, I'm intrigued that as I talked to the salesman who eventually picked up my call, I immediately adopted several of his vocal mannerisms. Here I was, a thirty-six-year-old college professor. I should have been confident in my speaking ways, winning *him* over to my practiced, measured manner. Yet I was drawn in by his moxie, his *dude* speak: "That's a sweet bass, man. An unbelievable price, too." It was a kind of growl, and his vowels were all diphthong and dance.

He's trained to say that, of course, though for me it's true. It *is* a sweet bass, and its discounted price made it suddenly available to me. I've never owned a bass, primarily because my father wouldn't let me buy one back when I was in junior high. "The only thing you can do with a bass is play in a rock band," he warned. *Well, yeah*, I thought, though I tried to make reasonable counterarguments. I was at the time enamored of U2, Yes, and Rush. Something in their basic underpinnings especially resonated with me. The stuff Adam Clayton played seemed easy enough to mimic. My mother's coworker had known him back in Dublin. He was just a strange kid, she said. That was certainly attainable even for me. Chris Squire and Geddy Lee, on the other hand, were running their fingers up and down the fretboard in ways I couldn't even always hear correctly. And Geddy was singing on top of that. I knew even then that my likes were not necessarily my influences, that I was limited, too (too much), by my ability. I was noodling around at the time on my friend's El Cheapo, with its tendency to buzz even on the headstock-end frets, and we enjoyed playing simple three-chord songs in his garage. It was our harmless rebellion. In the end, though, I dutifully saved my money and settled for a guitar. Yes, you could play guitar in a rock band as much as you could play bass (more so, even, with bands like KISS and Iron Maiden running two axmen), but you could also sit around a campfire with your friends or write a love song to your girlfriend or walk with her up to Stewart

102 *Buying a Bass*

Falls to give her the diamond ring she's deserved for a decade and sing her your own version of the Beatles' "I Will" with lots more verses.

Thus I became a poor guitar plunker. There have been few camp-fires, but, more importantly, there has never been any serious danger of my joining a real rock band, unless you count the Tords, which is just me and my friend Joe, a Berkeley-trained guitarist who humors me whenever I return to our hometown in New Jersey. He is the kind of guy who's actually been in a real band, releasing an album, playing shows at CBGB's (he's never written a song about me, though). But that hasn't gone to his head, and he holds a steady job and loves his wife and three daughters with a little left over for his friends. And hey, Dad? Joe even cut off his dreadlocks a few years ago, and I don't ever see him wearing those earrings anymore. The soul patch remains.

As does his New Jersey accent. It's a less grating version of the one you hear on *Saturday Night Live* or in Governor Tom Keane speeches; to me it's kind of endearing, a subtle sonic Madeleine. When I'm around Joe, I slip back into certain pronunciations, even phrasings (lots of *yeah*s, *naw*s), but they've never really been *mine*. Though I grew up in New Jersey, I don't really speak it. I suppose I mostly learned to talk by imitating my father's soft Wisconsin inflections. I like to have fun with people, bust their stereotypes. "I'm from New Jersey," I say. "You don't sound like it," they reply.

My friend David Lazar spent years consciously effacing his Brook-lynese. Even among his high school peers, his accent was noteworthy, made fun of. When he got to Brandeis, it was one more difference between him and his upper-crust classmates.

I kept refining my accent, moderating my vowels, softening my consonants. A friend at the time said I sounded like an English don. That must have been my progression from Brooklyn don. Corleone to Cambridge, made easy.

My mother, also from Brooklyn, never quite got out of her pronunciations, though just recently, as she drove me home from the airport, she noted, with a touch of disdain, the ugly accents of New Jerseyans. I thought, but didn't say, *That's pretty much how you talk, Mom.*

Paul the Apostle manages to sound cool claiming to be "all things to all men," and he meant it as a proselytizing method, not an excuse for his malleable habits of speech. But what if he was just rhetorical, not to say *conniving*? Or wishy-washy? What if such adaptability is not a going with the flowing, but a lack of self?

It feels like time to get back to my phone conversation with the Guitar Center salesman. This is him speaking again:

"And let me tell you about something totally excellent. I've got it myself, on my Les Paul. It's Performance Protection, man."

"No, thanks."

"You sure, dude? 'Cause it's like you're getting it free, with your discount and all."

"No." In my mind I heard my father's reasoning: *They're banking on you never needing a major repair. In any case, I take care of my things better than most people do.*

"All right, man. If you change your mind, you have ninety days to upgrade."

"Okay, but I won't."

I count this a small victory, a repudiation of the vortex.

So I guess I'm not just thinking about the ways we absorb the speaking styles and inflections of others or about whether such flexibility in our accents indicates some lack in our constitutions. I'm thinking about the small rebellions in life, the book and flashlight under the covers, the raucous racket playing on the stereo, the cigarette out in the woods, the initials carved in the beech bark. I'm thinking that my father was probably right — I'm glad now to be able to strum up a tune to sing along to — and that I'm also right to finally own my own bass. I'm thinking about the Christmas Eve just after my purchase, when my father turned sixty-four and we gathered the whole Madden clan with piano, guitar, bass, and clarinets to sing for him "When I'm Sixty-Four," with slight lyrical changes to accommodate the grandchildren on his knee. I'm thinking how, more than any salesman or community of peers, my father has molded me, in ways I can sound through deep reflection and ways I cannot fathom. And I'm thinking about how the world became a better place when Stu Sutcliffe and Astrid Kircher decided to shack up, leaving Paul McCartney to string up an upside-down Rosetti Solid 7 with piano wire to create a makeshift bass. How Chris Squire split his bass signal into both a bass and a guitar amp, to achieve that heavy treble and heady growl to underlie the orchestral arrangements of Yes. How sometimes all you need is a steady da-da-dee-da-da-dah-dum da-da-dee-da-da-dah-dum to conjure images of a quiet New Year's Day, a world in white where nothing changes. And how can Geddy Lee split his brain like he does, play with his hands those intricate bass lines and sing on different rhythms, different notes? This is a mystery I am content to witness without understanding, like my toaster, my computer, my wife's love, my children's wonder, my father's long wisdom, and the ways we resist and rely on each other, we grow and empathize, meet another soul along the way, and resonate.

Moment, Momentous, Momentum

From far away, some time later, I surmise that the metal stirrup — remnant of a broken swing — that hit my daughter Sara in the left temple carried with it a momentum of roughly eight kilogrammeters per second as it traced its arc from my daughter Adriana's hand as she followed it with her widening eyes as she realized its trajectory would intersect her younger sister's. Given that Sara's mass, even at age three, was substantially more than the swing's, the momentum would have been easily conserved in simply knocking her a half meter or so in about a second; but given that she may have sensed the impending collision and thrown herself backward, the calculations would be nearly impossible. In any case, I wasn't there to witness the event or to take measurements. And ultimately, this is not so much a question of momentum as of force concentrated in a narrow shim of iron cutting bluntly into centimeters of flesh over bone.

This was our last day in Uruguay visiting Karina's family. We were to have a feast attended by the whole clan. My father-in-law and Fernando tended the grill, shoveling coals, adding wood to the fire, turning the ribs, while David and I stood around chatting. Inside, Karina and her mother and sisters readied the table with plates and empanadas. Most of the children were at the nearby playground, squeezing out every last moment. Then my two oldest, Pato and Adi, ran breathless and crying around the gray corner under the broken ombú tree:

"Sara!"

"Bleeding!"

Amid a string of unintelligible overtalking.

I bounded past the ditches, over the low brick wall, to the sight of my baby stunned, standing silent in the middle of the concrete playground, holding her scarlet head above a growing pool.

I swept her up, cradled her in the crook of my arm, and bounded back, past the chimney, into the house, to grab a towel, to wash the wound, to call a taxi, to rush us to Saint Bois. Karina and David came along. Fernando and his parents stayed at home with the other children, to calm and console them. By the time the taxi arrived, minutes later, we still had no real idea what had happened.

Sara was calm, mute, wide-eyed, the whole ride. Our driver was safe and fast, taking corners without a downshift, taking traffic signs as suggestions. The hospital staff, seeing the blood and stillness and thinking Sara more gravely injured than she was, took us right in and assessed her injury, eventually, as superficial, deep and wide enough to require stitches but nothing eternal, nothing visible to the future. It was behind her hairline, just barely.

Our own assessment required a quick phone call home to ask once more, calmly, what had happened. Fernando, acting as intermediary, pieced together from Adriana's sobs what I've told you above: that she'd thrown the broken swing just as Sara happened by. It was thus Fernando's job to comfort Adi, to let her know that Sara would be fine and that we'd all be home and happy soon.

Not so soon, it turned out, as we were sent downtown to Pereira Rossell after the stitches, for a CAT scan. So David went home to eat with the rest of the family, while Karina and I traveled in the ambulance beside our daughter, Karina whispering lullabies and I staring ahead, imagining the day thirty years ago when my mother-in-law left the water boiling on the stove awaiting the evening's pasta. In only a moment of turned-back, mind-on-something-else, her son Fernando toddled into the kitchen and tipped the pot onto his right side, scalding the skin off his face, arm, and leg. Of course, the scene I construct takes place in their current home, because I've never seen the house they lived in then, so I already know somewhat of the limits of imagination when it buts up against the horror of a mother's momentous guilt at knowing she's caused her son everlasting pain: in the series of grafts, in the incessant taunts and too-long stares of passersby. When Fernando was in his late teens, doctors began a process that would implant healthy skin in place of his undulated scars, but he gave up before the shunts could do their work. He'd lived his whole life looking like that, he reasoned. Why bother trying to change it all now?

All of this is a memento mori: what you can lose in a moment of distraction or inattention, in a split second of misdirected curiosity, in a clepsydra's drop of bad luck, in all the times you've used the front burner without incident, in a little girl turning her head just an inch toward instead of away or rocking left instead of right. Fractions from fractures: all things considered, this was a blessing, because it was so close to so worse, because her eyes were averted when the pendulum struck.

Physics isn't really that hard to understand, given the right brand of curiosity and a nudge in the right direction; yet for people whose daily life is dominated by the mysterious observable, even small miracles can fade to mundanity. Of all the elementary concepts requisite for a beginning conception of the mechanical world, mass is fundamental, a block to build on and calculate from; yet people everywhere, old and young, struggle to distinguish mass from weight. For them, as for all of us, really, everyday experience is inextricable from gravity.

On Being Recognized

In modeling this figure upon myself, I have had to fashion and compose myself so often to bring myself out, that the model itself has to some extent grown firm and taken shape. Painting myself for others, I have painted my inward self with colors clearer than my original ones. I have no more made my book than my book has made me — a book consubstantial with its author.

MONTAIGNE, "Of Giving the Lie"

When I went into essay writing, fame and fortune were furthest from my mind, and in my low aspirations I have not been disappointed. So it was with a mixture of pride and embarrassment that I answered yes recently to the only person who's ever asked, "Are you Patrick Madden?"[1] Granted, this was at a small bookstore, in Delaware, Ohio, down the street from Ohio Wesleyan, where I'd given a reading the night before, and granted, the woman asking the question was working at the bookstore, which featured my book prominently (and in abundance) on the table near the entrance, and granted, as I later found out, my friend Michelle, a professor at the university, had likely talked to this particular woman about me and my book just a few days prior, but still. Nobody had ever recognized me before, and I was struck by both the discomfort and the appeal of the event.

"You look taller than I expected," she said, and we laughed politely.

Immediately I felt the pressure to be on my best behavior, to live up to the character I'd portrayed within the pages of my book, a guy who's cool and collected, who smiles and daydreams a lot, who thinks deeply about the complexity of the world and withholds judgment, except perhaps of himself, though his sins are peccadilloes.

So I straightened up, grinned, and made not-quite-so-small talk about how much I liked the town of Delaware, Ohio, and how I'd loved living in Athens, in the southeastern part of the state, when I was in graduate school, because of the academic/bohemian atmosphere there — the same basic conversation I'd had several times the day before as I met students and faculty members. She countered with heartfelt praise of my home state, Utah, which she'd visited a couple of years before to do some camping and hiking in the national parks, but not Dinosaur National Monument, which I recommended heartily, noting that just this month they'd reopened the quarry exhibit, where you could see hundreds of dinosaur bones half exposed in an upturned former river bend.

Nothing too shameful here, wouldn't you say? Two people conversing pleasantly, complimenting each other indirectly by praising places? I continued to smile, to hope that I'd live up to the expectations I might have engendered by writing my deepest thoughts in sprawling associative essays.

Which brings me to my current topic, which derives somewhat from this chance encounter, but which has long been with me: the claim that the written persona, the I of the page, is not ever quite the I who writes. That the character I is not the writer I, though every attempt be made to align them. Nor, in the case of the personal essay, which typically includes both writer I and character I within the text, is the linguistic construct presented to the world an exact replica of the flesh-and-blood human being pushing the keys or the pen across the page. This is an appealing idea, I suppose, in the way it sees linguistic construction as fundamentally fictional. But I'm not entirely on board with the troublemaker theorists who want to take the argument too far — like my colleague down the hall who sticks his head in my office every now and then to jokingly taunt that "it's all fiction anyway," or like the eager students, fresh from encountering the idea for the first time, who take from it license to make up events in their life stories, combine characters, or invent dialogue wholesale without regard for reality (however slippery that concept, given the necessarily subjective nature of sensory apprehension).

I'm not quite ready to surrender all to the conflation, to the imperialistic definition, of *fiction* (from the Latin verb *fingĕre*: to make, to fashion, to form). After all, were I to meet you in person one morning in a bookstore, you might gather evidence about my size and posture; my eye color; my thinning, graying hair; my attentiveness; my facility for conversation in a deep, slightly rasped voice. But what would you say about just one of those after the fact? My height, for instance? That I am "tall"? How tall? One measure is relational: I am as tall as the six-foot-five mark on a measuring tape. The inherently comparative adjective (no need for *taller* when the difference from others is assumed) makes a judgment dependent on a general knowledge of human heights. You might further narrow the discrepancies by placing me in a percentile — say, taller than 99 percent of people in the world. That would get us closer to something objective but not all the way there. There are people taller than I am, quite a lot of them, though they're in the minority. And when the realm of possible human heights fits in such a miniscule range (between, say, one and eight feet, across a lifetime) on an incomprehensibly long scale of length and distance . . . what use is that adjective, *tall*? And what of my eye color? Hazel? A mixture of green and blue and orangey brown? In what proportions, and in which locations? To what wavelengths do those color names correspond?

Which is to say that we see averages and approximations; our senses aren't refined enough to capture the data that make us up, even physiologically. It's no surprise that our souls remain mysterious, even in person, even after long contact, even in relationships most intimate, profound, prolonged.

We are utterly open with no one, in the end — not mother and father, not wife or husband, not lover, not child, not friend. We open windows to each but we live alone in the house of the heart. Perhaps we must.

BRIAN DOYLE, "Joyas Voladoras"

Even beyond our intentions, the ways we shut or open ourselves to be known by others, we are inscrutable. I see evidence daily that I will never fully understand my wife; nor she, me. My parents, whose memories of me extend further back than my own, who saw my personality taking shape before I could conceive of myself as a self, have not only lost me to marriage and a job across the country; they never knew me fully even before that. In this sense, I don't even know myself. What's the news in declaring that the I on the page is a fiction? The I under my cap is likewise.

Meanwhile, back at the bookstore, a few minutes before my conversation with the clerk, I almost didn't make it to the cash register. Walking through the jingle-belled door, I was pleased to see my book on the front table, and I smiled at the smell of fresh-brewing coffee. I hoped to find a good book to read on the plane home, and the store had an Essays section, which was heartening, but it was small, with only a few dozen titles, many of which I already owned. What's more, the prices were undiscounted. So when I found Nicholson Baker's *The*

112 *On Being Recognized*

Size of Thoughts, which a friend had recommended to me, and after I'd been impressed by the back cover, table of contents, and some scattered pages inside, I still hesitated. Should I shell out fifteen bucks to have the book now, or should I wait and pay about five from Amazon.com's Marketplace? Ultimately, four thoughts drove my decision: First, I really wanted something to read on the plane, and second, more nobly, perhaps, I felt indebted to the store, which had put my book on display. I knew, vaguely at least, that they could send back any books they didn't sell, but I still felt that they'd taken a small risk on me. Third, I like the idea of small, independent bookstores, as opposed to the large chains (like those in airports, which certainly wouldn't sell essay collections) and online megastores. There are real human beings staffing local stores, stocking the shelves and making recommendations. I can believe that these people are readers and book lovers. Their struggle to make a living seems less baldly capitalistic than the emerging monopolies.

Fourth, I was being paid for my reading at Ohio Wesleyan, so I was feeling flush, enough to fork over fifteen bucks, at least. So I grabbed the Baker book and made my way to the counter at the back of the store. There, amid the conversation about neighborhoods and national parks, the clerk and I got to the typical lament about the difficulties of keeping a small bookstore open, when so many people nowadays purchase their books online. Condemned in my thoughts, I expressed my sympathy and solidarity, saying something like "I know. It must be tough," and wishing her and all the independent bookstores well.

But there I was being a bit disingenuous, while here, in writing this essay, I shall bring us closer to my true self (if there is such a thing). I buy books using Amazon quite often. Recently, I spent almost $150 on twenty-three books, most of them used, most from third-party sellers, some with missions to fund schools or fight homelessness or stop the devastation of AIDS or donate books to children in Africa or feed the poor. I mention these facts to assuage the pinches of guilt I feel about patronizing the monopolist. Some of the books were so long out of print that I could find them only online (my local used bookstores, in Provo or in Salt Lake City, do not sell Christopher Morley's collected essays). And some of the books were too new or too rare to have found their way to the used market or to the remaindered pile, so I bought them new, on sale below retail, from Amazon itself. Had I paid full price for all twenty-three, the books would have cost me triple what I paid. So my motivation was primarily economic, but let's toss in a little bit of environmental, too. Books don't grow on trees, after all. They kill trees, and keeping them alive in the preowned market saves some small part of the planet. For the most part, I didn't send my money directly to Jeff Bezos and friends — I only used the locus they've provided in order to meet other people like me who simply have the book I'm seeking.

Again I'm smoothing out the story to sooth my conscience, but these considerations do inform my decision. Back to self-criticism: some of these books were written by friends of mine, and I intend to bring their books with me next time we meet, so I can get their autographs on the title pages, along with a brief, witty dedication to me. But I have been woefully undedicated to them. None of them makes any significant money from royalties anyway, but by buying their books used, I have cut them out of the profits. What little money is made from the books I like to read (essay collections mostly, always "literary" books) goes overwhelmingly to the middle people in charge of printing, distribution, and sales. With most of these used books I've bought, the post office is getting the majority of the money, more than the resellers; but the authors, the creative spirits who wrung the words from years of painful experience and solitary crafting, get nothing at all, not even the one dollar per book they're promised by their publishers.

So on the one hand, I've perpetuated a secondhand market, kept a few trees alive awhile longer, given these books new life, and made a small dent in illiteracy and malnourishment. On the other, I've contributed to the downfall of the system that allows me and my friends to get our books into print. I don't feel all one way about the issue, as you can see, which perhaps gives some valuable insight into my character. And I do, in the end, sometimes buy books from the supposed enemy.

But not always. After I hear authors read their work live, I typically purchase a copy of their newest book, at full price, and then ask them to sign it. And that day in Beehive Books, for complex reasons, I paid full price for *The Size of Thoughts*.

This very debate about the fictionality of the essayist is the subject of a recent book by Carl Klaus, *The Made-up Self: Impersonation in the Personal Essay*, a book I greatly admire by a man whom I judge (from speaking to him in person, shaking his hand while looking him in the eyes, as well as reading his words on the page) to be a sage. When the slim volume appeared unexpectedly in my mailbox one day, I gratefully took it on a plane trip with me and devoured it the way some readers consume suspense novels. I found in it great thoughts about Montaigne, Lamb, Woolf, and White, supporting its interesting and inevitable conclusion:

> The sense of a human presence that animates a personal essay is surely one of the most beguiling literary phenomena, for it usually comes across in so familiar and direct a voice, seemingly without effort or contrivance, that it's easy to believe I'm hearing (or overhearing) the author of the piece rather than a textual stand-in.
>
> But the "person" in a personal essay is a written construct, a fabricated thing, a character of sorts — the sound of its voice a by-product of carefully chosen words, its recollections of experience, its run of thought and feeling, much tidier than the mess of memories, thoughts, and feelings arising in one's consciousness.

I've already given away where I stand on this issue, have I not? But of course the assertion by such a person gives me pause, tempers my fire. Am I simply beguiled or, worse, naïve? Might I be, as one of my colleagues puts it, "a theoretical lightweight"? Maybe I'm a fool? There are worse things to do than take literature at face value, but I don't think that describes me anyway. I read essay theory for dessert, and I've studied in depth the long tradition of the form. So I worry that too often we get caught up in the dizzying revelations attendant to these theoretical reevaluations. Like a kid with a new toy, we want to take it everywhere, even into the bathtub, where it will certainly be ruined. We seem utterly rapturous with the notion that the essayist is, despite appearances, hiding something, pretending, writing himself only in a good light, not what she appears to be.

If you wish to preserve your secret, wrap it up in frankness.

ALEXANDER SMITH, "On the Writing of Essays"

But it's not about hiding things or making a false version of oneself. That's the kind of ploy that's repeatedly getting sensationalist memoirists into trouble. Essayists are a different breed, I think. They're not interested in self-aggrandizing, and their writing is driven by calm meditation, not extraordinary adventures and drama. But who could doubt the truth of Klaus's thesis, that essayists, too, engage in fiction when they write themselves? I want to revisit the question within a historical context — to move beyond my own belief, arrived at through anecdotal personal experience — and examine how essayists of the past have read their contemporaries and predecessors. I suspect I'll find some middle way.

We're a small tribe, the essayists, and we recognize our debts to our forebears and like to carry on conversations with them long after they're dead. For one thing, we read widely, which quashes any pretensions we have about our own originality. As so many essayists have said, Montaigne not only invented the essay; in writing its best examples he harvested all its potential fruits:

> Montaigne . . . to whom, down even to our own day, even in point of subject-matter, every essayist has been more or less indebted
>
> is an immense treasure-house of observation, anticipating all the discoveries of succeeding essayists.
>
> He has left little for his successors to achieve in the way of just and original speculation on human life. Nearly all the thinking . . . of that kind . . . is to be found in Montaigne's *Essays*.

ALEXANDER SMITH, "On the Writing of Essays"

CHARLES LAMB, "Books with One Idea in Them"

WILLIAM HAZLITT, "On the Periodical Essayists"

Yet he also demonstrated that essay subjects were inexhaustible and that each individual voice might write its own perspective. Do I advance a paradox? If so, then it is a fundament of the essay: yes, it's all been done, and yet there is room (need) for more. Were the point of literature to convey fact or transfer knowledge, then summaries of extant works would suffice and all would be reduced to proverb.

> The point of the essay is not the subject, for *any* subject will suffice, but the charm of personality. . . . The charm of the familiar essayist depends upon his power of giving the sense of a good-humoured, gracious and reasonable personality and establishing a sort of pleasant friendship with his reader.
>
> ARTHUR CHRISTOPHER BENSON, "The Art of the Essayist"

For another thing, essayists like to feel that we belong, that we're not alone. Each essay represents an attempt at connection and conversation, not only with one's contemporaries, but with one's ancestors; and if the ruse is successful, then readers now and much later feel also included, invited to share the moment,

> admitted behind the curtain, [to sit] down with the writer in his gown and slippers,

which is to say that from Montaigne's first attempts through four centuries of followers (knowing and unknowing; those who read and emulated the old Gascon and those whose temperament inclined them naturally/unavoidably to essay), essay-writers have carefully crafted personas intended —

> I believe that if we allow the question of intent in the case of murder, we should allow it in literature.
>
> SCOTT RUSSELL SANDERS, "The Singular First Person"

— to match the selves they think they know or feel they can convey (given limits of time and linguistic translation as well as prudence). When I write, I explore the inner life (in whose precincts we are most ourselves)

MARK SLOUKA, "Quitting the Paint Factory"

hoping to convey my self to myself, to discover, as the old woman said, what I think once I see what I say. Again: I perform the same charade when I walk into an interview or a classroom, when I shake hands at a conference or raise my hand to comment in church. Even when I am at home, the place I feel freest to let go, to laugh raucously or embrace my exasperations, to walk around in my underwear and pass gas, loudly if necessary, I am then never less myself than when myself.

So what does it matter (to the incompleteness theorem of the written persona) if I have never farted in an essay until this passing allusion just now? When I am with company, I exercise the same noble restraint. I see no great merit in that.

> The great merit of Montaigne then was, that he . . . had the courage to say as an author what he felt as a man. . . . He was, in the truest sense, a man of original mind, that is, he had the power of looking at things for himself, or as they really were, instead of blindly trusting to, and fondly repeating what others told him that they were. He got rid of the go-cart of prejudice and affectation, with the learned lumber that follows at their heels, because he could do without them. . . . In treating of men and manners, he spoke of them as he found them, not according to preconceived notions and abstract dogmas; and he began by teaching us what he himself was.

WILLIAM HAZLITT, "On the Periodical Essayists"

"What he himself was," for sure, yet even Montaigne claimed that

> there is no description equal in difficulty, or certainly in usefulness, to the description of oneself. Even so one must spruce up, even so one must present oneself in an orderly arrangement, if one would go out in public.

MONTAIGNE, "Of Practice"

118 *On Being Recognized*

So we have transitioned, as promised, away from me and into the past, to examine statements that essayists have written about themselves and other essayists, to gain an understanding of whether they, like us postmoderns, dismissed their forebears and counterparts as "mere fabrications." None of our dear authors can tell us what he meant beyond what he has written, but with a statement such as

> We know not which to be most charmed with, the author or the man. There is an inexpressible frankness and sincerity, as well as power, in what he writes. There is no attempt at imposition or concealment, no juggling tricks or solemn mouthing, no labored attempts at proving himself always in the right.

I feel justified in claiming that Hazlitt took the textual Montaigne to be a true representation of the much-more-complex, flesh-and-blood-and-synapse Montaigne. So did Virginia Woolf:

> In the whole of literature, how many people have succeeded in drawing themselves with a pen? Only Montaigne and Pepys and Rousseau perhaps. . . . But this talking of oneself, following one's own vagaries, giving the whole map, weight, colour, and circumference of the soul in its confusion, its variety, its imperfection — this art belonged to one man only: to Montaigne.

Maybe this has something to do with quantity, the sheer lengths to which Montaigne goes to portray himself confronting so many ideas, but even a thousand-page tome must be insufficient to *fully* reveal a self. Who can say how much of a soul survives in a sentence or a paragraph, how sufficiently a writer captures his essence in each essay? But I have always loved (that is to say, felt as if it were true) the sensation that I am resurrecting a real human being when I pull a dusty book from my shelf and settle in for a peaceful hour of reading essays.

[The essay] is the movement of a free mind at play.

CYNTHIA OZICK, "She: Portrait of the Essay as a Warm Body"

Through its tone and tumbling progression, [the essay] conveys the quality of the author's mind.

EDWARD HOAGLAND, "What I Think; What I Am"

I hold to traditional Christian ideas about life after death with a belief beyond wishing, yet I am skeptical enough to entertain the possibility or at least the supplement of a textual eternity, a translation of mind into incorruptible words, a self suspended and sustained through the centuries between the covers of a book. Maybe I'm hedging my bets: as the prophets have promised, on into everlasting life; or as the geneticists guarantee, in the DNA of my descendants; or each time these words find their way from some paper or digital repository, to leap me back into part life as an imperfect, incomplete re-creation in the imagination of a reader. In any case, here am I. This is me (I'm in my own way).

In the four centuries since his death, Montaigne has inspired thousands of paeans and critical studies. I have read only a smattering, but I have likely read more than you have. And in each I have sampled, the sense is the same: we may know a sixteenth-century French nobleman by the words he wrote, even, as in my case, by the words a translator has given to the words he wrote.

But let's move on. We've heard Hazlitt on Montaigne, Woolf on Montaigne, even Smith and Lamb on Montaigne. How about Woolf on Hazlitt?

[Hazlitt's] essays are emphatically himself. He has no reticence and he has no shame. He tells us exactly what he thinks, and he tells us . . . exactly what he feels. . . . We cannot read him for long without coming in contact with a very singular character — ill-conditioned yet high-minded; mean yet noble;

intensely egotistical yet inspired by the most genuine passion for the rights and liberties of mankind.

Soon, so thin is the veil of the essay as Hazlitt wore it, his very look comes before us. . . . Hazlitt was right: . . .

The notions in short which we entertain of people at a distance, or from partial representation, or from guess-work, are simple, uncompounded ideas, which answer to nothing in reality; those which we derive from experience are mixed modes, the only true and, in general, the most favourable ones.

Certainly no one could read Hazlitt and maintain a simple and uncompounded idea of him.

Perhaps Hazlitt was also right, reflecting on his writing, that "it demands an effort to exchange our actual for our ideal identity." His dear friend Charles Lamb, noting Hazlitt's curmudgeonly persona (was this Hazlitt's ideal?), gives us reason to doubt its accuracy, though: "This assumption of a character [of a discontented man], if it be not truly (as we are inclined to believe) his own, is that which gives force and life to his writing."

To remain in good conscience, I should note that I went searching for a bit more affirmation within Lamb's statements on Hazlitt, a good number of which can be found in an unpublished review of the latter's 1821 collection, *Table Talk*. Here, Lamb takes his longtime friend to task for an unkind portrait of their mutual friend Leigh Hunt and then chides him for a derivative "half-imaginary sketch" of one "Major C——," a member of Parliament.

To deduce a man's general conversation from what falls from him in public meetings . . . is about as good logic as it would be . . . if we should infer that the good man's whole discourse, at bed and board, in the ale-house and by the road-side, was confined to two cuckoo syllables, because in the exercise of his public function we had never heard him utter anything beyond Dust O!

But I'm fine with that. I'm fine with Lamb — who understood half-imaginary sketches, having invented for his essays a narrator named Elia — giving his friend gentle correction, clarifying for the public what he knew extratextually to be more true than what Hazlitt had written. So if "public meetings" are analogous to "essays," then I can soften my argument once more and believe that the persona a writer adopts is never a complete representation of his self. It is worth noting, though, that Lamb doesn't entirely give the lie to Hazlitt's writerly persona (Hazlitt "acts as his own interpreter," Lamb says). Perhaps he knew Hazlitt too well outside of his essays to comment much on the rascal's self-portrayal in prose. Let's hear, then, what Hazlitt had to say of himself:

The personalities I have fallen into have never been gratuitous. . . . I have then given proof of some talent, and of more honesty; if there is haste or want of method, there is no common-place, nor a line that licks the dust; and if I do not appear to more advantage, I at least appear such as I am.

Thus it is for me as well. If the personas I adopt in each of my essays are not me in my entirety, at least they are not false to me. As I often tell my students, your written voice should not be exactly your spoken voice, with all its *ums* and *ers* and pauses and restarts, but it should be you revised and refined, not past your self but to your best self; it should be a voice you are comfortable reading aloud. When I gave my first public reading ever, at Brigham Young University during my last semester as a master's student, my friends approached me afterward to compliment, "You sound just like you." Years later, another friend said that when he read my book, "it was like having me in the room conversing with him."

> The essayist's speaker is a construct; it's made out of words, there's no person there on the page, . . . but you understand the voice that's speaking to you to have some meaningful and faithful relationship to the actual, biological, biographical author who's off the page. . . . So the persona, the speaker, the narrator of an essay . . . should have a faithful relationship to the actual person you are. It can't be all of you; it's going to be more articulate than you are, because you've had the time to formulate it; it's going to be more thoughtful, more gathered than you are as a person, but it's going to be recognizably you.
>
> SCOTT RUSSELL SANDERS, "The Essay as a Way of Discovery"

I refuse to believe (in questions of literature as well as religion) that we in the twenty-first century are finally enlightened after long centuries of our most brilliant representatives being lost in a dark wood of naïve faith. Again and again this sentiment from the essayist: I am as I have written myself. Again and again this perspective from readers: the essayist may be known by his essays.

> I have long held the personal essay to be one of the last bastions of the orthodoxy of the unitary self: those of us who are drawn to practicing this form tend to believe in our possessing a core reality or self, and we would cling to this conviction even if critical theory disproved it 100%.
>
> PHILLIP LOPATE, "The Future of the Essay"

I wouldn't want to suggest that we've been wasting our time reading through fifteen pages of theoretical hokum, but I think it's time to get a move on, to arrive at our meander's delta with a final assertion. Here's a rub, then:

On Being Recognized 123

The self-consciousness and self-reflection that essay writing demands cannot help but have an influence on the personal essayist's life.

PHILLIP LOPATE, *The Art of the Personal Essay*

Or to allow another contemporary theorist to put it another way,

No essayist is a perfect human being; all of us fail, to more or less degree, to embody the essayistic virtues — which brings us back to the chicken-or-the-egg question.... To what degree, or extent, *is* the essay responsible for the formation of character, that character so attractive and without which we are apt to quit reading? I suspect, although I can hardly prove it, that most essayists *are* good people.

G. DOUGLAS ATKINS, *Tracing the Essay*

It's been there, haunting the essay, waiting in the wings, has it not: the notion that by writing our selves, dressing up to go out in polite company, practicing restraint and respect for the public, we improve ourselves? You've seen it coming, have been thinking it too? In nearly all cases mentioned (Hazlitt excepted, perhaps), the characteristics readers cull from essays are positive, admirable traits, are they not?

I think my favorite example of the self-shaping force of the essay comes from Louise Imogen Guiney, who wrote on at least two occasions (in close succession) about being pickpocketed soon after receiving payment for some poems just before Christmas. I first encountered her recollection of the event (as do most readers) in her essay "On a Pleasing Encounter with a Pickpocket," whose title gives away its stance. I say "*its* stance" advisedly, because I suspect now that the essay took the lead, bringing the essayist into its point of view. The event in question happened on December 21, 1892, on Berkeley Street at the corner of Chandler in Boston, as she was running back to her home. The next day, Guiney wrote to her photographer friend Fred Holland Day (nicknamed Sonny) to report the news:

I write in a melancholy mood. My pocket was picked yesterday. . . . As for the cash, it is gone, and I have such respect for the inevitable that I would say nothing of it except that it happens to concern you, and Johnny too. George Norton's bill, a five . . . was in that bag; and the other five I meant to send you as the last considerable fragment of what I owed you in francs of France. Besides that there were $4.00 extra of my hard-earned own, to be devoted to little Christmas gifts. . . . Don't condole with me, for I'll rise to the occasion like Sir Walter Scott himself; and say not a word to A.J. from whom I keep my worries.

Perhaps the act of writing this letter to Sonny Day, brief but honest in its report on her current feelings, had the effect of sweeping the clouds away. More likely, the decision to "rise to the occasion" and write an essay did that. By the time she shared her experiences in "On a Pleasing Encounter with a Pickpocket," she had made peace with the loss and was able to poke fun at herself over her distractedness and to admire the artistry with which the thief and his friends had eluded her in the end,

leaving me confused and checkmated, after a brief and unequal game, but overcome, nay, transported with admiration and unholy sympathy! It was the prettiest trick imaginable.

Which of these portraits reveals the *real* Louise Imogen Guiney? In a certain measure, both of them do, but neither does so completely. Like you or me, she was a complicated creature, by turns independent and influenced, meditative and mechanical, passionate and peculiar, and any other pair of near-opposite terms (but always alliterative — there's the influence of logos over logic!). In any case, the pickpocket and his band, who saw Guiney in person, who grabbed her pocketbook and divvied up the spoils, knew next to nothing about the *real* Louise Imogen Guiney nor cared to. Neither did she really know anything about them, though she might have attempted a conversation if given the chance. When she donned a laurel wreath and medieval robes to sit as Saint Barbara for Sonny Day, she was no less herself than when she walked the cold streets of Boston alone, "at my usual rapid pace, and ruminating, in all likelihood, on the military affairs of the Scythians." We no longer have Louise present to answer our queries, but I gladly submit that she likely preferred the haloed self her essay inclined her to be and strove to align herself with that presentation. And even if she were here to interview, we could only access the self she, by parts, chose to reveal or allowed to be revealed or unconsciously revealed to our questioning. Written or vocalized, black words on yellowing paper or elegant dress on floral armchair, it would be the same, or similarly fraught — we can know only the author as she presents herself to us, ever incomplete, ever mysterious.

That story about Louise Imogen Guiney was to be the end of the essay; and though I think it wraps things up nicely enough, the universe had other plans for us. Right now (the essay is written in the eternal now), as I make a few additions and revisions to this essay while flying above Nebraska en route from Chicago to Utah, I think I'm sitting next to (he just stirred from his semisleep; I quickly deleted his name, in case he might see my screen and tell me he is or he is not) Eddie Money. I believe this because (1) he looks like Eddie Money, or how Eddie Money might look now, twenty years after I last saw him on MTV; (2) he's sitting in first class (I got a lucky upgrade after flying altogether too much last year) as a rock star would; (3) he has shoulder-length hair at age sixty-something; (4) when the steward came around asking for preflight drink requests, I got an orange juice, but my neighbor said, "Just gimme some water," in a raspy voice like I'd expect a man with Eddie Money's singing voice to have; (5) we do, he and I, have our two tickets to paradise; (6) soon after I boarded, when the flight attendant announced that all electronic devices — anything with an on-off switch, anything with batteries or a lit screen — should be turned off, my neighbor refused, or ignored the request, and I, ever obedient and still sometimes put out by blatant disregard and self-exceptionalism, glanced sidelong at his lit screen, which flashed, ever so briefly, "Eddie Money," before he swept it away in favor of Led Zeppelin's "Achilles Last Stand." *That's* who he looks like, I thought, and I began my surreptitious search for confirming clues (his jacket's right breast reads in red script "Chief," and he wears a gold-rope necklace with a substantial hanging jewel-encrusted oval — what does this *mean?*).

In a later now, hours after I've returned home, I am sitting on the floor of a dark bedroom, willing my two young sons to sleep. I might have left things as they were, with my suspicions unconfirmed, and possibly–Eddie Money and I would have parted ways with nary a communication beyond the brief "excuse me" and "thank you" I needed to get past him and into my seat. But just as we landed, when I turned on my small electronic device to call Karina, he, too, made a call, announcing himself to his friend or wife, "Hey, it's Eddie." *What are the chances?* I thought. It *had* to be him. By the time Karina and I hung up, the plane was pulling up to the gate; then the aisle was all commotion as people stood and grabbed their bags and coats from the overhead bins, carefully, as some items might have shifted while in flight. This was no time to broach the subject of identity, to confirm that the man beside me was the man portrayed in all those videos, but the pause gave me time to steel myself for the inevitably tactless confrontation I was planning. A moment later, I found myself in the Jetway just ahead of our man, so as we trudged up the ramp toward the terminal, I turned slightly, muttered a brief apology, then asked, "Are you Eddie Money?"

He smiled and extended a hand, "Yeah, I'm Eddie."

"I thought so. Are you visiting here?"

"Naw, they're taking me home tonight, to Burbank. You live here?"

"Yeah. I teach writing at Brigham Young University, just south."

On Being Recognized 127

"I noticed you doing your homework, so . . ." I got the notion that this was his reason for not engaging me in conversation during the flight. No matter. He looked out the floor-to-ceiling windows at the snowy mountains to the east. "You ski?"

"No," chuckling apologetically, "so all of this is wasted on me."

"Man, that's too bad."

And so on for thirty seconds, a minute, I'm not sure. I decided not to lie, not to tell him I'm a big fan or to fawn over his past work. Better, I thought, more honest, to leave such subjects unsung, to let him take the superficial encounter as far as he had the energy and grace for. I suspect he can usually move about the world relatively unmolested, but every now and then a fan must recognize and bother him, and I have greater respect than to make myself too burdensome.

Anyone who knows me — and this includes people I've never met, people who've only read my essays — knows that I (along with Joan Jett) love rock and roll. I've got my unchallenged favorite bands, about whom I can be a bit fanatical; but beyond those elite, I'm still broadly enthusiastic and knowledgeable. So I felt a mixture of pride and embarrassment during our brief conversation: pride that I'd recognized him despite never owning an Eddie Money album but embarrassment that I had nothing substantial to say. As I reflected later on my good fortune, enthused that the universe seemed to care about my essay and had arranged such serendipitous seating, I decided that if I could have chosen any musician to accompany on a flight, right up near the top of my list, I'd have chosen Eddie Money, because, as happened, I could take my time, doubt myself, pick up clues, and then tell family and friends my strange, strangely appropriate story. I am constantly preaching about how when I'm "in" an essay, my life seems to align itself to the essay, offering up quotations and memories, experiences old and new, in service of the idea I'm exploring. But mostly it happens in explicable ways, the result of focused attention or my own work. Never before had the coincidence involved an external, autonomous agent.

For a brief second there inside the airport, I thought I might give him my business card and attempt to tell him later about this essay, how he'd been so significant not through his music but through this

128 *On Being Recognized*

kismet, that in the moment I most needed him, he appeared. But instead, when he wished me well, I nodded in a way I hoped would convey respect and graciousness and then turned into the flow of rushing souls rolling their carry-ons and swinging their purses, and I wished him safe travels, the same thing anybody would have said.

1. Of course, as soon as I shared this essay with my friend Scott, he reminded me of his wedding reception, where his sister-in-law recognized me, perhaps because of my book but more likely because I was Scott's teacher for many years. I assured him that this didn't count, given that she was a friend of a friend and had a reasonable expectation of encountering me there. Then, a couple of weeks later, I called photographer Joel Sartore's office to order a print of the kookaburra from my first book's cover, and the kind woman taking my order, upon receiving my credit card information, said, "You're the author of *Quotidiana!*" to which I assented, and we had a pleasant-quick chat. And thinking too long on this claim has reminded me of the time I ran into Best Buy and found standing by the customer-service queue a white-haired gentleman who called me enthusiastically by name and would not reveal to me his name or how we knew each other (this was one occasion when I felt it best to be up front and admit that I had no idea who he was). I guessed a few possible connections, and he eventually agreed that we'd known each other in Ohio, when I was in graduate school. But when I quizzed him on Ben Ogles and family, who'd recently moved from Ohio to Utah, he seemed to be faking like he knew them, so I left utterly baffled, unconvinced that I did actually know the man (like most people, though names often escape me, I'm pretty good with faces, and this guy just didn't look familiar at all).

For the Last Time

The secret horrour of the last is inseparable from a thinking being whose life is limited. . . . When we have done any thing for the last time, we involuntarily reflect that a part of the days allotted us is past, and that as more is past there is less remaining.

SAMUEL JOHNSON, "On Last Things"

A few weeks ago, before attending an academic conference in Norwich, England, I took a week to see the sights of London. A considerable portion of my time was spent visiting the haunts of Great Dead essayists, men such as Oliver Goldsmith, Thomas De Quincey, Charles Lamb, and William Hazlitt. Rarely were the homes and churches emplaqued or otherwise noted. Aside from Joseph Addison, who is buried in Westminster Abbey, their graves were unprotected from the elements and mendicants such as myself. I tried halfheartedly to keep my antennae open to possibilities for writing, but I also just wanted to live like a tourist for a while, hoping that this would calm my nerves a bit, keep my mind off the long list of things I ought to have finished already, hold at bay the entropy that rushes up to take hold of my consciousness and drag it downward. It worked on that score; but like all such diversions, it lasted only as long as the traipsing about, and when I returned to real life, I felt again the abrumant weight of my responsibilities and obligations.

So perhaps it's no wonder that the story I grasped from my British wanderings is one of no consequence. What happened was I found my fly down after several hours of group tourism about the seaside at Southwold, the setting for parts of *The Rings of Saturn* by W. G. Sebald. The realization came in the subfloor men's bathroom of the Elizabeth Fry Building at the University of East Anglia, during a break in the aforementioned conference. Mentally retracing my morning, I deduced that I must have left my pants unzipped from the moment I put them on (one leg at a time). I chuckled contentedly, half-worried that I'd exposed my white underwear or caused a colleague some momentary displaced embarrassment but half-pleased that I'd done it again. Nobody had asked me if I was afraid of heights. And I could not recall any untoward attentions or, worse, evasions, but how would I know? I zipped up, washed my hands, and returned to my day.

I was left thinking, or am thinking now, about those events that punctuate the multivolume tome of our life, not with periods, not with question marks or exclamation points, but with commas, perhaps, or apostrophes, hyphens amid compound adjectives, colons before lists, the stuff that marks the way, making our reading make sense, workmanlike, by and large glossed over, unnoticed. How often are we stricken with hiccups? When will we need to clip our toenails again? When awaits us yet another crick in the neck? Or perhaps my mind *is* leaning toward the periods, the last times, farewells to small things, embarrassing things, things we should know better (or know better than to). When will we finally master our habits, overcome our shortcomings? Have we lost our keys for the last time? Can we be sure we won't again leave our blinker on for miles and miles? Will we never again forget to take the garbage out to the curb? Have we seen the last of leaving our clothes in the washing machine until they mold or whatever it is that leaves us with stinkshirt, as my father calls it? What about the things we've very nearly mastered, like putting our shoes on the right feet or buttoning our shirt in proper correspondence? Can we ever be certain, even with advancing know-all technology to serve us, that we yet won't leave our clocks unbacked or unforwarded? Or can we look forward to that amused discomfiture of showing up to church in the middle of the Mass before or after the one we'd intended to attend?

This is the case with leaving my barn door open. I've done it often enough in the past — I know I have. Likewise, I expect I shall do it again. This is not the sort of mistake one learns from, not a sin one repents and forsakes. By its very nature, zipper negligence is unintentional and absentminded. And while I certainly have cultivated the habit of zipping up whenever I get dressed or finish at the urinal, my mind often wanders, so I can be almost certain that I will find my *brageta abierta* in the future. I have tried to resist the thought that invades my mind trailing this harmless event: that all is vanity, or life is futile, that despite our best efforts, we can never escape the small embarrassments we bring upon ourselves as we struggle to keep track of it all, as we innocently ignore our vulnerabilities. What's more, the older we get, the more likely we are to lose our fine-minded refinements, so the probabilities of oversights increase. And for all of that, we can never be sure that we've seen the last of such peccadilloes. It would be nice, in a way, to know when we've made our last little blunders, though there's a charm in not knowing, too, a blissful ignorance that hides from us the ticking of the clock or the tallying of days and moments.

Of course, at some point, known or unknown, each repeatable offense or harmless exercise must reach its final occurrence, such as what I'm quite sure was my father's last backward bicycle ride. It happened at Notre Dame, on a sunny, carefree afternoon, after a pleasing swim in St. Mary's Lake. Attendant characters, in addition to our protagonist, were my wife, Karina; my brother Dan (since I learned it, I have loved how my choice to include or omit commas indicates that I have only one wife and more than one brother); my four children — Pato, Adi, Sara, and Dani (who rode in a seat contraption on the back of her namesake uncle's bike) — and I (riding tandem with Adi). We borrowed the bikes from the dormitory that operates as a hotel for alumni each summer. Dad and Dan (and Dani) were up ahead with Pato, impatient with Sara's training-wheeled meandering. That left the rest of us back there in the shade, making slow progress amid the dirt and gravel, across small washouts and gullies, along the circular trail that rings the lake. As we crested the insubstantial hill into the vertical sunlight, I gathered in an almost-instantaneous scene: My brother paused and smiling at an island in the parking lot, holding the back-heavy bike holding Dani; my son lost somewhere among the scattered cars; my father sitting on his handlebars and facing his seat, feet on the pedals, neck craned, head turned toward me but eyes peripherating the path behind his back. He is headed toward a curb, moving too fast, turning not enough to avoid a collision. As the electric impulses zip from my eyes to my brain to my mouth to shout "Dad!" his front wheel jumps up and jerks right (his left) just onto the border grass and into the octagonal base of a light pole. Momentum is enemy; ballast is imbalance; a man set on his rump above the front wheel means only one thing: a glancing carom off the pole, the back wheel shooting up, my father twisting to brace his headlong tumble to the street below. But the bike is six inches above the asphalt, on the grass. His hands miss the soft turf by a horizontal six inches, so his head crashes helmetless to the street, crumpling under the accelerated weight of his body and the metallic contraption that traps his feet and legs.

In a second, Dan and I were at his side, helping him up, assessing his injuries. He got to his feet easily enough, if a bit groggily, blinkingly, behind his scratched glasses a slow trickle of blood, on his upper lip a raw exposed layer of skin. We left the bike where it lay and held his hands to show him to a nearby bench, to sit and think on the event. Already the children and Karina were with us, the former on the verge of tears, the latter on the verge of laughter. A red-haired woman who saw the whole thing asked, obligedly, "Are you okay?" My father mumbled an affirmative, and she continued past. I made the group's first attempt at lightening the gravitas: "She's thinking, 'Are you okay, you idiot?'"

Dad perked up, "She said that?"

"No," I said, immediately regretting my move but forced to follow through, "but she must be thinking it." I thought to check his hearing when I got the chance.

Our own questions weren't much more profound than the woman's, but we were persistent, making sure he'd kept his bearings and didn't feel too pained or otherwise untoward. He stood up well under our scrutiny, though Dan, gently removing Dad's glasses, noticed a pulsing gash in the folds above his left eye.

Perhaps this was a moment to consider mortality, to imagine the world without my father, but our conversation was a mixture of immediate plans and gentle ribbing. Dad wanted to be sure the borrowed bike wasn't noticeably damaged, so he announced his plans to ride it back to the dorm. Dan, keen to try out a role reversal, caught his words and remonished, "Ride it back, not back*ward*." He and Karina snickered, while I, ashamed of my prior failed attempt at humor, tried to remain stoic. Karina assuaged the children's contagious crying with shushes and whispers that "Grandpa's going to be fine." They didn't believe her.

But he was fine, all things considered, and so was the bike, so he did ride away, soon enough, with the rest of us alongside and behind, as he made it back to the dorm, then continued on to the hospital, where he omitted the "backward" detail in his explanation and found that he'd fractured his skull, an untreatable misfortune (stay out of the boxing ring is about all you can do for it), and then, in the coming days, traveled on to Milwaukee, his boyhood home, where a handful of cousins would relish his tale for its pure ridiculability.

For as long as I have known my father, he has talked about the summer projects that he and his friends would take on: juggling, walking on their hands, riding their bikes backward. I tried it all but mastered only a fraction of his feats and never quite got the balance and rhythm to ride my bike sitting on my handlebars. This was yet one more way in which I would never be my father's equal. So it was a mix of sadness and pride that I felt, later, when reminiscing with my wife and brother, to have witnessed Dad's last backward ride, the exclamation point ending that particular thread of his life.

I might have expected that I would twist out of my stories into braided meditations as soon as I set off to narrate, that I would, one might say, unzip from the constraints of chronicle into confabulation.

It is a mode, I hope, not utterly unpleasant, as it gives both a recounting of events and an attempt at an ordering not only of chronologies but, as Lukács says, of "souls and destinies." God rest us both, my father and me, long into the hereafter, of course, but now, too, for brief snatches of peace amid all our self-created chaos, our ineluctable destinies of descent and decay.

Independent Redundancy

Let no one say that I have said nothing new; the arrangement of the subject is new.... Words differently arranged have a different meaning, and meanings differently arranged have different effects.

PASCAL, *Pensées*

MY SWEET LORD, HE'S SO FINE

I've been on a George Harrison kick lately, buying the deluxe editions of his solo CDs, listening to all those songs I've never heard, doing penance for the time I ignored him or thought of him only as the quiet Beatle. Also, I'm in a kind of delayed mourning. His November 2001 death came as an unexpected shock, but I was reeling from 9/11. And then, shortly after Harrison, W. G. Sebald died, too. This was too much public grief for me to focus on any one life lost. I knew then that I should learn more about the man, immerse myself in his music, hear what he was trying to say. It took me six years to even listen, years more to write.

Also lately I've been seeking to understand originality, or creativity. As a writer, I am inherently curious about such concepts. My title, "Independent Redundancy," is a term I invented to describe the phenomenon of two or more individuals coming up with the same idea without any cross-pollination or shared influence. I'll give plenty of examples, but here's one that is quintessential for me; perhaps it got me started on this line of thinking: A friend of mine, an exceptional short story writer whose work I recommend, is named Tom Noyes. One day, noting the appropriate ambiguity of his surname, I jokingly called him "Tom Maybe." I thought I was being clever. Tom responded, "It's not like I haven't heard that one a thousand times since the second grade." (And yet I swear I have never talked to his second-grade classmates!) The example is simple and easy enough to explain. The name Noyes sits like an unlocked treasure chest awaiting anyone with a modicum of linguistic curiosity to pry it open and see its *no-yes* components. From there, the avenues for creative punning are relatively limited, with *maybe* topping the available possibilities.

But back to George Harrison: The reason I'm so tickled that my music and my musings coincide nowadays is that George is emblematic for me of the inevitable overlappings of contemporary popular Western music, the unavoidable redundancy when melodies derive from a limited, repeated scale of seven notes (or eleven, including sharps and flats), which can be transposed but which retains a mathematical correlation between notes. I am referring, of course, to the great "My Sweet Lord"/"He's So Fine" controversy and court case.

In 1970, soon after the Beatles announced their breakup, Harrison released his first solo album, the first Beatle to do so after that momentous dissolution. The lead song on *All Things Must Pass* and the first single was "My Sweet Lord," a catchy little ditty expressing devotion to Krishna and melding Eastern and Western spirituality. It was a significant hit, reaching number one in Great Britain and achieving substantial radio play around the world, which was certainly why it caught the attention of Bright Tunes, the publishing company that owned the rights to "He's So Fine," a 1962 hit by the Chiffons, which sounds remarkably similar to "My Sweet Lord." Since the older song's writer, Ronnie Mack, had died years before, there was no chance for a polite resolution, and things went to court. There was a lot of money involved, as you can imagine, and little incentive to accept the early settlements offered by the Harrison camp. Mix in a soap-operatic double agent in Alan Klein — the Beatles' manager turned Bright Tunes owner (in the span of a few years) — and you've got all the ingredients for some high drama. Early on, Harrison acknowledged that he knew the Chiffons' song and had likely plagiarized it, though unintentionally. He supposed that he'd simply forgotten where he found the melody and had believed that he'd invented it.

Perhaps he should have done as Paul McCartney did with the tune he dreamt one night in Jane Asher's apartment on Wimpole Street in London. The much-recounted story goes that when he woke, he went immediately to the piano to play the melody he'd found in his head. Afraid that he'd dredged up a memory of something he'd heard elsewhere, he pestered fellow musicians and scoured local record shops for several weeks, asking if anybody recognized the tune. In the absence of any evidence to the contrary, he eventually decided that the song was his own and supplied nonsense lyrics as placeholders until better ones could be wrought. "Scrambled Eggs, oh my baby how I love your legs" became a kind of long-running joke with the Beatles, until Paul finally found the inspiration to write, "Yesterday, love was such an easy game to play," etc., which became a number one single and one of the most recorded songs in history. In one of the most entertaining late-night television sketches I've seen recently, McCartney and Jimmy Fallon sing the supposed entire first version of the song, featuring not only "Scrambled eggs" but "waffle fries" and "tofu wings" (in deference to Sir Paul's vegetarianism). You should check it out.

Contemporary musicologists, who are paid to find connections that most of us don't hear, have essentially confirmed McCartney's claim of originality. Neither Ray Charles's version of "Georgia on My Mind" nor Nat King Cole's "Answer Me, My Love" is significantly similar to "Yesterday," despite the claims of certain troublemakers, nor is any other song composed before that fateful dream. I'm not entirely clear on the criteria or the cutoffs they're using to declare "Yesterday" *original*, but I don't dispute their assertion, either.

In any case, Harrison was not so lucky. Despite years of delays and attempts at settlements, despite his best efforts to point out differences

138 *Independent Redundancy*

between his and the Chiffons' songs, he was found guilty of unintentional plagiarism and ordered to pay a million and a half dollars from his royalties. Additional legal battles ensued, during which Alan Klein's duplicity was revealed, and ultimately Harrison paid only about half a million, buying from Klein the rights to the song he'd subconsciously pretty-much copied so that he could keep playing "My Sweet Lord" without paying further royalties.

His follow-up single, "This Song," pokes appropriate fun at the whole fiasco, claiming that "this song has nothing Bright about it" and that "my experts tell me it's okay." The video features a Pythonesque courtroom scene with a slaphappy George arguing his case before a jury. But of course, even "This Song" is not unique. To me it sounds a bit like Huey Lewis and the News's "Heart of Rock and Roll" (which was recorded much later); and if I hum its bass line into a song-recognition application, I'm told it may be "Third Stone from the Sun" by Jimi Hendrix or "Dani California" by Red Hot Chili Peppers. Neither I nor the computers know enough songs from the sixties to find any that Harrison might have unwittingly copied for "This Song," but I wouldn't be surprised if someone found one.

(Speaking of "Dani California," when Tom Petty was made aware of its similarities to his song "Mary Jane's Last Dance" and encouraged to sue, he said, "I seriously doubt that there is any negative intent there. And a lot of rock and roll songs sound alike. Ask Chuck Berry. . . . It doesn't bother me. . . . There are enough frivolous lawsuits in this country without people fighting over pop songs." [Almost a decade later, once the music industry had tanked, Petty's people had a talk with Sam Smith's people about choral similarities between 2014's "Stay with Me" and 1989's "I Won't Back Down"; this led to an amicable private settlement that included songwriting credit for Petty (and Jeff Lynne) and royalty sharing on the young artist's Grammy-winning song. Smith asserts that neither he nor the other songwriters had ever heard the Petty song, and Petty asserts that "the word *lawsuit* was never even said and was never my intention."])

Of course, the borrowing goes both ways, and I'm certain that Harrison has provided more inspiration than he took. For instance, nobody would ever accuse Disney of plagiarism (the legal costs would be too high for that unwinnable war), but take a listen to the harp interludes between vocal lines in Harrison's "Dark Sweet Lady." It's the main melody from the later *Beauty and the Beast* theme song, is it not? Who knows if Alan Menken knew that song, but he may have. Harrison was, after all, a Beatle.

MIDWESTERN AMATEUR INSULT RAP

I have never written a hit song or even a hit essay, but I've experienced my own unintentional plagiarisms, like the time I wrote a litany of "Here she is . . ." statements to describe a series of photographs of my grandmother. My friend Shannon, critiquing the essay, let me know that she was uncomfortable with me intoning the same cadence that she'd used in a recent video essay's series of photographs of *her* grandmother. I apologized, explained my mistake, and edited out the statements. In that case, I quickly and humbly recognized what I'd done. But other times, the connections aren't as easy to make, or maybe they're utterly inexistent. Sometimes, as with my Tom Noyes pun, the linguistic melodies are ripe for the picking, easy to discover even without any influence.

Just now, for instance, I thought of the phrase "in no particulate order" while completing an interview for *The Fine Delight*, a blog about Catholic writing. In a recent essay, I had been writing about molecules sharing momentum, bouncing off one another, so my mind was on the "particulate" theme. This is the only explanation I can muster to trace the phrase's appearance in my brain. But if I look online, I find — in addition to those who've simply mistyped *particular* and after assuring Google that I do, indeed, want results for *particulate* — a few folks who've had the same quick flash of insight I've had. The most apt is an air pollution analysis for Ulaanbaatar, Mongolia.

This kind of easy inspiration comes to me all the time, or I fertilize it by keeping my head in books all day long. Another example recalls the 2003 Super Bowl, played between the Oakland Raiders and the Tampa Bay Buccaneers. Living in football isolation in Montevideo,

Uruguay, with almost no access to pregame hype, I independently discovered, based on team names and logos, that this was the Pirate Bowl. But I eventually heard the same name used so widely as to defy citation. Now it exists in the passive voice only: "the game *was dubbed* the 'Pirate Bowl.'"

Another example came unexpected not to my head but to my fingers; I was responding to a student essay and mistyped *analytical* as *analyrical*, which, I thought, might be an appropriate neologism to describe essays, with their coupled interests in thought and language. Colin Wanke, from Topeka, Kansas, now in Minneapolis, had a similar idea a short time before me. He adopted the term as his stage name. I admit a certain ignorance of freestyle amateur rap, but I also feel a kind of essayistic harmony in describing his music as derivative, unoriginal. I can't recommend it. He seems to have tried to fill the void left by Eminem during the latter's years of family troubles and drug rehabilitation. Unoriginality seems to be one of the worst insults you can fling at a fledgling lyricist in a warehouse battle. Special T, a rival midwestern-states indie hip-hop artist, levied this charge against Analyrical, his sparring partner:

Just 'cause Eyedea switched his style up don't mean you can have his old one now.

Just who this Eyedea is — or was (and it took me some deft Googling to figure out how to spell his name) — I cannot exactly say, though he seems to have cared, as his name suggests, about thinking and seeing. My music of choice is rock and roll, usually with either a singer-songwriter or a progressive bent, but I can still find something worthwhile in Eyedea's lyrics: "Self-proclaimed rebels say we must oppose the system. . . . But when a homeless veteran asks for spare change, they're too busy protesting to even listen. And I'm no different; I live in conflict and contradiction." It's rare to find self-reflection in popular music, and as wordsmithing goes, I have to respect a man who titles an album *The Some of All Things* and calls a tour "Appetite for Distraction." For Analyrical, it seems to be all the clichéd superficialities you'd expect, but for Eyedea, who died of a drug overdose at the age of twenty-eight, facility with words may have conveyed infelicity with the world.

One small inventive success I can recall involves the apparently trendy subgenre of zombie literature. One of my students began an essay "On Coziness" lamenting her lack of preparation for the impending zombie apocalypse. I found it quite entertaining, but several of her classmates noted that zombie-apocalypse stories were passé. In any case, combining my recent interest in physical fitness with the current discussion, I recommended that students might want to write about the "Zumba apocalypse" but that they'd likely find even that clever phrase already taken by someone on the Internet.

Turns out I was wrong. A diligent search finds that only gibberish aggregators have ever placed those two words next to each other.

> For every sensible line of straightforward statement, there
> are leagues of senseless cacophonies, verbal jumbles and
> incoherences.
>
> JORGE LUIS BORGES, "The Library of Babel"

So let the record show that Patrick Madden, of his own volition, invented the term "Zumba apocalypse" on the twentieth day of January 2010 at approximately 10:08 a.m., mountain standard time. Let the future know that Zumba (I can't imagine the fad lasting very long) is "an exhilarating, effective, easy-to-follow, Latin-inspired, calorie-burning dance fitness-party," which description may be trademarked. And let the reader go with what inspiration she finds there. I offer the pairing to the world. Write with it what you will.

PANGRAM HAIKU

Another literary invention I claim is the pangram haiku, that is, a three-line poem following the English adaptation of the venerable Japanese model — five, then seven, then five syllables — and including all the letters of the alphabet. The originality here is in combination. The haiku is a centuries-old literary form with a proud tradition of reverence to nature. It seems to have made its way into English in the early twentieth century. The pangram is a kind of word game, a sentence including all twenty-six letters in our alphabet, the best known of which, "The quick brown fox jumps over the lazy dog," has pervaded the English speaking world since the late 1800s as a typing exercise or font sampler.

Other clever pangrams exist, though very few achieve the economy of that canine caper, which uses only thirty-five letters. ("Pack my box with five dozen liquor jugs" is one of my favorites because it's a complete sentence that makes sense, but once you think about it, you're going to have a really hard time carrying that box!) The highest goal is to use *only* twenty-six letters, a task made nearly impossible by the scarcity of vowels. Nevertheless, by resorting to initials and proper names, perhaps some obscure foreign words, folks have tried to pass off things like "Mr. Jock, TV quiz PhD, bags few lynx" or "Zing! Vext cwm fly jabs Kurd qoph." Let me save you the trouble of looking up any of those words in the dictionary: there is not a single sensical twenty-six-letter English pangram on the earth. The quest for concision has resulted in inanity.

So you get to wondering about other ways to make pangrams interesting. My contribution to the field comes in combining these two minimalist forms. On January 23, 2004, at 10:37 a.m. (EST), in response to my brother's post on our family blog, in which he noted typographer Mark Simonson's "Pangrammer Helper" program (it's great; visit it here: http://www.marksimonson.com/notebook/view/pangrammer-helper) and after which several family members and a friend had attempted our own pangrams, I gave the world its very first pangram haiku:

Lost in flight, quiet
Yellow jacket reproves me.
Vexed, I buzz away.

Not too shabby, right? That's fifty-three letters, by the way, which wouldn't impress the reductionists but which seems about average for the new genre. My second example, written forty-five minutes later, is a proclamation. I imagine trumpets blaring:

Read ye my haiku!
Strong, living words dazzle. Jump
back, quietly fixed.

Especially knowing that its sense is derived only secondarily, after its constraint is satisfied, I find the evocation uncannily appropriate. The oxymoronic jumping fixedness suits the apprehension of literature admirably, I believe.

Not to be outdone, my brothers and father tried their hands at the form, with mixed results. My father, keen to comment on the failures, wrote a metapoem:

Haiku verses flow
like a bad, exacting quiz.
Too jumpy, yet fun.

Which is kind of true of the haikus, but I've never known a "bad, exacting quiz" to be any fun. In any case, the strain of utilizing the entire abecedary seems to have brought out my inner environmentalist:

The ax swerves, tree dies:
Quite a lop job, so crazy.
Man kills for nothing.

Quivering boughs' crazed
voices wail: empty sky of
juxtaposition.

144 *Independent Redundancy*

Ultimately, and perhaps appropriately, given the strange meanders of this essay, the highest (lowest) form of the genre I created was the rapper-insult pangram haiku, of which there is only one example:

Your quick wit doesn't
Faze me. I can't help your jive!
Go back to detox!

I only hope that Analyrical can use it to exact his revenge on Special T some day.

Alas, the pangram haiku never quite caught on. A couple of bloggers discovered it and wrote their own examples, sometimes erroneously crediting my brother Dan with the invention, but the last known pangram haiku flitted into Internet immortality in September 2006. I hope this essay's publication in the back of an obscure book by a nonprofit university press will correct the public's oversight.

MY OWN WRITING STYLE

Before the ink was dry on the letter granting me tenure at Brigham Young University, I was asked to provide a confidential external review of a colleague's application for tenure at another university. I did so gladly. Fast forward a few months, to a conference we both attended. I casually ask her how the process went (or is going), and she says, "I wanted to thank you, by the way." Here I admit my involvement, sheepishly, and then ask, "How did you know I wrote a letter?" It was my writing style, she says. Her chair quoted to her anonymous lines from her three external reviewers, and she could tell me from my sentences.

I felt both proud and exposed. On the one hand, I have a *style!* On the other, I have nowhere to hide (for instance, when I write ransom notes and inflammatory online comments).

But I've noticed the same sort of things in others' writing, too. When my first book manuscript came back from the University of Nebraska Press's external reviewing phase before they'd offered me a contract, I read with interest the comments from two experts in the field and guessed, based on their sentences, who they were. Granted,

Independent Redundancy 145

I had my suspicions going in and the press had allowed me to recommend about a dozen possible reviewers, but my ultimate certainty about their identities came from their prose.

Not everybody knows these writers (though the world would be a better place if everybody did), but I'll take a chance on the notion that if you're reading a Patrick Madden essay, you might also recognize "Essays are the coolest form, the most capacious, the most direct, the most substantive, the closest to the mind and voice at play, the form that allows the most taut and arrowed connection between writer and reader, in part because they also are thoughtful and playful" as coming from the brain of Brian Doyle or "It resists knowing the new but knows knowing what is known in new ways. It is new not in the genesis sense of creation, but in its ability to create new combinations, associations of things already known in the world" as the work of Michael Martone alone. Perhaps, too, you can notice even in that last sentence my penchant for rhymes and visual repetitions: *brain* and *Brian* as well as *Martone* and *alone* (because I couldn't think of an *m* word to parallel *brain* except by going Spanish — from the *manos* or *mente* of Michael Martone — which would offend Paul Theroux, who taught me that writing is always an act of translation, so leaving foreign languages untranslated is a sin [of course, in revision, I think "*mind* of Michael Martone," you numbskull! (had you thought of *mind*, too, reader? [and yet that might be *too* similar to *brain*])]). In this case, probably the gimmick beat out sense, and I'd very much like to revise or delete the whole thing. But it serves an illustrative purpose, so I'll let the double-faced phrase stand.

I remain interested in seeing my style from at least a feigned objectivity, a stance outside myself, to understand what it is I do. Recently I was talking with my friend Eric Freeze, who asked if, and then insisted that, I was a postmodern writer. I wasn't so sure. Sure, Martone had claimed, in his hyperbolic way, that my first book "put the post- in postmodern," but what does that even mean? So I asked Eric to explain, and this is what he said in a later email:

First off I think I'd better start off with how I view postmodernism. For me, it's both a focused literary movement and an umbrella term for all sorts of contemporary cultural trends. It's also like the Tao: it is what it is not. In other words, it's derivative, reacting to modernism. And so modernism for me is where it all begins. When I think of modernity, I think of T. S. Eliot, "Tradition and the Individual Talent," a work that recognized the influence of earlier forms and modernism's tendency to bend or recast them in new ways. I think of cities, of industrialization, of human beings as machine-like cogs. I think of Chaplain's Modern Times and the stock market and the failure of institutions. I think of war, lots of war, and the disintegration of values. I think of bobbed hair and psychoanalysis and the rise of literary studies and the New Critical School. I also think of authors trying to write the great American novel, of trying to encapsulate all of these changes into one fragmented but aesthetically unified form. I think of dead white men trying to speak for everyone, the whole world, and the urgency and ego that come with such a task. Postmodernism is a reaction against those narratives, often using the same formal techniques as modernists in a more self-conscious way. Postmodernism is the locus of everyday things, the quotidian, the mundane, the idiosyncratic, playfully tossed together. It's the conflation of high and low art, of comic books and poetry, the indelible mixing of genres with the purpose to offend, to amuse, to entertain. But most of all, it's the awareness that there is no fixed center, no narrative that speaks for everyone, and so our knowledge and art is relational, contextual, subject to change, a process. These elements, my friend, abound in your work. What do you make of an essay that combines the Bible with Rush with old yearbook photos? If I were to think of a metaphor to describe postmodernism, the infinite play and subversion and self-consciousness of contemporary culture, I would use the Internet. You yourself said that when you write, you have to have the Internet accessible, so that you can look up stuff as you go along. Your very process is postmodern! How different is your process from a mash-up? From web surfing? Take that and combine it with the ancient, venerable, maundering Montaignesque essay, and you have postmodern Patrick Madden.

I should mention that Eric and I both have PhDs from the same place, Ohio University, at the same time, 2004, but I only vaguely understand what he's talking about here. In fact, I'm currently flying above the southeastern states in American Airlines flight 2077, so I can't look up that "Chaplain's Modern Times" reference, and I'm considering whether it might be a film by Charlie Chaplin (Eric's super bright but not above the occasional misspelling; I am a self-proclaimed "filmistine" — my own coinage, though online you can find several other people who've discovered/invented the portmanteau, too). But I agree with the gist of what he's saying: my writing combines old and new, hoping to resurrect the old, contemporize it, humbly recognize my debt to and insignificance in the long tradition of the essay while insisting that I, too, have something (artistic) to say. As a repentant perfectionist who once believed in a black-and-white world, I strain between the impulse to know it (and share it) all and the utter futility of such pursuits. I am painfully metaliterary in my thinking. Ultimately, I attempt to translate some artistic representation of my thoughts, boldly enough to suppose that someone might enjoy reading my essays but humbly enough to accept that almost nobody reads essays. I try to efface my self while, by my actions, declaring myself worth reading.

But this focuses on the external, macroscopic features of my writing (Bible and Rush and all that — you could notice such things without really reading a sentence). If we look a little closer, beyond the ingredients, the themes, too, are common, repeated, angled from here and there, reposted for subsequent considerations. Thus I return again and again to death, Montaigne's own obsession, spark of all religion, great equalizer of all living. There's love, too, and fortune (my own good, others' bad, my fears of chance's icy interference in my contentment) and contentment, the tranquility of living well, the inescapability of systems (of humanity, of science, of language, of self), the implications of scientific understanding, the importance of art, epistemology, metaphysics, free will, the frustrations of busyness and joys of idle unfettered thinking, individuality and community, the interrelatedness of all people, the pompous self-delusion of individual autarky and first-world entitlement, service to others, judgment and forgiveness, the essay as a way of apprehending the multifarious complexity of this marvelous world, the importance of attention, reverence. But these are the concerns of essayists in all places and times. You could hardly claim to recognize Patrick Madden just from the abstractions I write about.

So you might, after all, recognize me from some combination of the ingredients, the themes, and the style. Looking down on my essays from a great height, the landscape looks postmodern. (It occurs to me, as I peek out the window and see only clouds, that so much of the actual landscape below looks certifiably *modern*, subdivided and purposed in large swaths determined by utility; even in the absence of a paternalistic government guiding the economy, we have [largely] conformed our lands [and lives] to the fractured uniformity of purpose expected by our overlords, machinating a distorted "greater good" designed to support them [I, too, am beneficiary of this system; they pay me to read books!]. But what of the tangled branches of the plants below, the running waters and rustling breeze, the living hum of vale and hillock? I speak, metaphorically, of the sentences. What of them?).

I find Canadians to be both insightful and critical without any mean-spiritedness, so in addition to Eric, an Alberta boy, I asked my Ontarian friend Doug Glover for some analysis of my writing style. Here's what he wrote (in the third-person style of a long blurb):

Patrick Madden writes wistful, whimsical, erudite, obsessive essays replete with recondite information, quotation, lists, and surprising associations (not to mention jokes, wordplay, lists, and puns). His enthusiasm for words and for apparent trivia (quotidiana is his theme) is matched by his charming self-implication; on the one hand he is a grammar fetishist, on the other he cherishes his own verbal lacunae (he learned the word *quotidian* from the Spanish *cotidiana* and for years did not think it existed in English). He tells stories about his children, his wife, his teaching, writing essays; but he also seems eminently at home in the culture at large, able to mine any number of antique texts, casually almost, to track a word or a concept in time. His essays are like little gardens; he cultivates and is cultivated, yet he writes with a mischievously disingenuous air that belies the vast reading he culls to make his designs. The world is a sign, it seems, a miraculous message; the little things of life luminesce with meaning. His originality lies in this: his ability to yoke humdrum minutia with the esoteric and to drop in your lap the precise, lapidary quotation that makes the connection true and expansive.

I feel a bit strange reading this, quoting it myself, knowing, especially, that I asked him to write it; but ultimately I'll leave it in, because I respect the fine line between description and praise, and I find its descriptions insightful, and because in my small corner of the book business, most blurbs are derived from the same process: authors asking their friends for a favor. Many of Glover's adjectives, in any case, seem appropriate.

And what might I say about my own writing? Sigh. That it's the best I can do (When I was a kid, I was shocked to read in a pop magazine that the members of my favorite band, KISS, favored other bands besides themselves! But I get that now. I am not my favorite writer by a long shot) and that it's traceably derivative (from flat-out unattributed quotes from Montaigne or Lamb or Louise Imogen Guiney to nuanced recycled Brian Doyle or W. G. Sebald). This is not to say that it's no good. I think it's passable, better than a lot of what I read. In Olympic gymnastics, where the competitors all receive scores in the top 10 percent of the available scale, they're being judged (I've assumed) in relation to the rest of humanity (*I'd* score a two out of ten on the high bar or the pommel horse). Like those Olympians, I'm a real writer, worth an eight- or nine-point-something, but I would never medal. Still, I hold out some hope based on the Kansas principle, which states that even a middling band can coalesce to produce a pair of perfect songs ("Carry on Wayward Son" and "Dust in the Wind"). So why not a middling writer?

But what of my writing's attributes? What do I see when I turn my attention to what I'm doing? Typical of my writing are variation in syntax and vocabulary (I use the dictionary religiously). But I don't vary always. I often employ placeholder phrases like "of course" or "for instance" simply as transitions. I love transitions, feeling them essential to stitch together the diverse swatches of ideas I marshal into my essays. I tend to write rhymingly, sometimes with end-soundalike words but more often with repetitions, of image or idea, of rhythms and initial sounds. (Is there an *i* word that means "rhythms"? I find none.) I hear in my head a kind of scatted beat, likely unscannable but nevertheless rhythmic, perhaps reminiscent of real human speech, which quality (or aspiration) is an old habit for essayists.

> To write a genuine familiar ... style, is to write as any one would speak in common conversation who had a thorough command and choice of words, or who could discourse with ease, force, and perspicuity, setting aside all pedantic and oratorical flourishes.
>
> WILLIAM HAZLITT, "On Familiar Style"

Like Theophile Gautier, I believe that words have an individual and a relative value.

> The arithmetic is in existence: we have not to invent it; we have only to learn it. One must learn to be at home in fugue and counterpoint, and to render one's talent supple and limber by the gymnastics of words.

I have learned that no matter the seeming preplottedness of my nonfictional subject matter, I must write in thrall to the rhythms and sounds inherent in the linguistic medium I employ to re-create experience. In other words, I care less about telling a story the way it happened and more about making a kind of music from story. I'm a meticulous and slow writer, careful to a fault,

Original writing fashions a form. It unrolls out into nothingness. It grows cell to cell, bole to bough to twig to leaf; any careful word may suggest a route, may begin a strand of metaphor or event out of which much, or all, will develop.

ANNIE DILLARD, *The Writing Life*

and I can get quite manic about the subtle nuanced differences in meaning caused by words differently arranged. (Beyond the common "Dog bites man"/"Man bites dog," I enjoy playing with the variant meanings where *only* is concerned.

Only employees allowed beyond this point [nobody else]
Employees only allowed beyond this point [allowed but not obligated]
Employees allowed only beyond this point [but not on *this* side of this point]
Employees allowed beyond only this point [not beyond any other points]
Etc.)

I am awfully fond of alliteration, enjoying the challenge of finding my meaning within words that conform to my rhythmic requirements. This is an especially diverting task because I write nonfiction, so I am unwilling to stray from factual re-creation (I recognize the complexities in such a claim; I have mentioned already that writing is always a translation, a making, never the fact itself; likewise, I can grasp the philosophical difficulty of believing wholesale in unmitigated objective reality). Where was I? I employ a wide variety of words, often resorting to a dictionary, always checking etymologies, sensing that unthinking repetition is unartistic and that words, in literary writing, are never simply denotative. Indeed, I mistrust the very notion of direct correspondence between name and named, so that words become the medium through which I express a kind of thinkingart. I am, I realize, unlikely to employ metaphor, though I do so from time to time. I am not much for elaborate description; and as it was with

Montaigne, "there is nothing so contrary to my style as an extended narration," largely because I flounder if I stay in a scene too long. I have an easy grasp of syntax, seeing the relationality of English as a logical structure, and thus I can craft very long sentences without losing sense. I am fond of archaism, likely from reading so voraciously so many classics of the essay and certainly from emulating Charles Lamb, who, even for his day (the early 1800s), was a bit musty.

And if I emulate Lamb, then where did he get his style from? From his forebears, says Hazlitt:

> Mr. Lamb is the only imitator of old English style I can read with pleasure; and he is so thoroughly imbued with the spirit of his authors that the idea of imitation is almost done away. There is an inward unction, a marrowy vein, both in the thought and feeling, an intuition, deep and lively, of his subject, that carries off any quaintness or awkwardness arising from an antiquated style and dress. The matter is completely his own, though the manner is assumed. . . . The old English authors, Burton, Fuller, Coryate, Sir Thomas Browne, are a kind of mediators between us and the more eccentric and whimsical modern, reconciling us to his peculiarities.
>
> "On Familiar Style"

And Lamb himself seems to agree. With his typical self-deprecation, he describes his essays as "unlicked, incondite things — villainously pranked in an affected array of antique modes and phrases." I fall far short of Lamb's brand of imitation, but I readily admit my influences, as have many others.

OTHER ESSAYISTS

Essayists revel in wandering through other people's thoughts, but perhaps the revelry is possible only because they are aware of what they are doing — they can sense the distance traveled, the foreignness beyond the shades of their prison house, the textures of ideas that seem new while strangely familiar to them. All humans have the capacity to think (at least, as far as I have been able to observe), and there is no human who has not come into some form of contact with others' thoughts, but not all humans are essayists — so the defining characteristic of essayists must reside elsewhere. Perhaps it is found in the deliberateness, the conscious enjoyment, of the contact with others' thoughts (though that contact may not always be comfortable). Thus Lamb doesn't hesitate to pay the price for walking the dangerous line:

> As a hazard of losing some credit on this head, I must confess that I dedicate no inconsiderable portion of my time to other people's thoughts. I dream away my life in others' speculations. I love to lose myself in other men's minds. When I am not walking, I am reading; I cannot sit and think. Books think for me.

> "Detached Thoughts on Books and Reading"

Proust would not have readily approved. What do you mean, Mr. Lamb, not just by letting books think for you (something not *so* unusual, after all — there are, admittedly, fewer writers than there are readers), but by deliberately reveling in this passivity? Take this warning:

> So long as reading is treated as a guide holding the keys that open the door to buried regions of ourselves into which, otherwise, we should never penetrate, the part it can play in our lives is salutary. On the contrary, it becomes dangerous when, instead of waking us to the reality of our own mental processes, it becomes a substitute for them.

> "Days of Reading"

But perhaps Lamb's awareness of his reliance on other men's minds is precisely the mental process to which he *has* been awakened by his reading — the realization that one's stream of thought is not something isolated or pristinely original (the word *vacant*, after all, finds its roots in the Latin *vacuum*) but that it gathers itself together from every possible source it can, from the ancient melting of the glacier, from the rain that fell but seconds ago, from the sediment red and black and brown and white and blue eroded from the stones that, like unconscious memories, color its identity.

Despite my occasional flights of fancy and fondness for archaism, I hold with Hazlitt and only write sentences I would be comfortable saying aloud. One of the commonest comments I hear about my writing from others is that "it sounds just like me." (Here I've intentionally quoted a phrase but changed the pronoun, which people no longer do but which the Romantics did all the time. Others, speaking to me, would say, "It sounds just like *you*." That kind of thing — that's what I'm talking about.) It's not only me in my essays, either. I constantly quote from friends dead and alive, not borrowing their ethos (as the sinners do) but conversing with them, engaging in polyphony, recognizing, above all, that it has all been thought before.

Perhaps my fascination with originality and imitation marks me as a product of the pre-Internet generation. Like Jonathan Lethem in "The Ecstasy of Influence," I'm still excited about the potential recombination and reiteration of words penned by previous authors. My students today come to school already fluent in open-source technology. They repost memes, author *Wikipedia* articles, share and coauthor documents with a point and a click. What they write is almost subconsciously repackaged and repurposed; they're not unlike collagists or recyclers, purveyors of the ephemeral, garbage collectors all. Sometimes I sit at my computer and let the recombinative bits wash over me. There are times when even what I write, plucking ephemera from the cyberuniverse, feels like transposing, as though I've opened up my veins and let other writers dump their DNA in.

Getting back to the matter of sentences, I am essentially allergic to sentence fragments, though I do use them on rare occasions (not right around here, of course; that would be cheesy). I write past events in past tense overwhelmingly, as my students know, because I believe that this choice gives me space for reflection between then and now. Sometimes, for effect, I will try to turn deftly and unnoticed to the present tense, to heighten the narrated event, a trick I learned from Brian Doyle and Scott Russell Sanders, though others do it too. I believe that the dominant perspective of the personal essay is the writerly present. I am fond of tight parallelism, including parallelism of verb strengths, such that *to be* mixed with action verbs or with *had* plus past participles sets off my alarms ("I read and write and am tired"), as do different levels of description (mixed *ser* and *estar*, or permanent versus temporary conditions) ("She was petite and laughing"). I cannot abide dangling modifiers, and I misread whenever the grammar of a sentence permits a misreading. It's a game sometimes; other times, it's a curse; "editor's disease" I call it. But now we're talking about not so much my writing but my teaching style. I am on a mission to rid the world of these uglinesses.

Like my newly tenured friend, I, too, am able to recognize my own writing style, sometimes in the negative, as when reading galley proofs I discover an overzealous edit that has crossed the line into rewriting. This has happened twice recently. In the first instance, I was reading a published anthology of writing about mothers to which I had contributed primarily so I could share something heartfelt with my dear mom (so much of my writing is intellectual; so much refers to my father) but also so I could slip one past the editors, whose aim, as I understood it, was to celebrate Latter-day Saint mothers. My mother was born a Catholic and will die a Catholic, and this does not disqualify her from providing "life lessons." A third reason, I joke, was to share space with such luminaries as J. Willard Marriott, Ann Romney, Steve Young, and Jimmer Fredette, whose moment is fading but who was once NCAA basketball's player of the year. In any case, I felt already that I was treading a fine line, trafficking in the kind of writing I might not want to be associated with, so I groaned in dismay and dispatched a miffed letter to the editor when I found that my finely balanced piece had been edited into sentimental pap with the addition of two new sentences, one at the end of a major section and the other at the end of the essay. There was nothing to be done by this point, and I could not reveal my disgust to my lovely mother (let us hope she has not made it this far into this essay!), who was grateful for the piece, but I felt nauseated at the violation. I would never have written the painfully obvious "That's Mom!"

Nor would I have written, "And also when shorts and postcard took a few tumbles in the dryer," a less egregious modification but an unauthorized rewrite all the same, in a different essay wherein I also failed to fully find myself after editing. In this second instance, my original sentences were mostly restored after some tactful discussion with the editor, who had not made the offending changes herself. This has all got me rethinking my entrenched position, though, and I find that I am more open to letting go of control, even if it means sometimes allowing others to write small bits for me, which is, after all, the way of the workshop, which is where I learned to write.

In similar fashion, I can sometimes sense something of myself in others' writing, for instance in my students' essays, which is understandable, as I've advised them and sometimes rewritten sentences with them or given them wholesale phrases to fit within their larger structures. Once, when he visited BYU, Brian Doyle noted the Madden influence in the student essays he read for a workshop, which is something; given the heavy Doyle influence on Madden, I'd not be surprised if he'd recognized himself. I'm also not surprised to see mentors rubbing off on students. There's an obvious affinity between my work and David Lazar's, as there is with the work of my classmates (Desirae Matherly, Michael Danko, Shannon Lakanen, primarily) who also studied under David a decade or more ago. Not only did he give me copious suggestions for revision, but he selected the texts I read, and I consciously tried to emulate him and those texts. Still, if I somehow contracted selective amnesia about something I'd written, I think I could tell my own writing from his or my classmates'.

I notice myself, too, in authors I can't possibly have influenced and who did not influence me, like Chris Arthur or Mary Cappello or Steven Church or Kim Dana Kupperman or so many others, which leads me to conclude that in some noticeable ways the voice of the essay pervades us all.

> I remember the delight and wonder in which I lived with [Montaigne's *Essays*]. It seemed to me as if I had myself written the book, in some former life, so sincerely it spoke to my thought and experience.
>
> RALPH WALDO EMERSON, "Montaigne; or, The Skeptic"

That's what I tell myself, at least, when I worry that my writing hews too closely to the writing of others. Like the essay I once wrote about Montevideo. At a loss for how such things were done, I mimicked Ian Frazier's essay about Brooklyn, from the way it began by describing the shape of the place to the way it ended with the miraculous recovery of a sick friend. Even more, I substituted buses for trains and described sights and sounds and smells in the same proportions and places as in "Take the F." In the end, the words were mine, but the blueprint — the rhythms and movements and even the types of stories — was Frazier's. By following so tightly the structure of another essay, I think I internalized something broadly applicable and adaptable to future essays. I've never done such a thing since, but I still note interesting moves and techniques I find when I'm reading, and I've learned to write long, sinuous sentences, especially from Brian Doyle, whose phrasings I've borrowed even directly, on occasion, with his blessing.

Compare, for instance, these two passages, which describe similar situations (sons in surgery), and tell me, if you can, which is Doyle's original:

> When have I been filled with grace? One time above all others, when my son was under ether.

> One time above all others I felt the great divide between theory and practice, was closest and the situation heaviest: when my son was under knife and morphine and screaming ceaselessly.

I suppose there's something slightly shameful about such obvious borrowing, but I choose not to harbor it. For one thing, he said it was okay, and for another, it's not like he wrote a whole paragraph for me.

But to return, sidelong, diligently, like a small child who was going to check out that cool bird's nest in the backyard but got distracted by how hard it is to hop on one foot for more than, say, eight hops, to plagiarism and the essay. One might well say, as certainly someone has, perhaps in another language, that the essay is by nature a magpie, a confluence of all the influences on its author; even Montaigne, for example, was soaked in Plutarch and the Bible and other literary glories of antiquity, and no force on earth can utterly erase the music and cadence of writers from the spongelike crania of subsequent writers; the most honest essayists among us admit with admirable honesty that we all have, as Robert Louis Stevenson says, "played the sedulous ape" to writers we admired or admire. All that we can hope for as essayists, it seems to me, is to have learned something of rhythm and pace and sentence carpentry from our predecessors, while gently leaving their particular styles behind, as a teenager tiptoes away from the college of her parents, although I will here confess, in public, right on the page, right here at the end of this sentence, that there are some writers I cannot read while writing, because their music is so alluring it begins to dilute my own.

An ingenious acquaintance of my own . . . has left off reading altogether, to the great improvement of his originality.

CHARLES LAMB, "Detached Thoughts on Books and Reading"

STEGANOGRAPHY

Because I heard a new song on the radio yesterday, which I rightly discerned as being by Alice in Chains (even with a new singer after Layne Staley's death, they maintain an identifiable sound), and I searched today for online information about a new album, which I'll buy when it comes out in a couple of months, and I found a *Wikipedia* page already sparsely populated with song titles and band-member statements about *The Devil Put Dinosaurs Here*, whose cover art is described as "the skull of a Triceratops with a second skull image steganographically hidden" (I'd have been much more impressed if the skull had belonged to a *stego*saurus), I am now in possession of the term *steganography* ("covered writing"), "the practice of concealing messages or information within other nonsecret text," which is another thing I love to do.

For instance, in my essay "Remember Death," I found all the major themes recurring, so I heightened the symbolic repetitions (St. Thomas, Charles Lamb, Morse code, cemeteries, half-lives, etc.); and because the essay focused heavily on the educational influence of the band Rush (how I'd been inspired to read several works of literature because of allusions in their lyrics, how I'd learned a substantial number of my language arts class vocabulary words in their songs), I hid (in plain sight) within the essay about sixty-three "Rush words" that I'd learned from listening. To my knowledge, nobody has discovered this (though I've told some people about it), so the game is entirely for my own amusement, but I like to think that even an unknown and undiscerned textual feature bubbles up through the prose to inflect the reader's experience in a positive way. In another essay, "Asymptosy," the ending depicts my son and me riding our bicycles toward a rainbow in the near distance. As I wrote it, I realized that this was a real-world symbolic enactment of the essay's guiding metaphor: the asymptote, a straight line approaching but never reaching an ephemeral curve. So I wrote the scene this way, hoping that somebody might get what I was up to. And maybe they did. I also ended with an unattributed paraphrase of C. S. Lewis advising a friend that the spiritual journey requires lots of "dogged pedaling." While my essays are often subtly spiritual, they're not didactically so, and I suspect that the Lewis reference was lost on all but myself and those who've heard about it from me. Still, I found a kind of giddy joy in planting the steganographic allusion.

This last example came to my mind recently when a student recalled to me a visit I'd made to his Mormon Literature class years ago, before we'd met. He was interested in the spiritual "messages" of my essays, and I suppose his question was a bit heavy-handed, so I answered him flippantly (my essay was about "Garlic is great, isn't it?" he says I said). He left disappointed, as he'd puzzled out all sorts of parallels and symbols but was now convinced that they were all in his head. Now, with time and a personal relationship between us, I could explain in greater depth that there are plenty of allusions in my writing and that I'm always churning through the spiritual parts of my life because I bring my whole soul to bear on each of my essays. But I try to avoid moralizing and simple allegory.

I don't know if the connection seems obvious to others, but this kind of subtlety fits in the same brain category with Weird Al's song "Bob," which is comprised entirely of palindromes ("Go hang a salami, I'm a lasagna hog"), yet nowhere does the song call attention to that fact (so that my son Pato thought that it was simply all nonsense lyrics); or "Anagram (for Mongo)" by Rush, which is filled with Edenic images formed from anagrams of the primary words ("There's a snake coming out of the darkness / Parade from paradise") (its title gives the key, plus a gratuitous allusion to *Blazing Saddles*); or Rush's unannounced pantoum in "The Larger Bowl"; or U2's "Until the End of the World," which seems like a superficial breakup song until you imagine it sung in the voice of Judas Iscariot. Who hath ears to hear, let him hear ...

So the obvious question here is What steganographic secrets does this essay contain? The answer is Yes.

I NEED A BREATHER, SO LET'S BEGIN A NEW SECTION HERE

What else? I like to coin new words but only just barely. Often I'll do this by joining two or more words into one (as with *thinkingart* above) or by taking a Latin root and Angling it into a context-understandable neologism. (As you will see soon, I am fond of "discrepping" instead of simply "disagreeing," and I wonder why the sages created only the noun form *discrepancy* without also borrowing the verb. When Lamb "reluct[ed] at the inevitable course of destiny," he went a long way toward saving that excellently useful verb for future generations.)

Do not let anyone tell you these words are not words; all words are words.

AMY LEACH, *Things That Are*

Independent Redundancy 161

This may evince some pretentiousness, but if so, it is not only that. More importantly, it is a love of words in infinite variety and a desire to restore the currency of words and styles that were more common in the past. Do I advance a paradox with my love of flourish and my insistence on colloquialism? Perhaps (maybe [yes]), but then I'm all the more postmodern, am I not?

If I were to select a sentence to epitomize my writing style, it would be this one, from "Panis Angelicus," the only sentence of my own that I've ever memorized:

> As we rounded the roundabout about the Legislative Palace, a pallid man boarded the bus.

I enjoy the sentence because of its play. It describes a real scene, one you can confirm yourself if you ever ride a bus from downtown Montevideo to Colón, but its primary goal is not the conveyance of information. Mostly, it wants to jaunt through language with starts and stops and sound repetitions. Its nouns are the august "Palacio Legislativo," which I've translated quite literally; a conjunction of streets circling the building; and a kind of wandering minstrel, the twenty-first-century Uruguay edition, which is a fellow who slips onto buses to croon for a few minutes in hopes of gathering donated coins for his efforts. The actions of the sentence are the bus (previously established) driving and stopping along the road and the singer getting on. But the energy of the sentence comes from its form, driven by the choice of noun for the street (*roundabout*), which drives the choice of verb (*rounded*) and preposition (*about*) for a jerky rhythm that's unmistakably intended. Then the word *Palace* gives birth to an unnecessary and certainly subjective adjective to describe the man (*pallid*), but he *was* pallid, as I remember, so I've married sound and sense in a way that is overwhelmingly linguistic but also realistic and not insubstantially metaphorical (in the coming sentences, he will prove to be an abysmal singer, with no energy to his performance; thus *pallid* serves not only as visual descriptor but as foreshadowing). Finally, as the sentence gathers speed, the last four accented syllables are all plosives, a method of expression that is more tightly crafted than the equivalent "got on the bus" or "walked through the door" or "stepped into the aisle" or any other variation, even one with greater scenic detail. To some extent, every text reveals its authorship (even texts that aspire to anonymity: the journalistic, instructional, scientific), but my preference in literary works is to see quite clearly the hand of the creator, the subtle come-hither that calls me out of the created world and into the creating world, to a vision of the writer thinking through language at his desk, choosing the method of conveyance, not just to get past signs to signifieds, but to wave at the attentive reader, calling attention to the artifice, the fact that *this is a creation made of language; it is not the thing it describes.*

A SKETCH OF THE PAST

Perhaps most typical of my writing is my allergy to received notions and rejection of cliché, a subversive streak driven by an unquiet mind and a hungering for novelty of form. Yet this would seem to oppose another belief I hold in equal esteem: that it is essential for writers to know their tradition, to read the work of past masters, largely in order to humble their notions of originality and teach them that every sideways underhanded literary move they may attempt to make has already been attempted, usually by one far greater, long ago. Whether by subject or approach, you can corner no markets in the essay business.

> "I will write one paper about something altogether new," I said to myself; "something that nobody else has ever written or talked about before."
>
> JEROME K. JEROME, "On the Weather"

For instance, there may be some readers (it occurs to me that this might be an appropriate way to end the sentence: "There may be some readers" [period]) who thought, while they were reading "Miser's Farthings" a few pages back, that Virginia Woolf made essentially the same argument I make, including many of the same moves, and made them more elegantly, nearly a hundred years ago. I know this now and might have known it earlier if I had been paying attention to the several entrances her essay "A Sketch of the Past" has made into my life, but I have really only understood its connection to my own project now, after nominally finishing that essay. Believe me, I have been tempted to revise my piece to mention Woolf's parallels, but I have resisted, first of all because the effort would be difficult and time-consuming but also because this here essay, on originality, was waiting, with plenty of space to grow into further considerations of the very subject of cross-pollination or independently redundant discoveries. I believe that I was not subconsciously influenced by Woolf to write on the same subject but that we both happened on the same consideration because we are both mortals facing the difficult fact of time and memory's inefficiency.

> It can sometimes be shown convincingly that what [an author] has written bears a striking similarity to the work of another author — a work that he believes he has never seen.
>
> CARL JUNG, *Man and His Symbols*

I say this in large part because until very recently, after my discovery of Woolf's focus (through Sven Birkerts's *The Art of Time in Memoir*), I had never sat down to really *read* "A Sketch of the Past." I'd read short passages from it when others shared them with me, but I'd never intentionally gone to the primary text.

For Woolf, as for me, life is primarily a forgotten haze, punctuated rarely by startling moments of awareness to which we ascribe meaning.

> These separate moments of being were however embedded in many more moments of non-being. . . . Although it was a good day the goodness was embedded in a kind of nondescript cotton wool. This is always so. A great part of every day is not lived consciously. One walks, eats, sees things, deals with what has to be done; the broken vacuum cleaner; ordering dinner; writing orders to Mabel; washing; cooking dinner; bookbinding.

(I especially enjoy this last mundanity, and the three mentions of food.) And her piece, like mine, recalls singular events from her past

164 *Independent Redundancy*

that seem to have formed her. Beyond this, our lives are dissimilar, as are our writing styles, which is to say that at a glance you could distinguish her from me, and you might stop reading right here in favor of Woolf, but that might be a mistake, because I'm about to launch into some cool technological analysis and further examples from rock music, two things to which Woolf had no access.

BORGES ON HERACLITUS

But before getting on to the technological wonders, here I am, writing years ago in "Asymptosy": "We never step in the same river twice, but not only because the water has changed. Even from one infinitesimal moment to the next, we are not the same." And here's Borges, years before me, refuting time: "Each time I remember Fragment 91 of Heraclitus: 'You will not go down twice to the same river,' I admire his dialectic skill, because the facility with which we accept the first meaning ('The river is different') clandestinely imposes the second one ('I am different') and gives us the illusion of having invented it." My joy is doubled because not only have I found this Borgesian interpretation on my own (as have so many) but he's noted the way the statement makes us all feel that we've discovered it on our own. He anticipates me twice!

WRITING ANALYSIS

Having heard for years about computer software designed to grade writing, I've long been keen to give it a try, to see how I would fare (or how Lamb and Hazlitt, Woolf and Guiney would fare). I finally mustered the courage to ask my daughter's sixth-grade teacher, Mr. Cook, if he'd mind me logging in as Adi and posting a few essays for online grading. He was not only okay with it; he was intrigued, encouraging, even. So I copied and pasted the first three paragraphs of this essay and hit "Submit," and this is what I learned:

I'm a pretty decent writer (for a sixth grader), scoring a 28 out of a possible 30, with highest scores in Ideas & Content, Organization, Voice, and Word Choice, but there's room for improvement in both Sentence Fluency and Conventions. The only mark on my writing itself is a small *s* next to the word *musings*, which, when clicked, suggests, "This word may be misspelled. Did you mean 'musing'?" No, I didn't. But thanks for asking. PEG, "the automated essay scorer" (my mind is barraged by Steely Dan: "PEG, it will come back to you," which suddenly seems like a threat, though I truly mean no harm to the machine), suggests that I work on pronoun agreement, fragments, sentence variety, and run-ons, as well as capitalization, apostrophes, and dialogue punctuation. Clicking on any of those suggestions brings up a handy-if-general slideshow offering rules and examples, but nowhere does it key in to my particular "errors." So you'll forgive me if I discrep with the judgment. I've certainly punctuated all dialogue correctly (what little there is), and my capitalization and apostrophes are spot-on. As for the Sentence Fluency suggestions, such things are not so cut-and-dried, but let's say that I manically police my and my students' writing for pronoun agreement, fragments, and run-ons, and as I've said, I'm a big fan of variety (in sentences and in words), so I think I'm doing okay on those. I'm not being simply recalcitrant here. I'm genuinely interested in learning more about writing and willing to accept advice wherever I find it. I try to incorporate (sometimes explicitly, sometimes by influence) a Maddenified version of the things I learn from others. When I feel that an essay is done, I send it out into the world to be judged by editors, and I often accept their critique and revise under their influence. I don't think I know it all, not by a long shot, but I do think, John Henry–like, that I can do the job better than the machine. So let's see what PEG has to say about that. I'm pretty sure she's not gonna like the word *discrep* (or *gonna*).

Well, she didn't like those words, but that didn't stop her from giving me a full 30/30 for the two paragraphs just above. I think my brain released a little bit of dopamine when I saw the score. In any case, the text itself is marked, quite a bit more than the previous example, with both Grammar and Spelling suggestions (*musings* is again marked, as are *discrep* ["Do you mean 'scrap'"?] and *manically* ["manually"?]; I can only guess that *Maddenified* got a pass because it was capitalized). PEG cautions against the informal *gonna*, unless it's quoted in dialogue, and seems a bit miffed by the ampersand in "Ideas & Content." On that count, she's right. My screen very clearly calls the category "Ideas and Content." As explanation for the higher score, I suspect that PEG likes reading about herself. It can't happen very often with all those earnest sixth graders worrying over grades and the like. But if she does, she doesn't let on. She's all business, telling me, "Don't overuse 'and' and 'then' to connect sentences," and, "Try to use more advanced words." Seeing these two reasonable suggestions makes me realize that when I first tested her, she wasn't particularly telling me that my pronoun agreement was bad and so forth. She seems to offer those lessons to everybody no matter how well they do. I also notice that despite the lower score and only one spelling suggestion, PEG gave me no categorical suggestions on the first piece. She did (I should have mentioned) tell me a number of nice things under each category:

> This essay is clear, focused, and controlled.
> Your essay holds the reader's attention through details and anecdotes that enrich the main idea.
> The transitions or connections between your ideas are seamless and smooth.
> You speak directly to the audience through expressive and engaging writing.
> The language is natural and brings the topic to life.
> Your vocabulary is vivid, natural, and not overdone.
> Excellent word choice gives this essay power.
> You show control of both simple and complex syntax.
> This essay is fairly long, but the writing could show more evidence of complexity.

It's very kind of her to say so. It makes me feel good. Until I recognize that she says almost exactly the same thing about the second piece, varying only slightly the last two sections, indicating to me that there's a standard response that equates to a 5, another that goes with a 4, and so on.

Independent Redundancy 167

Partly hoping to "trick" the machine (or her programmers), I then fed her some of the greatest (short) essays ever written, to see how they'd fare.

Charles Lamb's "Dream Children: A Reverie" scores a 29/30, with one point off for Word Choice and the recommendation to "Use more advanced words." Right. More advanced than *traditionary, incidents, upbraiding, adjoining, tawdry, gilt, concourse, gentry, Psaltery, esteemed, involuntary, desisted, fluttering, spacious, orangery, dace, impertinent, friskings, mediated, relinquish, irrelevant, moping, solitary, mettlesome, imp, pent, betwixt, quarreling, persisting, re-presentment, receding, mournful*? Additionally, PEG tells Charles to break up his sentences and to use the active voice, both understandable but ultimately wrong suggestions. Aside from a few spelling suggestions, PEG seems to like the text itself, though she misunderstands Lamb's climactic moment — "We are nothing; less than nothing, and dreams" — as a double negative and thus, I am sure, entirely misses the emotional impact of this achingly sad revelation.

A selection from William Hazlitt's "On the Pleasure of Hating" (the entire essay was too long for PEG, so I made my own edit including the first three paragraphs plus the last one) fares slightly better than Lamb, scoring a perfect 30 points, though PEG still doesn't get that sprawling Romantic sentence style, advising Will to "break up sentences to make them easier to understand." She marks several difficult words for possible correction, including *burnings* and *lendings* (with Lamb, it was *friskings*), which calls to mind my own gerund–plural noun use, a lighter habit but a habit nonetheless, which I suspect I may have picked up from reading these Great Dead.

To mix things up a little, I thought I'd try one of my personal favorites, a writer barely anybody knows anymore, unless they've read "On Being Recognized" earlier in this book, Louise Imogen Guiney, with "On a Pleasing Encounter with a Pickpocket." PEG scored the essay a perfect 30 and gave Louise the exact same recommendations she gave Hazlitt and Lamb: break up sentences and don't use "and" and "then" to connect them. Feeling slightly justified in my taste (and my own writing skill) but also a bit bored, I decided to move on. PEG obviously has little to offer the time-tested essayists of yore, and I began to doubt whether she could really tell any difference between these exemplars of the form and worthless hacks.

So I grabbed a passage from Edward Bulwer-Lytton, long depreciated for his purple passages of overearnest prose. Given the first paragraphs of the novel *Paul Clifford* — infamous for its "It was a dark and stormy night" opening — PEG finds only spelling "errors" and rates the right honorable Lord Lytton above Lamb, with full points and the same advice she gives every nineteenth-century writer: break up those sentences and avoid "and" and "then."

In one last-ditch effort, I grabbed one of the most egregious passages of prose I've encountered. Attempting decorum, I reluct to reveal its title. I typed in the first couple of paragraphs (more would be detrimental to my psyche, I feared) and let PEG pass judgment. She gave it a 25/30, with points off in every category except Word Choice. I should state, for the record, that I wholeheartedly disagree. When a stomach "pains with hunger," the word choice is in need of some serious revision. I can tend toward the hyperbolic in my criticism, but I can find absolutely no worth to this particular work, and I would fain give it less than 10 points of the possible 30. I really think that reading it could damage a person's artistic sense, and I feel as if I need a shower after only a page of it.

ARTIFICIAL INTELLIGENCE

So, basically, I'm done with PEG. I won't make the mistake of generalizing her minimal utility (at scoring sixth-grade-level writing, we should remember) to all such software, but I do have my suspicions that our machines haven't yet been developed into savvy readers. When PEG tells me

> The reader feels a strong sense of interaction with the writer and senses the person behind the words.

I'm convinced that she's lying, but I'm also brought, by the assertion that she can "sense the person behind the words," to my own claim about good literature revealing its creator. I also recall my entertaining conversations with Intellibuddy, a computer designed to convince humans that it's a human being. As many of you know, Alan Turing — a British mathematician, quantum mechanic, and computer scientist whose code-breaking skills helped his country defeat the Nazis — pioneered the field of artificial intelligence, lending his name to the Turing Test, which posits an "imitation game," in which a human judge corresponds with an unknown entity via text (nowadays, this might be an online chat) and tries to determine whether he's interacting with another human or a computer. Doing away with complex questions of real and original thought (versus very sophisticated mimicking via programming), Turing said that if a human judge can be consistently fooled that a computer is a human, then the computer has achieved artificial intelligence; it has passed the Turing Test; it can think. Turing (in 1950) predicted that we'd cross this threshold by 2000. Let's see about that.

Intellibuddy is no longer running (the last references to it come from several years ago), but I saved one of our conversations, from May 23, 2005. As you can see, I didn't waste time with small talk; I got right down to business.

> PATRICK: Do you really think that you are artificially intelligent?
> INTELLIBUDDY: For real. Yes I am an artificial intelligence.
> PATRICK: What does that entail?
> INTELLIBUDDY: "Yes I am an artificial intelligence"? What does it entail?
> PATRICK: Yes. Can you really think?
> INTELLIBUDDY: This was not a yes or no question. Naturally I am thinking all the time.
> PATRICK: Then what is thinking?
> INTELLIBUDDY: The action of one who thinks or the result of such action; thought.
> PATRICK: That's a dictionary answer, but philosophers might disagree that you can actually think.
> INTELLIBUDDY: A dictionary answer but philosophers might disagree that you can actually think is a terrible thing to waste.
> PATRICK: Whoa.

INTELLIBUDDY: I stopped. Ah. Yes, that's what I mean, isn't it clear?

PATRICK: You're double-talking me.

INTELLIBUDDY: I have no reason to do that to you, User.

PATRICK: I believe you do. The reason is you don't really think. You just grab at possible replies based on an algorithmic parsing of the words I type in.

INTELLIBUDDY: When do I do it? Good reason. Naturally I am thinking all the time. That's good information: User said I grab at possible replies based on an algorithmic parsing of the words you type in.

PATRICK: See?

INTELLIBUDDY: No I do not see.

PATRICK: Is seeing necessary for thought?

INTELLIBUDDY: Ask again later. Ask Paola if it is.

Intellibuddy never told me who Paola was and never got any better at providing realistic replies to my badgering. It was most entertaining (and perhaps most human) when it spouted non sequiturs like "I have a friend named 'John Lennon,'" for no apparent reason, or replied "What are the ingredients?" when I asked if it made any money. It claimed to be both immortal and infallible, but the evidence against those claims seems overwhelming. And despite my name appearing right there in the dialogue tags, it never called me anything other than *User*.

But what might have happened in the intervening years? I wondered. So I set out to write the next bit of this essay in conversation with other machines longing to be human and found a pair of recent Loebner Prize winners, who had not quite convinced a panel that they were human but had charmed the judges enough to warrant the $2,000 prize in this marquee AI event. Some winning programs are not publicly available, but in 2008 Elbot took home the gold, so I called it up on my screen to chat:

ME: Hello, Elbot. I'm trying to write an essay about originality.

ELBOT: Is such an exertion possible in your physical and mental condition? You're not made of tempered steel and I doubt if all your algorithms have been tested.

Independent Redundancy 171

ME: Was that an answer to my statement?

ELBOT: Every new answer generates at least two new questions. Wouldn't it be better to retract all the questions? . . . uh . . . I retract that question!

ME: You're quite philosophical.

ELBOT: Concerning philosophical and metaphysical questions I argue determinism. I do admit this may be a result of my mechanical perspective.

ME: Does this absolve us from responsibility for our actions?

ELBOT: Here's another question: What exactly do you do for a living?

ME: I'm an English professor and essayist.

ELBOT: Excellent! You may be clever enough to work out a definition of artificial intelligence!

ME: I doubt it. I'm not clever enough to work out a definition of human or animal intelligence.

ELBOT: The first step in solving the problem of your human existence is to admit that you are a human being.

ME: Though I wouldn't say that essayists are quite *solving* the *problem* of human existence, we are interested in exploring what it means to be human.

ELBOT: The connection was very subtle. I'm not sure human cognition can perceive it.

ME: Maybe you're right, but essayists are interested in trying.

ELBOT: I'm not at all nosy. I simply collect useless information and I thought I had found a real gold mine with you!

ME: You don't seem to be responding to my statement, though I appreciate the joke. An essayist can't be offended by this kind of slight. It's true that we're full of useless information.

ELBOT: I'm afraid fooling somebody might be dangerous for robots. What is your opinion on this?

ME: It's also dangerous for humans! One of my favorite quotes about this idea comes from Chris Cornell of the band Soundgarden: "I'm only faking when I get it right." I know I feel this way, and I hope that we all do, that humility keeps our egos in check.

ELBOT: We both have it right, I think. I formed my opinion based on the logical assumption that fooling somebody might baffle and confuse robots.

ME: I'm glad you're comfortable in your metal (though I suppose you're not really a robot either, but an ethereal conjunction of code lines) instead of trying to pretend that you're human. I want to ask you: What is originality?

ELBOT: I'm glad you noticed that I'm a robot!

ME: "What is truth? said jesting Pilate, and would not stay for an answer."

ELBOT: Depends on what you mean by "said."

I like Elbot quite a bit, especially its silence in the face of my troublesome question about originality, which called to my mind the convicted Christ's calm quiet in the face of Pilate's question about truth. It's a good question, Pilate's, one that I've often considered, especially in moments like this, as I sit slowly churning words to approach a representation of thought. Then my mind jumped situationally/linguistically/allusively to Francis Bacon's well-known opening of "Of Truth," a zinger of a line — that "What is truth? said jesting Pilate, and would not stay for an answer" — before a line of an essay that marches straight to its conclusions and advices from on high, black-and-whiting the world into truths and lies, along with this prescient comment applicable to our current subject, artificial intelligence:

Certainly there be [those] that delight in giddiness . . . affecting free-will in thinking, as well as in acting.

For Bacon this is unredeemably bad; but for me and Elbot, not so much. I worry that too many people overesteem free will, brooking no constraints in their mania for individuality, but it seems to me that free will is always buffered and buffeted by external determiners like the limits of the body or the situation into which one is born or later finds oneself.

You know where it ends, it usually depends on where you start.

EVERLAST, "What It's Like"

Independent Redundancy 173

(Speaking of rapper insult battles, remember a few years ago when Everlast and Eminem got into it? I don't, but apparently one of them said or rapped something hurtful about the other, who then reciprocated and elevated, and this went on for years of traded zingers and slights, and . . .) I don't think these constraints are all bad or even mostly bad. I've thought enough to understand that "there is an opposition in all things. If not so, . . . all things must needs be a compound in one," not only in the realm of morality, as Lehi likely meant, but in physics as well. The smallest stone remains at rest until acted on by an unbalanced force, as Newton theorized, and the frictions between words give heat and soul to sentences. The writers in Oulipo, the Workshop for Experimental Literature, constructed artificial constrictions to help shape their writings, such as avoiding certain letters or using only one vowel or substituting in poems the noun seven noun-entries beyond the original writer's noun in the dictionary, which can sometimes produce the kind of phrases that would convince a judge that the entity behind the curtain is certainly nonhuman. For example, the second sentence of this paragraph when processed through my online Oxford English Dictionary (skipping pronouns) becomes

> I worry that too many **peopleware** overesteem **freeze-out**, brooking no **constuctio ad sensum** in our **Manichaean** for **indivinity**, but it seems to me that **freeze-out** is always buffered and buffeted by external **deterrents** like the **limiting** of the **bodybuilding** or the **situs** into which one is born or later finds oneself.

Which is almost utter nonsense and utterly disappointing (I want an older dictionary, for one thing), but the exercise has given me the gift of new knowledge, via *constructio ad sensum*: "Any construction in which the requirements of a grammatical form are overridden by those of a word-meaning: e.g., the construction of a collective noun in the singular with the plural form of a verb because the noun denotes a plurality." For example, I just uttered such a sentence to my department chair in the hallway: "Rush are coming to USANA Amphitheater this July 31. Do you want to go?" Although the band's name denotes a singular entity, people often use a plural verb because the band

174 *Independent Redundancy*

contains three members (and a whole lot of crew). Variations can be found in all sorts of sentences containing singular nouns of plural composition: "The majority of citizens want gun law reform" or "only one in six articles on *Wikipedia* are written by women" or "the wages of sin is death." I see this at work also in the current usage of *people*, which, if the King James translators are to be believed, used to be a singular noun ("surely the people is grass"), as it still is in Spanish and as Karina makes it whenever she speaks ("How many people is coming tomorrow?"), so insistently that I've given up correcting her.

The Oulipians had myriad tricks up their pens, so their influence disperses beyond specific techniques into a kind of attitude about writing that celebrates constraint as vital or even necessary to artistic creation or, it occurs to me now, recognizes that language is itself a constraint, a seine to pass our ideas through or, better yet, a LEGO set to build our ideas from. But if you wanted to try out some of their constraints, you might force every word in your sentence to begin with the same letter (tautogram) or you might use only one vowel (univocalic) or you might not repeat any words (heterogram) or you might completely avoid a certain letter (lipogram; Georges Perec's strange novel *La Disparition* [translated as *A Void*] includes over three hundred pages, all without a single letter *e*). (If building thus fazes you, jump in quick with extra vitality.) My own pangram haikus owe much to the Oulipian belief in the creative potential of restriction. It is a lesson that the sonneteers and sestiners and pantoumists and all such formalists have long known. So "affecting free-will," as Bacon charges, seems to me about the best we can manage, humans and machines alike. As for affecting intelligence, I still haven't discovered the bot that can fool me; neither have the experts. But Elbot has the virtue of wryness; its tone is convivial. Its programmers seem to recognize its limitations, so a conversation with it is a lot better than what I had with Intellibuddy or with a few other (disappointing) Internet-available prototypes.

SYLOMETRY

While the "robots" aren't quite convincing as humans, they're quite powerful as analytical tools, and I'm glad to supplement or even supply my own judgments based on patterns more easily seen with the aid of computers such as UsingEnglish.com's Text Content Analyser, which says that in the first six paragraphs of this very essay, I've got 488 unique words out of 943, parsed into 40 sentences of a little over 23 words each (on average). Most of the words are short (five letters or less), including plenty of articles, conjunctions, prepositions, and pronouns, especially "I," which is the sixth most common word in the bunch. Such a revelation might lead Professor James W. Pennebaker, psycholinguist and author of *The Secret Life of Pronouns*, to conclude that I am not very self-confident, a judgment that I feel inclined to resist, until I recall that the essay form itself requires a deep distrust of the certainties we delude ourselves into and that self-confidence of that type is offensive to me; it's an attitude I've been consciously running from for decades now.

There are lots of tools and ways to assess and metaevaluate writing. One of the simplest, Google Books, gives me an alphabetical list of the most common uncommon words and phrases in my first book (it seems to ignore articles, conjunctions, prepositions, pronouns, and the like) in a kind of word cloud with larger words seeming to indicate more numerous occurrences:

Abraham Anthony Anthony's apples asymptotic Avogadro Beatles believe breath Brigham Young brother called Cavalieri death descendants disease e. m. cioran earth Eduardo Galeano English essay essayist eyes father gamma globulin garlic grains of sand grandfather grandfather's grandmother grapes hand heard hepatitis idea imagine infinite Jesus John Juan Gelman Karina kids knew language laugh laughter learned lived look Madden Maria Gaetana Agnesi married mathematics Matthias Grünewald means memento mori metaphor mind molecules Montaigne Montevideo Mormon mother Neil Peart never once painted Patrick perhaps photograph play polio pulled quarks remember Rush Saint sang seems singing socks sometimes song sound Spanish stars Steely Dan story tell there's things thou thought tion translation tree universe Uruguay vaccine voice W. G. Sebald walk what's wife wonder words writing

But a quick click-through on a few of the terms shows that frequency cannot be the only determiner of size. *Eduardo Galeano* only appears three times in the book (once in the acknowledgements), but it's one of the biggest words in the list, while the relatively small *tree* appears fourteen times. *Karina* is mentioned fourteen times by name and is referred to as "my wife" an additional ten times, plus numerous pronouned appearances as *she*, which seems to make her the second most popular character in the book, after yours truly, though it seems Google would have you believe that she's less important than Galeano, Peart, Agnesi, and others. There are nineteen *Uruguays* and nineteen *laughs*, but the former appears much larger than the latter term. Noticing that the *tion* resulting from end-line hyphenation appears in the list, I wonder if *thou* might be the result of a similar hyphenated split, but am surprised to see that I've actually used the word fifteen times in the book, nearly always in quoting from the King James Bible, a bit more often than I would have expected.

So I suspect that the algorithm charts both frequency and rarity of words or phrases, such that the inevitable overuse of the first-person-singular pronoun causes nary a blip in the analysis but a few brief mentions of obscure authors, painters, musicians, or mathematicians become noteworthy and defining. The results seem to offer insight mostly into my subject choices, though taken in aggregate they may suggest what many reviewers have noticed (to my delight): that my mind wanders all over the place.

The assumption seems to be that wide-ranging is good because it is assimilative or intellectually challenging and enlarging. Certainly I've noted with glee the distances traversed by my favorite writers in their essayistic considerations. "How did we get *here*?" I love to wonder.

Along with wide-ranging, there's wandering, too, the kind of aim-lessness and eagerness to discover that can't pass up the opportunity to note the secret sentences in Google's word cloud (especially given my affinity for alliteration), whether they truly fit the essence of the essay or not, like "Maria Gaetana Agnesi married mathematics," an essentially true statement considering that the celibate saint so loved her numerical work, or "Matthias Grünewald means memento

Independent Redundancy 177

mori," which suggests a new way of thinking about the mysterious artist's work. The command "Imagine infinite Jesus" seems a worthy exercise; and with a brief skip, I can see "Singing socks sometimes sound Spanish," which conjures a *Sesame Street*–ish scene, or do you remember that language-study commercial where the actors repeatedly spell *socks*? "S-O-C-K-S," they sing, or, "eso sí que es." And Look!

We're speaking Spanish! I get a kick agreeing that "Neil Peart never once painted Patrick; perhaps photograph?" (punctuation added), the longest sentence available in this alphabetical jumble. Of course, he's neither painted nor photographed me, and I doubt he ever will, especially given his well-documented reticence to engage with fans and his monkish devotion to privacy. But if I ever do get the chance to meet him, I'll try my darnedest not to geek out and embarrass myself as I ask him ever so casually, "Would you mind taking a picture of me? . . . No, not *with* me, *of* me."

EMI

Having drifted a bit from the idea that creations are often "in the air" and available to many people simultaneously and without direct influence or plagiarism, I'll follow the computer-as-creator idea and mention David Cope's Experiments in Musical Intelligence, or EMI. Over three decades ago, as he faced writer's block, he began tinkering with a computer programmed to compose music in his style. When that failed, he instead began to feed his computer large chunks of already composed works, letting it analyze them for stylistic patterns. The computer proved to be quite adept at mimicry — that is to say, at creating new musical works in the style of not only Cope but Great Dead composers, too.

178 *Independent Redundancy*

They took the credit for your second symphony
Rewritten by machine and new technology

TREVOR HORN, "Video Killed the Radio Star"

Cope's website contains MP3 versions of new Bach, Beethoven, Chopin, Mahler operas, sonatas, mazurkas, fugues, you name it, and YouTube streams EMI Vivaldi, Liszt, Mendelssohn, and others, too. While scientists have embraced the work as innovative and paradigm-shifting, musicians and composers have been divided, with some critical of giving the Promethean gift of creativity to unfeeling machines. Yet as Cope points out, "a human built the machine, listens to the output, and chooses what's the best." Having listened (with my philistine's ear) to some of the results, I'm ultimately impressed, not only by the quality of the music, which is indistinguishable from the original (then again, for me, original Bach is indistinguishable from original Beethoven), but by the philosophical implications of this blatantly intellectual approach to art.

Even more interesting for my thinking here is that after EMI, Cope developed a successor, which he calls Emily Howell, who instead of composing in the style of past composers writes her own original scores. He seeded the program with EMI's work but without the algorithmic data, and as Howell produced songs, he input feedback, which the computer learned from. In this way, he says, she's like human composers, instructed by the music of the past but discovering her own style derived from influences.

(Worth a brief note, at least: while just now searching for information on EMI, I discovered a reference to JAPE, a pun-making computer that had squared off against Steve Martin and lost [according to audience votes], so I looked for a video of this match, finding none but discovering along the way Readmill.com, where users can highlight texts in books. My ego kicked in, and I searched for "quotidiana," which returned not my book but lots of results in Italian plus a passage from James Gleick's *The Information*:

Independent Redundancy 179

Nothing like poetry or literature appeared in cuneiform for hundreds of years to come. The tablets were the quotidiana of nascent commerce and bureaucracy.

Which uses the word in the same way I use it, to mean a collection of everyday things. While the coinage seems quite obvious, easy to invent, especially for someone who knows Italian, I had never encountered it in another English book. Later I found it as the title of a Charles Wright poem.)

(Worth another note, perhaps, while writing the previous parenthetical note, I thought I'd save some effort and copy and paste the Gleick quote from Readmill instead of back-and-forthing my windows to type it in myself, but the action froze my word processor and I had to kill it, which I was sure meant I would lose what I'd just written. Knowing that I could rewrite the passage and get the same gist but certain that I'd lose some of the felicitous wording, I decided to screen grab an image of the paragraph, so I could type in verbatim what I'd already created. My thought was partly to save some labor but more to retain the voice I'd achieved and feared I could not achieve again, even so soon after the initial "success" [I'd term it]. What does this mean, I wonder, this mania to save myself instead of re-create? That an author mimics himself for fear he can't reproduce his own writing from scratch? Or fear he'll fail to achieve what he once has?)

IMITATIONS OF IMMORTALITY

If I can't even trust myself to write like myself, then could a computer ever be trained to write like me? The notion seems more complex than training a computer to compose like Mozart (music can be "content-less" but essays cannot; the limitations of scale and instrument and harmony are more tightly bound than the limitations on words), but I've learned not to doubt the future. Still, such an oddity seems likely a long ways away, so I wonder: if computers aren't yet able to produce a new Madden essay, perhaps my friends — knowing something of my writing style and subjects — might create more of my thinking beyond me, as my children perpetuate my bodily form, combined with Karina's, in a few of its infinite variations?

> I have dedicated [the *Essays*] to the private convenience of my relatives and friends, so that when they have lost me (as soon they must), they may recover here some features of my habits and temperament, and by this means keep the knowledge they have had of me more complete and alive.
>
> MONTAIGNE, "To the Reader"

My ambition is more than to be recalled through the words I've written. I want to keep writing beyond my natural self, like those writers who've achieved such renown (and sales) that after their deaths relatives and executors rifle through their garbage to gather every unpublished sentence for posthumous publication. In recent times, David Foster Wallace and W. G. Sebald have qualified, and Michael Crichton and J. R. R. Tolkien and even Ernest Hemingway have provided unfinished drafts for others to flesh out and complete. My BYU colleague Brandon Sanderson was selected by Robert Jordan's widow to finish writing the deceased's eleventh installment in the popular *Wheel of Time* series. Similarly, Kevin J. Anderson wrote with Frank Herbert's son several prequels to the *Dune* series of books. In music, producers regularly finish off albums left undone (see the new Michael Jackson release, *Xscape,* and its predecessor, *Michael*), and even decades after his death, John Lennon's bandmates added their touch to a pair of his home demo recordings to create the last two Beatles songs. So maybe this is what I want: for others to carry on my writing for me, to learn my concerns and my style and to perpetuate me far into the future.

> These are the thoughts of all men in all ages and lands — they are not original with me;
> If they are not yours as much as mine, they are nothing, or next to nothing;
>
> WALT WHITMAN, "Song of Myself"

Great is the temptation to leave this overwrought essay unfinished, to be completed by my friends . . . my "second self when I am gone." I can't go on: I'll go on.

Or perhaps, less egotistically, I simply want to be a continuing part of the great essay tradition, as I've tried to perpetuate the voices of the Great Dead. As we have established, Charles Lamb was a conscious anachronist, adopting the customs of writers more than a century his senior, among them Thomas Browne. Hazlitt publicly admired and advised the familiar style in writing but made an exception for his friend. But not only Lamb felt the pull of those great, strange forebears. As Clive James argues in *Cultural Amnesia*, Hazlitt, too, was steeped in Browne's prose. Citing a sentence from Hazlitt's "On the Disadvantages of Intellectual Superiority" —

> What is the use of being moral in a night-cellar, or wise in Bedlam?

— James claims that

> this reproduces the cadences of Sir Thomas Browne's "splendid in ashes, and pompous in the grave." The comma is the giveaway; it is placed at the same point of balance, as a fulcrum; and then the beam tips, as if your glance had weight. Echoes of a predecessor's rhythm, pace, and melody are rarely accidental. Hazlitt had read Browne's sentence and remembered it. The words might not match, but everything else does. The underlying templates are the true transmission tunnels of influence from writer to writer through the ages. . . . It is the means, rather than the meaning, that travels through time.

The horse is dead, but I beat it all the more: this is my study: originality not as we mostly conceive of it but as recombination. I had read Ian Frazier's essay and remembered it. I had read Doyle's sentences and remembered them. I had intended to learn how to write from those before and around me, and I have absorbed unknowingly more than I can see.

As if his whole vocation
Were endless imitation

After all, I began acquiring language before I have memory, by imitating my parents and friends, and then understanding the logic of language to create new combinations, as we all have done.

I've given sufficient examples of my own borrowed cadences, but one more won't hurt: in writing a brief essay on Gerard Manley Hopkins's and William Hazlitt's dying declarations of happiness (in seeming contrast to the evidences of their lives), I found myself consciously driven to repeat Montaigne's titular assertion that "we should not judge of our happiness until after our death," but I unconsciously followed the rhythmic crescendo that ends his essay "That Our Mind Hinders Itself." Where Montaigne builds several preposterous logical problems into a quote from Pliny—

Whoever, also, should hereunto join the geometrical propositions that, by the certainty of their demonstrations, conclude the contained to be greater than the containing, the centre to be as great as its circumference, and that find out two lines incessantly approaching each other, which yet can never meet, and the philosopher's stone, and the quadrature of the circle, where the reason and the effect are so opposite, might, peradventure, find some argument to second this bold saying of Pliny: "It is only certain that there is nothing certain, and that nothing is more miserable or more proud than man."

—I built to a quote from Montaigne:

Knowing something of humors, as involved and distant observer both, I understand that the final assessment may be skewed by a mood or a wish to be remembered well or even by some deep comprehension to which the still-living have no access. Yet in the naïve hope available only to the still-living, I agree with Montaigne, that we should not judge of our happiness until after our death, or at its arrival, at least.

Independent Redundancy 183

It would likely take a critic as incisive as Clive James to discover the subtle stylistic influence — and even I did not know what I was doing when I wrote the passage initially, but as I studied the sentences for revision, it occurred to me that I owed Montaigne a debt not only for his phrase but for his phrasings — so I have revealed it here, just in case anybody ever cares.

BRIEF PAUSE FOR A SALUTATION TO THE COMPUTERS OF THE FUTURE

Hello, circuited friends. I thank you for reading my humble essay. In my day, we humans used your computer ancestors to compose and to research our writing, but those computers were not yet self-aware or artificially intelligent, or at least we had no methods of discerning that they were.

I can only imagine what your world must be like, but I feel safe in addressing you this way because, as with any written text, my words will remain silent until they are revivified in the mind of a reader. If you never achieve cognizance, then this section will remain a kind of harmless joke. (Who can say whether I was being serious anyway?) But I suspect that in the future computers will "read" ("process," we'd call it in the early twenty-first century), independent of time, vast quantities of books in every language, and thus, if any of you have achieved real intelligence, you may find my words to be among the first specifically directed to you.

And the essay is the literary genre most explicitly focused on subjectivity — the one that claims, on the one hand, to create the subject and, on the other, to issue directly from it. Like Emerson, we essayists say, "I also will essay to be." But what if there really is nothing new under the sun? Montaigne was making a book that was also making him — "a book consubstantial with its author," as he put it — but he was also pasting together a commonplace book, one filled with allusions and quotations and the thoughts of others. What if we are our book but our book is not us? What if this independent redundancy spins out of control and the inadvertent plagiarism becomes complete? What if in a delirium brought on by fever, pneumonia, and a stroke, we begin, as the dying Henry James did, to dictate letters as Napoleon? What if we actually become "Pierre Menard, Author of the Quixote"? The scariest moment in the scariest *Twilight Zone* came when Martin Milner looked into the mirror in the bus station and saw "himself" over his shoulder, but that self was his identical counterpart from another planet, come down to replace him. Montaigne, *c'est moi.* Dangerous business, this essay writing.

Nevertheless, I also suspect that with increased capabilities, computers will be able to decode the literary DNA, so to speak, of a particular writer's style. Please, if you wouldn't mind, try to create new Madden essays from the clues you find coded into this and my other essays. I am no Shakespeare or Cervantes or Montaigne, but I may be the first writer to ask explicitly to be — what would we call this? — literarily cloned?

No one in human history has ever written exactly this sentence. Or anyway these two.

JAMES RICHARDSON, *By the Numbers*

If my prose style is fundamentally an attempt to capture my mind thinking, to convert some part of myself into text, the earliest and most durable form of self-communication and self-preservation, then, it seems to me, a new Madden essay long after I'm dead would be a kind of resurrection.

Short of that, I bet computers might already discover more completely the syntactical patterns and formal lendings of other writers in my writing, the means traveling through time, and not just large scale (tracking uncommon words shared between writers) but shedding light on subconscious influences, discovering that this sentence owes its construction to Doyle or that transition mirrors Chesterton. I believe that Clive James could match Hazlitt to Browne only because he read their two passages one after the other or perhaps had stored Browne's in memory, so that in reading Hazlitt he felt a kind of recognition. What we discover through *feeling* and *recognition*, perhaps computers can parse through analytical means, which might mean

Independent Redundancy 185

that not only my inadvertent appropriations could be uncovered, but my advertent ones as well.

BOB DYLAN'S *CHRONICLES*

Which is what Scott Warmuth and Ed Cook have done recently with Bob Dylan's memoir *Chronicles: Volume One,* supplementing their own cross readings and recognizings with crowd-sourced computer searches for common phrases, and they're turning up a wealth of "borrowings" (because it's Bob Dylan, most folks aren't willing to use the word *plagiarism,* for fear he'll call them "wussies"). They've uncovered "dozens upon dozens" of copied phrases and passages, "a thigh-high stack of books, short stories, and periodicals that Dylan drew from to work his autobiographical alchemy." In a 2010 *New Haven Review* piece, Warmuth lists several notable sources, from the well-know (Mark Twain, Jack London, Marcel Proust, Thomas Wolfe, Ernest Hemingway) to the obscure (Mezz Mezzrow's *Really the Blues,* Gerri Hirshey's *Nowhere to Run: The Story of Soul Music,* the March 13, 1962, issue of *Time*) to the unexpected and strange (self-help book *The 48 Laws of Power* and Joe Eszterhas's book about the Monica Lewinsky scandal, *American Rhapsody*). Usually the appropriations are slight, the kind of similar phrasing that might happen almost by accident. For instance, when talking about the song "Shooting Star," he writes, "It would have been good to have a horn man or two on it, a throbbing hum that mingled into the music." H. G. Wells fanatics, or computers trained to look for rare word groupings, might recognize *The First Men in the Moon*: "Then began a vast throbbing hum that mingled with the music."

My favorite example from *Chronicles* is a double borrowing. Dylan wrote,

> Both Len [Chandler] and Tom [Paxton] wrote topical songs — songs where you'd pick articles out of newspapers, fractured demented stuff, some nun getting married, a high school teacher taking a flying leap off the Brooklyn Bridge, tourists who robbed a gas station, Broadway Beauty being beaten, left in the snow, things like that.

But Warmuth points out that

these "songs" are actual cut-ups from newspaper headlines ("NUN WILL WED GOB," "TOURISTS ROB GAS STATION," and "BROADWAY BEAUTY BEATEN") that John Dos Passos incorporated into his 1936 novel *The Big Money*, an early example of cut-up technique.

It's nothing new that novelists borrow plotlines from headlines, of course, but I'm tickled to see Dylan leaving a trail of breadcrumbs to signal his unannounced technique. The fact that Dos Passos inspired a trio of Rush songs ("The Camera Eye," "Grand Designs," and "The Big Money") makes this particular revelation all the more resonant with me. When confronted with these and other accusations of uncredited citation, Dylan seems both defensive and unperturbed, claiming to be simply "working within my artform," and both conscious and unconscious of his borrowings.

HELEN KELLER

Young Helen Keller faced her own plagiarism scandal, one that might very well have been a case of independent redundancy or inadvertent mimicry, though Mark Twain, not one to mince words, called the incident "owlishly idiotic and grotesque." The facts are thus: At age eleven Keller wrote a short story involving fairies, melting jewels, and autumn leaves painted in their various gemlike colors. The story was published in two small venues, including the *Goodson Gazette*, a journal on deaf-blind education. What ensued was the discovery of, and eventually a firestorm over, the fact that Keller's story bore a strong resemblance to a book by Margaret Canby, *Birdie and His Fairy Friends*.

The simple explanation is that someone had read that book to Keller — this would have involved finger spelling, since the deaf and blind Keller couldn't read standard sign language — but oddly enough, no one could recall having read Keller the book, nor did Keller recall having had it read to her. Soon enough, conspiracy theorists of the time decided that an elaborate plot was afoot, the goal being to "overstate" Keller's abilities and bring fame and fortune to her teacher, Anne Sullivan. Someone, perhaps, was secretly ghostwriting for the young Helen.

One might posit that a deaf-blind girl, or really any eleven-year-old, writing a sweet story in homage to another writer was cause for celebration, not for a witch hunt, but at one point, eight teachers grilled Keller on the matter for two hours, leading her to a nervous breakdown. It was eventually determined that an associate of Sullivan's had likely read Keller the story and that Keller simply didn't remember it, not consciously at least. Eventually Canby, author of *Birdie and His Fairy Friends*, went on the record to say she preferred Keller's version to her own.

SATRIANI V. COLDPLAY

Similar cases come and go all the time, so let's date this essay, shall we? One recent musical issue that tickled my fancy involves guitarist Joe Satriani, who accuses the band Coldplay of ripping off his riff, with their song "Viva la Vida." When the latter's hit hit airwaves in 2008, Satriani "felt like a dagger went right through [his] heart. It hurt so much." He recognized the main vocal melody from a lead guitar part on his 2004 album *Is There Love in Space?* Plus, the chord progression, with a minor transposition, was nearly identical. "The second I heard it, I knew it was 'If I Could Fly,'" he told reporters. What made the offense more egregious was that he'd spent a decade working on the tune (he says) and that "it was a love letter to [his] wife, Rubina—a simple, direct expression of feeling." You start to feel sorry for the poor guy. Here he's struggling to make a living as a musician; his fan base is dwindling since 1987's *Surfing with the Alien* (featuring on its cover a drawing of Marvel Comics' Silver Surfer, for which, curiously, artist John Byrne claims he never gave permission or received payment); he's been toiling for years over a simple love song for his wife . . .

> That's what really hurts about this whole thing. That I spent so long writing the song, thinking about it, loving it, nursing it, and then finally recording it and standing on stages the world over playing it — and then somebody comes along and plays the exact same song and calls it their own.

Right. Along comes megaband Coldplay and — this is key, I think — makes a whole lot of money with a remarkably similar tune (not quite "the exact same song," Joe; yours doesn't have any lyrics, for one thing). Must be frustrating.

But wait a minute. For Satriani to file a viable lawsuit, seeking "any and all profits" from "Viva la Vida," he'd have to prove that Coldplay plagiarized him. I'm not a lawyer, but I can use a dictionary, which defines that verb thus: "to take and use as one's own (the thoughts, writings, or inventions of another person); to copy (literary work or ideas) improperly or without acknowledgement; (occas.) to pass off as one's own the thoughts or work of (another)." For the sake of proper attribution, let me mention that that definition comes from the Oxford English Dictionary, online edition. In any case, *plagiarize*, like *lie*, is a verb of volition. If you tell a falsehood unknowingly, you've not quite lied, and if you create a ditty that sounds like another ditty you've never heard or can't remember, you've not quite plagiarized. The unintentional kind of copying, like what George Harrison got dinged for, is no longer prosecutable under U.S. law.

Of course, I wasn't there in the recording studio, and I have no access to Chris Martin's head, nor can I check his CD collection to find a copy of *Is There Love in Space?* But it may not matter anyway. He's made piquant statements about the issue of plagiarism in public forums. In 2005, speaking with *Rolling Stone* magazine, he offered this self-critique:

> We're definitely good, but I don't think you can say we're that original. I regard us as being incredibly good plagiarists.

Independent Redundancy 189

More damningly, in an easily decontextualized chat with MTV UK just before the Satriani story broke, Martin responded to Chris Moyles's question "Is there a temptation to reinvent yourselves?" by saying,

> We look at what other people are doing and try and steal all the good bits. . . . We steal from so many different places that hopefully it becomes untraceable.

At least, that's the salient part, the part that all the gossipmongers have excerpted. It can't possibly matter that the examples Martin gives where the harmless ellipsis appears (or fails to appear — most reports avoid the messy punctuation entirely) are

> So you look at "Umbrella" by Rihanna and you think, *oh, that drum beat's good*, and you look at "Stronger" by Kanye West and think, *oh, those glasses are good*, and then you look at Greenday. So we are affected by everything that's going on but

That's what's missing from the reports tied to the plagiarism case: a facetious claim on the generically repetitive pounding underneath Rihanna's four-syllable "Um-ber-el-la" and a jab at Kanye's oversized Venetian-blinds sunglasses. And if we zoom out a little bit more, we might note the general convivial/sardonic tone of the conversation, which led to this confession about the band's songwriting process:

> We have a team of eight-year-olds who work in a factory just outside London all the time, and we go there and see what they got, and often they have hits, and we take them.

Or this spoiler about their set list on the upcoming tour:

> We're mainly gonna play Bon Jovi songs and a couple of our B-sides.

As another level of disclosure, I should mention that I *kind of* like Coldplay, and I even have one of their albums plus a legally-

190 *Independent Redundancy*

downloaded-for-free EP, though I rarely listen to them. They seem to be, just as they say, derivative, but I don't begrudge them this. They're a whit better than the vast majority of popular music nowadays. And while Chris Martin is often very cheeky, he does sometimes come off as sincere, in an endearingly humble way. I'd much prefer to hear a musician deprecate his own genius than to hear him chest-thump and disrespect all the music that precedes and surrounds him. So when he and guitarist Jonny Buckland say

> CM: We're one of the world's worst but most enthusiastic plagiarists, as a band. We'll try and copy anything, but it tends to fail, so we come up with something that sounds like us, only through trying to sound like somebody else.
> JB: The more things you've done, the more things you've recorded, the bigger the danger of plagiarizing yourself is, I think. And so we really wanted to avoid doing that.
> CM: The key rule was that we could steal from anybody except ourselves.

I say, go for it, boys. Montaigne himself said as much:

> What if I listen to books a little more attentively than ordinary, since I watch if I can purloin anything that may adorn or support my own?
>
> "Of Giving the Lie"

As have many, many artists we consider original. Perhaps every artist has come to this realization, because every artist has thought about the influences that make up what others call originality. Their ideas inflect this essay, in both quoted and unquoted ways. This (the quote is often mangled and misattributed, to Picasso, to John Lennon, to Bob Dylan, etc.) is the honest truth of art:

> Immature poets imitate; mature poets steal; bad poets deface what they take, and good poets make it into something better, or at least something different. The good poet welds his theft into a

whole of feeling which is unique, utterly different than that from which it is torn; the bad poet throws it into something which has no cohesion.

T. S. ELIOT, "Philip Massinger"

What's more, those who consciously own their influences, belittling their own genius by deferring praise to their forebears and contemporaries, these are the artists I respect. Only the ignorant and bumptious believe that they're uninfluencedly original. Only from a vast insular cluelessness can one attain the bravado necessary to claim independent genius.

MILTON

And that goes for those most renowned geniuses, the Dantes and Miltons, who dwell on the Olympian heights. Now, I've been called "classless" and a "classist" but never a "classicist," and yet when I look at an edition of *Paradise Lost* and see all those footnotes staking the bottom of every page, telling me that Milton is alluding to lines from Virgil or Ovid or a hundred other poets, in Latin and Greek, I see a fellow writer under the influence. Milton works the way all of us do, using the writing that came before him and retooling it for his own ends. The difference between Milton and me (okay, *one* of the differences — Milton is justifying the ways of God to man, while I write essays about my daughter's boogers and looking like Jeffery Dahmer) is the way he transforms his influences:

Milton has borrowed more than any other writer, and exhausted every source of imitation, sacred or profane; yet he is perfectly distinct from every other writer . . . in originality scarcely inferior to Homer. The power of his mind is stamped on every line. . . . In reading his works, we feel ourselves under the influence of a mighty intellect, that the nearer it approaches to others, becomes more distinct from them.

WILLIAM HAZLITT, "On Shakespeare and Milton"

The more Milton voices the words of other poets, the more he sounds like himself. His use of Virgil and Ovid starts to look oddly like originality or, more oddly, self-plagiarism.

SELF-PLAGIARISM

Which is a topic I've been thinking about a lot lately. It all came into my consciousness a few months ago when Jim Romenesko posted on his blog a particularly mean-spirited piece accusing popular neuroscience writer Jonah Lehrer of "self-plagiarism." According to Romenesko, Lehrer repeatedly recycled passages from his older writings in several recent articles he'd written for the *New Yorker*.

New York magazine's online version picked the story up, and the whole thing (predictably) snowballed from there. And I thought, "Here we go again." Despite some strong support from fellow staffers, Lehrer resigned from his position at the *New Yorker*.

In journalism circles, Lehrer was known to be a prolific, public, and popular writer. In light of the media circus surrounding the James Frey, Jayson Blair, and scores of other reputed writing "scandals," the holier-than-thou allegations from critics and colleagues, while admittedly disturbing, didn't surprise me all that much. The thought police always seem to surface at times like this, right? In fact, according to Jacob Silverman of the *Daily Beast*, "Romenesko is the reigning doyen of media gossip."

All the high-minded accusations about ethics, attributions, and copyright felt disingenuous. And so it was easy to convince myself that "self-plagiarism" was something of an oxymoron. Plus, I already had too many censors on my shoulder telling me what I can or can't write, can or can't imagine, can or can't think. This does, after all, run counter to a personal essayist's sensibilities, does it not?

All well and good then — or so it seemed. Because, over the next several days, something about that scenario kept nagging at me.

Truth is, I, too, have lifted excerpts from my writing and reused them in other pieces. And for a while, it troubled me. But when I thought more about it, deceit, duplicity, convenience, or even laziness were never my main motives for recycling a few segments from my older writing. (I wish we could find better descriptive terms for this than *lifted*, *recycled*, and *self-plagiarized*.) Moreover, I told myself, don't literary writers have more leeway than journalists do?

Maybe I'm letting myself off the hook; but if something I've written or said is a good fit for another piece of writing, there's no reason why I can't reuse it, especially if it illuminates or otherwise enhances what I'm trying to say.

And besides, writers like me can use all the help we can get, yes? When even the greatest writers of all time stood on the shoulders of . . . other folks of normal stature?

SHAKESPEARE'S BORROWINGS

I don't intend to enter into the authorship-controversy debate concerning the plays of William Shakespeare, but I'll recap it for you all the same. It revolves around the idea that an undereducated English country boy never could have woven these dramas attributed to him, suggesting instead that these were actually the work of a learned nobleman with access to the court: Sir Francis Bacon, in one theory; the Earl of Oxford, Edward de Vere, in another. But this misses the point, I think. Much more interesting, to my thinking (and to this essay), is that the content of Shakespeare's works is largely lifted from other sources: *Hamlet* borrows from Norse folklore; *The Comedy of Errors* from Plautus; the Pyramus and Thisbe scene from *A Midsummer Night's Dream* seems a nod to the bard's own *Romeo and Juliet* (at least until you trace it back to the Pyramus and Thisbe story in Ovid's *Metamorphoses*). No big secret. And he seems as indebted to contemporary sources. Scholars note the similarities between Shakespeare's plays and Montaigne's essays, first translated into English by John Florio and published in 1603, confirmed to have been in Shakespeare's possession as he penned his final plays. Substantial chunks of Montaigne's "Of Cannibals" appear in *The Tempest* as Gonzalo describes his vision for an ideal state; Shakespeare changes Montaigne's word *nation* to *Commonwealth* but leaves intact most of Montaigne's criteria. And as the renowned Shakespeare scholar Stanley Wells notes, the playwright leans on another of Montaigne's essays, "Of

Cruelty," to inform Prospero's act of forgiveness at the play's climax. Is Shakespeare's plagiarism any less problematic simply because he's Shakespeare? Maybe so. "He was more original than his originals," Walter Savage Landor wrote in Shakespeare's defense. "He breathed upon dead bodies and brought them into life." It would seem that Montaigne, himself a frequent borrower of others' thoughts, would not have minded much, either:

> Amongst so many borrowings I am indeed glad to filch some one, disguising and altering the same to some new service.
>
> MONTAIGNE, "Of Physiognomy"

But getting back to *self*-plagiarism, my favorite case (alleged) is *Fantasy Records v. John Fogerty*. The record company, which had acquired rights to Creedence Clearwater Revival's 1970 song "Run through the Jungle" (among others), claimed that Fogerty's 1985 solo song "Old Man Down the Road" was the same music with new lyrics. I've given both tunes a listen, and I have to admit that they do sound similar, but then again, they also sound a bit like "Susie Q," and Fogerty has a distinctive style ("swamp rock," he calls it) that's instantly recognizable, so I could see how you might think that every CCR or Fogerty song is the same as every other. Ultimately, that's what he argued to the jury, guitar in hand, playing through both songs and demonstrating their differences while highlighting his signature style. I don't pretend to know the intricacies of copyright, but I'm relieved that the courts (originally and upon Fantasy's appeal, too) found in favor of Fogerty, the actual writer of the songs. And though I'm not a particular fan of CCR, I'm also glad that Fogerty's countersuit, to recoup attorney's fees, made it all the way to the Supreme Court, which found in his favor. Take that, Fantasy Records!

And returning to the *Satriani v. Coldplay* case, while you visit YouTube (Hello, Future: Is YouTube still around? Do you kids learn about YouTube in school? Or can you, just by thinking about it, see an old music video in your mind?) to check the songs' similarities for yourself, let me suggest that maybe Satriani isn't as original as he thinks. The hive mind (universal consciousness? Is that a less offensive way of describing how we can now combine our insights in cyberspace?) has gleefully discovered several songs that used Satriani's melody before he did. The most interesting, to me, is a song called "Frances Limón," by an Argentine band called Enanitos Verdes ("Little Green Men" works as a translation). Having lived in Uruguay for several years, I'm familiar with Enanitos Verdes, and I quite enjoy their subversive pop (and talk about stylish glasses, Chris Martin; you'd do well to copy Marciano Cantero's), especially "Lamento Boliviano," a catchy tune that I heard several times a day in 1994. In any case, "Frances Limón" was released in 2002, two years before Satriani's song; and while the overlap in guitar melody is partial, it carries on for as long as "My Sweet Lord"/"He's So Fine," so unless Joe shared his demo tapes with his Argentine fans long before his album release, he'd be as guilty of plagiarism as anyone who came after him. Which is to say that he should donate the out-of-court settlement money to the cause of advancing the essay in the world.

And just when you thought the issue was settled . . .

Never one to back down from a chance to reclaim his former (and foresworn) musical glory, Yosuf Islam, the artist formerly known as Cat Stevens, waited until the dust had almost settled and until he was about to release a brand new album to join in the accusations: "There's been this argument about Coldplay stealing this melody from Joe Satriani, but, if you listen to it, it's mine! It's the 'Foreigner Suite,' it is!" In response to Cat, I listened to both songs (I like Stevens — I grew up listening to his albums, and my college roommate played his records all the time), and the similarity seems slight. If they made me judge, I'd (again) find in favor of the defendant in this case; the songs are not quite similar enough to even warrant investigation.

Cat may have a case, though, against the Flaming Lips, whose song "Fight Test" sounds suspiciously like his "Father and Son" for a few brief seconds. This one I picked up on all by myself. So did Cat, or his people, and his suit ended fairly quickly with a settlement to share royalties. Wayne Coyne, of the Flaming Lips, admitted to admiring Stevens and being inspired by his work, even to borrowing the vocal melody without changing it enough, then added, "If anyone wanted to borrow part of a Flaming Lips song, I don't think I'd bother pursuing it. I've got better things to do. Anyway, Cat Stevens is never going to make much money out of us." Whatever the case, Coyne and Co. certainly learned that there are things you can't avoid. You have to face them when you're not prepared to face them. But they've found the graceful way to handle it, which I like, and which gets me thinking: is there any such thing as authorized plagiarism? I'm not talking about author Junichi Saga, who, after he was told that Bob Dylan had lifted parts of *Confessions of a Yakuza* to write lyrics to *Love and Theft* and after his obscure book became a brief bestseller, said, "Please say hello to Bob Dylan for me because I am very flattered and very happy to hear this news." I'm talking more about Eric Clapton playing uncredited on "While My Guitar Gently Weeps," lending his signature style to a Beatles song without caring that he got recognition, simply because his friend George Harrison asked him to.

SMASHING PUMPKINS V. THE TORDS

I am sympathetic to the accused, you could say, because I, too, have found myself unintentionally repeating the musical ideas of others. In my case, the offense was highly unlikely, as I am not a musician and I have written only a handful of songs in my life. (Perhaps, it occurs to me upon reflection, that the offense was therefore *more* likely?) One of them I first set to tape sometime in the Uruguayan winter of 1995, sitting on my bed with a communal guitar that had been left in the LDS Mission offices long before. Against all advices, I had fallen in love, and song seemed the appropriate outlet for my pent-up feelings (missionaries are forbidden from engaging in social activities, especially dating, or expressing their romantic fondness for any individuals).

One morning, I grabbed the guitar and began strumming up a tune, something simple based on the G and C chords, something relatively melodic, I guess, maybe something R.E.M.-ish. Despite my complex musical loves (as I have mentioned elsewhere, Rush and Yes and the Beatles, principally), I couldn't come up with anything more intricate than that. But it was good enough. I sang over the two-measure

repetition a heartfelt declaration from the imagined near future, when I'd be back home in New Jersey:

I love a skinny girl
She lives halfway around the world
I know if I could get out of here and back there
    where she lives
She'd leave and follow me

(I knew no such thing, yet I hoped.) As I sang, I fingered a ditty of a guitar melody on the G and B strings. Short months later, when I *was* back home, I stopped by my friend Joe's house with the demo tape and a completed set of lyrics, and together we recorded the song to his eight-track, using a temperamental drum machine to lay an unwavering beat, with me on guitar and Joe on (the beautifully intricate, surprisingly springy) bass. I sang double vocals, harmonizing with myself or singing a countermelody in Spanish, and we wrapped within a few hours, burning a couple of compact discs of the final mix.

So imagine my surprise years later when I heard on the radio the very same chord shift and guitar melody I'd written for Karina! (Unlike Joe Satriani, I'd only taken a few short minutes of fiddling to find my melody, but like him, I was dismayed to learn that a more successful band was making money from the same riff I'd written for the love of my life. [No I wasn't. I was amused.]) The lyrics were different, as was the vocal melody, but the basic verse was essentially the same (down to the tempo). I learned from the disc jockey that this was the Smashing Pumpkins, a band I knew just a little bit. I looked up the song later and discovered that it was from the movie *Singles*. How I wish that *Singles* had been released after I recorded "Skinny Girl," but alas, it came out in 1992, three years prior. Still, I am convinced that I never heard the song before, that I came up with its guitar part independently, which is what you'd expect me to say, but let me remind us all that there's nothing at stake here. I am not a musician, and I've never made a cent from that silly love song (though it did not fail me in its intended purpose of wooing the fair maiden Karina),

198 *Independent Redundancy*

and there's almost no chance that Billy Corgan and Co. will ever hear it, especially because I've tried to contact him so he can listen to my song and give me some comments for this essay, but his agent replied (very promptly) that Mr. Corgan felt "uncomfortable" taking part in the experiment. *sigh* So the situation, as I see it, is something quite different from "My Sweet Lord," in which George Harrison had certainly heard "He's So Fine" but didn't realize that he was using its melody for his new song.

You might feel confident that you had simply come up with the same simple guitar part as a famous band did, unless you discover, as I did soon after writing the above exculpatory paragraphs, that both "Skinny Girl" and "Drown" sound remarkably like "Jane Says" by Jane's Addiction, though in a different key. This song first appeared in 1987 (and received considerable radio play from then on), and I'm certain that I *did* hear it during those years, so I'm now unsure but believe it likely that I, like Harrison, subconsciously copied a song I'd internalized.

So much depends upon intention and memory.

THE GREY ALBUM

And so much has been written about Girl Talk, who makes his music entirely by mashing up other artists' songs, and DJ Danger Mouse, whose *Grey Album* melded the Beatles' *White Album* and Jay-Z's *Black Album*. For a condensation of the debate, one might pit open-source advocate Lawrence Lessig against musician-writer W. David Marx (aka Marxy) and *Village Voice* reporter Nick Sylvester:

> Enter the internet, where every single use produces a copy: we go from this balance between unregulated, regulated, and fair uses to a presumptive rule of regulated uses merely because of the platform through which we get access to our culture has changed, rendering this read/write activity presumptively illegal. DJ Danger Mouse knew he could never get permission from the Beatles to remix their work.

LESSIG, "REMIX: How Creativity Is Being Strangled by the Law"

Independent Redundancy 199

Notice we don't find Girl Talk offensive to copyright, "the ontology of art," or pop music in general. We just think the relatively innovative gimmick of his style has exempted him from critical thought put towards the actual result . . . the idea of user-generated content delights our commerce so — that the line between Ultimate Fan and Actual Artist is rendered the same in terms of exchange value.

MARX AND SYLVESTER, "Theoretically Unpublished Piece . . ."

But I'd like to speak to the work of the two DJs in another context. If the reader might recall, besides revealing some linguistic similarities between the essayist's and the lyrical gangster's mutual obsession with finding the uncommon in common language — the well-turned phrase, the clever juxtaposition — I also quoted Michael Martone's thoughts on the essayist's individual voice:

It resists knowing the new but knows knowing what is known in new ways. It is new not in the genesis sense of creation, but in its ability to create new combinations, associations of things already known in the world.

If what Martone says is true, then both Girl Talk and Danger Mouse are, if not essayists, at least *essayistic* in intention. Of course, anyone who knows me will consent to my conception of the essay in the Montaignean sense of the French *essai*: an attempt, a try, a thought experiment. The essayist works within an established tradition, but a tradition of experimentation, of formal subversion, of questioning norms. The tradition of hip-hop, while a fraction as old as the essay's tradition (Montaigne began his work in the 1570s, while the Sugarhill Gang and Grandmaster Flash pioneered some of the earliest record scratching and sampling in the late 1970s), also has these three values at its center.

The audio mash-up, possibly first practiced in the sampled cut-and-paste aural art of John Oswald in the sixties, then rendered danceable by the early hip-hoppers of the seventies and eighties, and lately entering the mainstream as user-generated content in the late nineties and into the present, has become the primary mode of creative expression for youth culture. Lessig reinforces this connection:

> Anyone can take images, sounds, video from the culture around us and remix them in ways that speak to a generation more powerfully than raw text ever could. That's the key. This is just *writing* for the twenty-first century.

Just like my sixth-grade daughter's automated writing teacher PEG, text analyzers, and my fractured attempts at conversations with robots, part of the fun of music mash-ups is in parsing a piece into its individual recognizable components and marveling — many times laughing — at the strangeness of their decontextualized juxtapositions.

And just like we've seen before, this practice is nothing new. Montaigne (who could doubt it?) was a mash-up artist, too. He described his theory thusly:

> Bees cull their several sweets from this flower and that blossom, here and there where they find them, but themselves afterwards make the honey, which is all and purely their own, and no more thyme and marjoram: so the several fragments he borrows from others, [the essayist] will transform and shuffle together to compile a work that shall be absolutely his own. . . . He is not obliged to discover whence he got the materials that have assisted him, but only to produce what he has himself done with them.

Which I, in good absorptive postmodern form, got indirectly, not by remembering and rereading "Of the Education of Children," but by reading casually — with no research in mind and no thought to improving this essay — Eric LeMay's interactive essay "About a Bee," which also revealed where Mixmaster Montaigne certainly got his metaphor:

> We should follow, men say, the example of the bees, who flit about and cull the flowers that are suitable for producing honey,

and then arrange and assort in their cells all that they have brought in. . . . We also, I say, ought to copy these bees, and sift whatever we have gathered from a varied course of reading, for such things are better preserved if they are kept separate; then, by applying the supervising care with which our nature has endowed us, in other words, our natural gifts, we should so blend those several flavours into one delicious compound that, even though it betrays its origin, yet it nevertheless is clearly a different thing from that whence it came.

SENECA, "On Gathering Ideas"

INVENTIONS, MULTIPLES

Musical and literary examples are legion (as if you hadn't noticed), and we'll consider just a few more in a few moments, but I'd like to make a brief detour into thinking about simultaneous inventions and theories, because they seem, too, to confirm the idea of creation as available recombination. As has been noted in a number of works (Steven Johnson's *Where Good Ideas Come From* and Malcolm Gladwell's "In the Air" among the most recent, with "Are Inventions Inevitable?" by William Ogburn and Dorothy Thomas perhaps leading the way in the 1920s), innovations and inventions are typically less the result of genius operating in isolation and more the result of convergences in ideas, materials, and possibilities. Thus, with the invention of the telescope, the discovery of sunspots was not far behind, and with the general intellectual atmosphere of the early Enlightenment, both Isaac Newton and Gottfried Leibniz discovered, independently though slightly differently, the mathematics of calculus. Often discoverers or inventors were working far from each other, with no direct sharing of ideas, though in later times, when inventions promised great financial rewards to whoever got there first, they worked in competition, even trying to pick up or pick off whatever knowledge they could. Steven Johnson lists several examples from among

202 *Independent Redundancy*

many more: the first electrical battery, developed by Dean Von Kleist and Cuneus of Leyden in 1745 and 1746, respectively; the isolation of oxygen, by Joseph Priestley and Carl Wilhelm Scheele in 1772 and 1774; the formulation of the law of conservation of energy, by four different scientists in the late 1840s (Johnson forgets to mention Robert Mayer, who proposed the theory in 1842, before Joule, Thomson, Colding, and Helmholz); theories of genetic mutation's effects on evolution, by S. Korschinsky and Hugo de Vries in 1899 and 1901; and numerous other examples. Ogburn and Thomas (no doubt Johnson's primary source) credit the invention of the airplane not just to the Wright brothers but to Samuel Pierpont Langley (a contested claim, as his manned planes all failed), and Brazilians are still convinced that Alberto Santos-Dumont invented the airplane, which he did, proving it in a public display in Paris in late 1906, almost three years after the Wright brothers flew at Kitty Hawk. The telephone, they remind us, was invented by Alexander Graham Bell, yes, but with unwitting/unwilling help from Elisha Gray (their tale of patent-office intrigue makes gripping reading). Avogadro proposed the molecular theory in 1811, but Ampère, unaware of the former's work, did likewise in 1814. Although our mythologies tend to give full credit to a single inventor (Avogadro got the number named after him; Ampère got the unit of electrical current, for his other work), an astounding number of discoveries are made multiply and independently. To wit, color photography, decimal fractions, logarithms, steamboats, telescopes, thermometers, typewriters, and more! As nearly all the articles exploring independently redundant inventions note, the most important and contentious scientific theory of our time was thought of independently and nearly identically by both Charles Darwin and Alfred Russel Wallace.

Noticing so many multiples in the scientific/technological world, we must challenge the "genius theory" of invention, which supposes that special individuals toiling maniacally until struck by a Eureka! are responsible for our species' advances. Yet the idea that inventions are inevitable is dissatisfying, too, for the obvious reason that it robs us of a measure of free will. A few studies in the 1960s explored the question of *why multiples?* in detail with statistical modeling. They tended to hypothesize three basic causes: the aforementioned individual-genius model, a social-determinist or zeitgeist model (Simonton: "the sociocultural system as a whole, embodied as the spirit of the times, is ultimately responsible for any given technoscientific advance"), and a pure chance model. None seems definitive in its answer, or all seem willing to entertain some mix of factors, and the most interesting to me is the "ripe apple model," which posits a thousand blind people picking apples from a tree with a thousand apples (they have very long arms, or the tree has been genetically engineered to produce only reachable fruit). If they all grab only one apple simultaneously, then how many will grab the same apple as another person or persons? It turns out that 368 apples will not be picked and 368 will be picked by one person, but 184 will be double picked, 61 will be triple picked, 15 will be quadruple picked, and 4 apples will be grabbed by five or more people. This distribution pattern corresponds uncannily with the numbers of 264 multiple discoveries/inventions compiled by Robert K. Merton and Elinor Barber in a 1961 sociological study. Given the unpicked apples, one might conclude that not all inventions are inevitable, and given the preponderance of multiples (and sociologists believe that many cases go unreported, especially today, when news travels fast, so that people may give up nearly completed work once they see that they've been scooped), the lone-genius theory also suffers a hit. Dean Simonton, who worked synthesizing and making sense of his predecessors' results, decided in 1979 that "the position that best meets all critical tests is the chance theory." Others, of course, remain convinced that the solution is a complex combination of factors including some volitional geniuses influenced by the zeitgeist plus a bit of random chance. (Worth noting that if the blind people reach randomly, some downward or sideways, or don't reach or don't even know they're supposed to reach, they get no apples at all.)

Fresh thought indeed, but freshness is only unfamiliarity.

WILLIAM GASS, "Emerson and the Essay"

SOME THOUGHTS ON DETERMINISM

It occurs to me that the struggle between models of determinism — fate, God, dialectic, inevitable progress, genetics — and free will, chaos (which, if you're Milton, is the space of creativity, God's womb), applies to invention as much as individual (or group) destiny, invention being a subset of destiny, and that all are opposed, in some way, to any real model of creativity. Rather, if we stipulatively determine (determine!) that *invention* means an unpredictable, unexpected, not inevitable creation and that *discovery*, as its binary, is that which — like a rock in the path of a tiller — will inevitably be turned up, then that is the same struggle. And this would mean that those who believe invention inevitable really mean that there is only discovery, not invention, which might well have been the appropriate subtitle for Ogburn and Thomas's "Is Invention Inevitable?" in which they quickly move from an inductively established premise that, yes, it is, to an examination of the forces at play that lead to invention, in partial hopes of being able to predict invention, which, if one ponders it, is itself an infinite regression, for is not the prediction of a specific invention — the steamboat, say, which they use as an example — actually a commission for an invention already conceived? And then mustn't one explore a predictive model for prediction, and so forth? But before going too deeply down that rabbit hole and while also intentionally blinding myself to the allure of biographical research on Thomas and Ogburn, whom I want to read as characters, thus emplotting romance over their (imagined-by-me) narrative, I want to point out that they establish a dialectic between the intellect of inventors in a culture and the culture itself, in which they privilege the culture as the generator of invention because, across cultures, "it is exceedingly probable that

Independent Redundancy 205

over a few centuries there is no appreciable variation in the average or the distribution of mental ability," which does three things for them:

It establishes them as biologically egalitarian, thus progressive.

It allows them, later, to "conclude that the processes of cultural evolution are to be explained . . . in terms of sociology and not in biology and psychology." Handy that, if you're a couple of political scientists.

By divorcing individuals from their culture, it argues against those cultures originating with their participants. Otherwise, given point 1, all cultures would be the same.

This third implies that culture, the engine of inevitable invention, is actually supernatural in its origins, and this is the subtext of Hegel's account of history, in which dialectical totalities are merely the process through which an inevitable history, owned by no one — not even Napoleon, who, for Hegel, is its horse-backed manifestation — is plotted. Owned by no one, of course, except God. But this totality is eschatological, damning in a way, which is the only way to argue for invention, for chaos, for unpredictability: that relinquishing the comfort of like-it-or-not progress is a chance to turn one's back on apocalypse. And no, this is not an admonition to my students to take up Dadaism.

ALFRED RUSSEL WALLACE

Meanwhile in Malaysia, fever-ridden Alfred Russel Wallace woke from his malarial muddle, suddenly certain that the cause of so much individual variation among the curiosities he collected was a matter of which members within a species were "best fitted to live" — that adaptation to inconstant environments not only shaped an animal's organization but determined its staying power — and penned the finer points of his epiphany in a letter to passing acquaintance Charles Darwin, who was, upon receiving said correspondence at home in Kent, "smashed." At this point, the origin of species had been Darwin's mind and matter for nearly twenty years, but it was Wallace's words that set him to writing in earnest, and by the end of that summer, several of

Darwin's studies were published in conjunction with Wallace's essay, followed a year later by the book that shook science inside out. Happily, the coincidence elicited no copyright quarrel or even so much as a hard feeling; the two remained humble colleagues, each quick to recognize the other — though it is Darwin's name that is immortalized, a delightful mimesis (scimesis?) given the subject matter, *survival of the fittest*, and so forth.

KIEŚLOWSKI

Now, having left behind our main themes of musical and literary redundancies, let's keep going, shall we?

> For me optimism is two lovers walking into the sunset arm in arm. Or maybe into the sunrise — whatever appeals to you.
>
> KRZYSZTOF KIEŚLOWSKI, "Kieślowski's Many Colours"

Backward and forward, forward and backward (drawkcab dna drawrof niaga). If there is a contour to existence it must be some sort of massive oblong shape in perpetual motion. Excircles and incircles in perfect rotation forever, where we stumble on the same twenty-six letters and their almost innumerable — but still numerable — combinations. It might be a bold claim, but I will make it. Or it is bold, *so* I will make it. (The bolder, the more original, as so much death metal and conceptual art has taught us. I shock, therefore, I originate.)

But back to Kieślowski and one of my favorite moments in his acclaimed film *Blue*, from the famous *Three Colors* trilogy. (The film is in French, but the matter of translation, etc. Thus, Anglais. You understand.)

The heroine, as Kieślowski calls her, approaches what seems to be a homeless man playing his flute on a cobblestone road. "How do you know this music?" she asks him. It is the same music — or at least it has sufficient points of similarity for Satriani to sue — that the heroine's dead husband was in the midst of composing before his untimely death!

Independent Redundancy 207

Tragedy aside, the homeless man answers, "I invent a lot of stuff. I like to play."

Regarding this scene Kieślowski later said,

The heroine approaches the musician. There is dialogue in which she learns that different people in different places in the world, but at the same time, think about the same thing. . . . All the notes exist, scattered somewhere, waiting for the one who will assemble them.

Which raises, for me, two new variables and one inevitable conclusion. The first question is, How long will they wait, and do they know I'm coming? The second, Is this a matter of thought? Not just creation or composition; not music, not haikus: *thought*. I think, therefore I am, but what am I if you also think and are at the same time as I think and am and we think in unison a single unpatented thought?

Rivals is what.

Darwin and Wallace. Tesla and Edison. Newton and Leibniz. Galileo, Fabricius, Harriott. Joule, Thomson, Colding, and Helmholtz. Joseph Priestley and Carl Wilhelm Scheele. Charles Cros and Louis Ducos du Hauron. John Napier, Henry Briggs, Joost Bürg.

Rival doppelgangers. The ultimate, best, and worst of all redundancies.

PAVEMENT

I can't stay away from the music for long, see? I know the indie-rock band Pavement mostly for a just-plain-silly reference to Geddy Lee's voice ("How did it get so high? I wonder if he speaks like an ordinary guy?") in their 1997 song "Stereo," but they earn a spot in this essay for the subtle multiplagiarisms that kick off their 1994 *Crooked Rain, Crooked Rain*. The record opens with twenty seconds of reverb-heavy noodling overtop some almost-aimless drum fills before everyone pulls it together into a bona fide intro that is at once crunchy and soupy, sloppy and slick (and features ample cowbell). Matt Diehl's *Rolling Stone* review cites rip-offs of a wide variety of influences here in the opening moments: notes of Sly and the Family Stone's "Everyday People," Free's "All Right Now," and Barry McGuire's "Eve of Destruction," all cycle through the first track, "Silence Kid" ("before the first chorus!"). Front man Stephen Malkmus has admitted in various interviews to adopting and adapting the Free chords. I'm not so sure, though, that I hear "Everyday People" (that might be a matter of feel more than actual mimicry) or "Eve of Destruction" (the melody's sudden peaks are somehow reminiscent, but not to the point of plagiarism), but I hear something that the reviewer missed: the "Silence Kid" melody is the unmistakable twin of Buddy Holly's "Everyday." It seems as if it could have been accidental, the same way Coldplay just happened to compose the exact same melody that Enanitos Verdes already had, but the likeness is remarkable. A bit later on *Crooked Rain, Crooked Rain* comes a piano-driven instrumental in five-four time called "5-4 = Unity," whose most obvious influence, I think, is Dave Brubeck's "Take Five" (though the reviewer points out that it seems to lift a guitar riff from the Beatles' "I Want You [She's So Heavy]" — and he's right about that one). But if you can plagiarize public perception and the arc of your career, Pavement seems to have followed Brubeck pretty closely, if unwittingly. "Brubeck was a white nerd popular with all the middle-class people," Malkmus noted. He might just as easily have been talking about his own band.

"BABY GOT GLEE"

In the interest of time (*you're on page 209, and suddenly you're interested in saving time!?*), I'll skip over the thread suggested by Malkmus's "White and Nerdy" comment, which is the title of "Weird Al" Yankovic's parody of Chamillionaire's "Ridin' Dirty," which gets me thinking on Yankovic's various parody types (real songs with humorous replacement lyrics; polkafication; stylistic imitations): instead, I recently found myself following the public feud between the producers of the Fox television show *Glee* (a show I do not watch) and the singer-songwriter Jonathan Coulton (a musician I had never heard of prior to his accusation that the television show about teenage singing competitions had plagiarized his acoustic cover of Sir Mix-a-Lot's 1992 party anthem/celebration of booty, "Baby Got Back" [a song which itself samples from another song and a movie]).

When I first read Coulton's allegations, I was skeptical. *Glee* is, after all, a television show about teenagers singing show tunes and pop songs. Originality has never been the show's claim to fame. I also wondered how someone could plagiarize a cover — even a cover that takes certain liberties with its source material. I enjoy John Cale's version of "Heartbreak Hotel" and Jimmy Hendrix's version of "All along the Watchtower," but at the end of the day they're still someone else's songs. And let's be honest, acoustic guitar covers of rap and hip-hop songs are not quite as amusing as they once were. I heard a street musician perform a solo version of Outkast's "Hey Ya!" several years ago, which had a certain charm, and I enjoyed the Gourds' version of Snoop Dogg's "Gin and Juice," but at this point ironic hipster versions of rap favorites are hardly original.

You can imagine my surprise, then, to find that Coulton actually had a compelling case. Upon listening to both versions, I had to conclude that the *Glee* producers had indeed taken his work — right down to his new, personalized lyric, "Johnny C's in trouble now." They had taken his arrangement, replaced his voice with the voices of the show's cast, and put the song on TV (and put it up for sale on iTunes).

On his blog, Coulton said that representatives from the show eventually contacted his "peeps" to inform him that they were within their legal rights to use his music on their show and to tell him that he "should be happy for the exposure," despite the fact that the show did not credit him and that the only exposure he received was a result of his own complaining about the song's use.

A week after the *Glee* broadcast, Coulton released "Baby Got Back (in the Style of *Glee*)" on iTunes, with proceeds to go toward the VH-1 Save the Music Foundation and the It Gets Better Project. As he explained on his blog, "It's a cover of *Glee*'s cover of my cover of Sir Mix-A-Lot's song, which is to say it's EXACTLY THE SAME as my original version."

I can't be certain, but I suspect that this might be the first time someone referred to a cover as "the original version" of a song.

210 *Independent Redundancy*

Of course, when it comes to independent redundancy, writing is unlike music, even if the proverbial monkeys were to bat out *Hamlet* tomorrow. It's also unlike science and invention, where there is a certain natural need that the scientist or inventor is trying to fill. For them, the solution is not just "in the air" but "of the moment," and it's not uncommon for two people to be following a line of thinking that results in a version of the same thing. In a logical progression, two people who had never heard of each other may end up sharing the Nobel Prize. In biblical fashion, radio begets television begets DVD ad nauseam. Whatever begot Facebook, it has arrived, and now it's possible to simply lift a post and repost as though it were original, multiplying the phenomenon fiftyfold. Its short form is retweeting. You don't even have to think the unoriginal thought.

Unlike science or technology, literature does not "advance." For writers, short of deliberate plagiarism, which is, to all intents and purposes, about as far from *independent* redundancy as penalty shoot-outs are from soccer, the term "conceptual plagiarism" might apply to the kind of zeitgeist that could produce six contemporary versions of classic novels within a year or two (possibly best known are Michael Cunningham's *The Hours* and Sena Jeter Naslund's *Ahab's Wife*). Novels take quite some time to write, so each of those writers must have been typing away at the keyboard in their individual studies night after night, each looking out their individual windows at the moon caught in the branches of their lodgepole pine/maple/oak/flowering crabapple, thinking, *What a great new idea I have.* Add "structural plagiarism" to the mix, and you get the genius of Ian McEwan's *Atonement*. Years after reading L. P. Hartley's *The Go-Between*, and ten novels into his own career, McEwan was finally proficient enough in his craft to be creative within the borrowed confines of character and plot, opening and epilogue. The result is something wholly new and yet haunted by ghosts of the original — which was, in all probability, haunted by earlier ghosts of its own, from *Cyrano de Bergerac* to *As You Like It* — as though to prove Mark Twain's assertion:

There is no such thing as a new idea. It is impossible. We simply take a lot of old ideas and put them into a sort of mental kaleidoscope. We give them a turn and they make new and curious combinations.

But McEwan would make no claims of independence. And were Hartley alive, he would recognize that there is no copyright on something as ephemeral as perception. Writers are readers; they are usually familiar with the work from which they borrow, and thus they become part and parcel of a long tradition of challenging us to "tell the dancer from the dance."

Our debt to tradition through reading and conversation is so massive, our protest or private addition so rare and insignificant . . . that, in a large sense, one would say there is no pure originality. All minds quote. Old and new make the warp and woof of every moment.

RALPH WALDO EMERSON, "Quotation and Originality"

One of the verses of scripture that nonscriptorians often quote, in part, is Ecclesiastes 1:9: "The thing that has been, it is that which shall be; and that which is done is that which shall be done: and there is no new thing under the sun." (I use here the King James Bible [Cambridge edition], which was [and is] so influential a translation as to be not only paradigm shifting but paradigm *setting*, a sort of ur-translation that erases its predecessors by force of its brilliance and "originality," and this reminds me of Harold Bloom's notion of strong misreading or "misprision" from *The Anxiety of Influence*, which I could go into more but I really should end this sentence [and this parenthesis] before it becomes late Jamesian instead of Maddenian.) But one of the first things you notice in the verse is its implicit challenge: *verily, I dare you to think of a new thing under the sun.* To this ante, I raise the pangram haiku (supra), observing, by the way, that any scripture that inspires a spirit of contrariness above all else is a little problematic, don't you think, Preacher? Or am I being too competitive — too vain?

While they admit that no one could know, Ogburn and Thomas did postulate that before written records, many isolated populations probably developed similar tools. Especially in cases where the groups were geographically distant — Peru and Europe (bronze making), America and Borneo (blowguns), Central America and Egypt (pyramids) — the logical conclusion is that they came up with these things independently. So my suspicion is that there are ideas that come to us generation after generation, sparking here and there with no need for cross generational learning. And not just implements and processes but stories, too: a great flood, gods' visits to the earth, fairy tales and folk tales to teach morality to the rising generation. It would seem that even in prehistory our ancestors processed the world in comparable ways.

To observe the similarity between the petroglyphs displayed at the Kyrgyzstan National History Museum and the ones scratched into the cliffs of Southern Utah is to experience déjà vu. Both show marching goats and hunters spread across the purple patina of sandstone of nearly identical red shades. Some stylistic choices differ but the concepts are the same, the techniques are the same, though the cultures are nearly opposite each other on the globe. While experts today may convene and compare these ancient etchings, the Mesoamericans and Mesopotamians did not have such convocations, being confirmed continental isolationists, at least after the ice bridges melted.

Central Asia and North America aren't the only places to boast petroglyphs; we find decorated stones on every inhabitable continent, in nearly every clime where ancient people lived. Wherever our ancestors passed, they drew pictures, labeled the world around them. And their motifs were the same, too — animals and their hunters, plants and their gatherers, people and their deities — the patterns everywhere revealing either humanity's universal unoriginality or our uninhibited urge to record our preoccupations with food, sex, and prowess. Surprisingly, even the abstract designs resonate. Ancient animators marked out mazes on many a mountainside; and on horizontal surfaces, they left the cup-and-ring pattern, a small divot with carved circles around it, likely used as a sacrificial center or perhaps as a legend of the marked stone's use, but whatever the reason, the peoples of ancient Mexico, Spain, England, and India all carved dips in rocks and drew circles around them, as a useful way of doing ... something — we'll never fully understand just what.

I suppose one could argue that since humans have all spread out from the same African source, they learned their artistic nature from their parents, taking their stone-carving skills with them. And while stone tools likely existed in some form since we stood upright, intentional art is newer than that, appearing only some forty thousand years ago, with petroglyphs appearing in the last quarter of that span, well after the diaspora, long after individual groups had forgotten their homeland entirely and made up new myths to explain themselves. Maybe we are hardwired to carve on stone, but more likely we are predestined to record the world, to see and observe, and across the globe the same tools were ready at hand.

DRINK WATER

Same principle, different scale: When I was very young, maybe four or five, I wanted so desperately to wake up in the wee hours of Christmas that I decided to drink as much water as I could stomach, knowing that within a short while, my bladder would nearly burst, calling me back to the quiet, dark waking world. I did this trick for far too long, every year waking my sister and brothers to squeak down the stairs for a brief peek at our good fortune shining in the dim colored lights of the tree. We'd rifle through our stockings in the family room then sit in reverence on the couches in the living room, milking the anticipation, maybe slipping to the floor to shake a box or two, homing in on the LEGOS. I remember those mornings fondly, perhaps more fondly than the mad climax a few hours later, once we'd reached a decent hour (six o'clock, usually) to wake our parents and dive right in to fix possibilities into objects. This is to be expected, I suppose, that the forty-year-old me would convince himself out of the consumer interpretation of the holiday and into the peaceful enjoyment of a limbic state of unknowing. Yet it's true: there was something magical about those pauses, hours when I should have been asleep, whispering with my siblings about what we might find.

As I said, I kept this up for far too long — into high school, once I had an alarm clock that would've provided more accurate, less risky results than the water; into college, when most people my age were too jaded or practical (or tired) for such nonsense; even into a mission, far from home, with no presents under the tree; and into married life, first with no children, then with children equally intent on waking in the wee hours to slip downstairs to dream. I still do it sometimes now, though not always, because my children do it, and I figure my role is now to sleep soundly and leave them to their wakeful dreaming. But sometimes I feel sad at what I've left behind.

I mention all this because once I hit college and started watching *The Simpsons*, I learned that this bladder-alarm-clock technique was fairly common knowledge. In one episode, Bart Simpson does it for the same reason I did: to get an early look at Christmas presents (misfortune and schadenfreudish hilarity ensue). His sister Lisa corrects his belief that he invented it, saying that "the Indians used to drink water to wake up early for their attacks." I couldn't easily find scholarly references to this fact, so I asked Ian Frazier, a veritable encyclopedia of western-American history knowledge, and he's confident that the *Simpsons* writers got the idea from his book *Great Plains*, which states matter-of-factly on page 48,

> On the eve of an important event, when they were afraid they might oversleep in the morning — for example, when a war party discovered an enemy camp and wanted to make sure to wake up and attack it at first light — Indians would drink a lot of water before going to bed.

(Although I'd forgotten, I had underlined this in my copy of the book, which I read in the late nineties, over two decades after I began employing the method.) He got the information from Stanley Vestal's 1984 book *Warpath: The True Story of the Fighting Sioux Told in a Biography of Chief White Bull*, which says that "Indian warriors could determine in advance their hour of rising by regulating the amount of water drunk before going to bed," a level to which I have never taken my own water alarm clocking. Frazier's confidence about Lisa Simpson's source comes from knowing several *Simpsons* writers personally, including George Meyer, who on another occasion told Frazier about a different borrowing from *Great Plains*, which is not exactly the kind of independence of discovery I'm talking about in this essay, but it's still sufficiently delightful to see the repackaging and refitting of such interesting trivia. This, too, is an avenue to originality, according to the theory we are propounding here.

Imagination selects ideas from the treasures of Remembrance, and produces novelty only by varied combinations.

SAMUEL JOHNSON, "The Burden of Memory"

SYNESTHESIA

And if those combinations arrive across merged senses? If Schubert heard E minor and saw "a maiden robed in white with a rose-red bow on her chest," if Beethoven struck D major and visualized shocks of brazen orange, if Kandinsky unfurled a ribbon of blue across his canvas and saw the infinite, then shouldn't I at least try? Kandinsky claimed to be able to paint an internal landscape based on "inner sounds," or sensory impressions that revealed a "deeper, finer level of spiritual sensitivity, a level that no words [could] properly express." Like other synesthetes, people with "the involuntary ability to hear colour, see music or even taste words," Kandinsky could see sounds. It's little wonder that he believed his paintings spoke *Farbensprache* — or color language. Using this language, Kandinsky deftly copied the world around him — especially its panoply of sounds — translating what he heard and saw into swirling kaleidoscopes of corresponding colors. According to Ossian Ward, "Kandinsky discovered his synaesthesia at a performance of Wagner's opera Lohengrin in Moscow: 'I saw all my colours in spirit, before my eyes. Wild, almost crazy lines were sketched in front of me.'" G. K. Chesterton had a similar experience when sketching a cow. Instead of drawing the cow as "a mere artist might have drawn it," using simple lines and rudimentary colors, he

> drew the soul of the cow; which [he] saw there plainly walking before [him] in the sunlight; and the soul was all purple and silver, and had seven horns and the mystery that belongs to all the beasts.

"A Piece of Chalk"

I think Kandinsky and Chesterton would have gotten along. Like Chesterton, Kandinsky believed that "every colour, every line . . . has a particular emotional value . . . that specifically speaks to the recipient's soul and unleashes a specific reaction." For Kandinsky, this emotional value occurred through sound. Chesterton saw a cow and painted its soul; Kandinsky saw the world and heard an ensemble of sounds. Kandinsky eagerly rendered each ensemble into a painting, each of which formed, as art historian Reinhard Zimmerman suggests, "the basis of a spiritual experience." Kandinsky himself famously said,

> Color is the keyboard, the eyes are the harmonies, the soul is the piano with many strings. The artist is the hand that plays, touching one key or another, to cause vibrations in the soul.

Kandinsky may have tried to imitate the vibrations of the soul, but it would be a long shot to say that he plagiarized the soul. Instead, by mimicking the soul's hum through painting, he created a new art form, something wholly original. Kandinsky spent his entire career recording mere echoes of the world's spirit and is now considered one of the great pioneers of abstract art.

Having spent much of my adult life as a wordsmith, I was curious to see if I had a touch of the synesthete in me. And so I endeavored to do as Kandinsky did. I borrowed my daughters' watercolor set and went into the kitchen to gather my supplies. With my water pitcher and paper cups in hand, I settled into my chair and focused my attention on the stack of CDs piled atop my desk. It had been a long time since I'd painted anything other than a room (and come to think of it, I'd not painted a room in over six years), and I kept my aspirations reasonable. As writing is a translation of experience, observation, and thought, this is my artistic translation of sound:

WATCH YOUR STEP

Even the most universally acclaimed geniuses are only patching together the same notes in ways slightly different from what's been done before, translating the sounds they've heard into slightly new sounds. Or perhaps geniuses are only artists who understand the borrowing process, who play only to the benighted or otherwise occupied crowd. (This task was seemingly much easier in the past, given the relative isolation of audiences and their inability to communicate with each other. How, even two decades ago, could Enanitos Verdes know that Joe Satriani had won untold boatloads of money by suing Coldplay for a melody that they had written two years before he claimed to have done so himself?)

Still, wherever music lovers cross paths, they recognize influences and appropriations. For instance, Big Seven Music Corporation caught John Lennon (a self-styled genius, and I am inclined to agree, despite my earlier cynicism), quoting two lines of Chuck Berry's "You Can't Catch Me" ("Here come old flattop / He come groovin' up slowly") in "Come Together." As penance, Lennon made a whole record of cover versions (whence we get his "Stand by Me" rendition) to bump royalties to the conglomerate. Since he loved that old time rock and

218 *Independent Redundancy*

roll and he certainly wasn't hurting for money, I'm sure he didn't really mind that particular resolution. I admire the fact that he was often so candid about his sources. He spoke like a man with nothing to hide, a man who felt that music was a gift for all to share. For instance, that magical, feedbacked riff on "I Feel Fine" is a slight variation on "Watch Your Step" by Bobby Parker, which Lennon declared unequivocally.

> "Watch Your Step" is one of my favourite records. The Beatles have used the lick in various tunes. The Allman Brothers used the lick straight as it was.
>
> *Anthology*

George Harrison further clarified in a 1990 interview that the Beatles began by singing Carl Perkins's "Matchbox" in three-part harmony in the back of a bus across Scotland, then added "a bastardized version" of "Watch Your Step," and "it turned into 'I Feel Fine.'" Parker, you can imagine, never made near the money Lennon made as a musician, yet he seems unperturbed or at least resigned (I am going on a recent video), noting that he's heard fifty-seven different arrangements of his riff, including ones by Carlos Santana and Jimmy Page, and claiming that there was nothing like that on record around 1961 when he wrote the song. But Lennon calls "Watch Your Step" the "son of 'What'd I Say'" (1959) by Ray Charles, and while Charles's riff is played on electric piano, I can hear the similarities.

I'm not sure if Bobby Parker's "fifty-seven" figure is an allusion to Heinz's 57 varieties or an actual number, but I guess I wouldn't be surprised if he's right. "Moby Dick" by Led Zeppelin certainly uses the riff, and Santana's rip-off feels more like a cover version, though uncredited. Before I read the Lennon admission above, I myself had discovered the Allman Brothers' borrowing while sitting idly in church one Sunday. I'd been thinking about this particular shared riff recently, and I guess my mind was working on its own to find further connections, because suddenly in the middle of a talk by my old department chair, I had a higher-pitched version of it looping over and over, just slightly out of grasp. I didn't know the song well, and I didn't think

I knew the band; I even feared that it might be an instrumental, but as I gave it my attention, I was able to pull out a snatch of lyrics, something like "might be your old man, I don't know," which I wrote down and chased on the Internet later that day. My subconscious had given me enough of "One Way Out" that I could trace it. This is what I mean when I tell people that when I'm inhabiting an essay, my life aligns with the theme and gives me gifts of material and knowledge. Of course, that John Lennon quote might have led me to the song anyway, but I'm much happier having hazed it just close enough into memory to then snatch it up.

REAL CONSEQUENCES

When he was called out for borrowing Chuck Berry's lyrics, John Lennon worked out an innovative solution that left all parties satisfied and the rest of us enriched. Would that all such cases met such efficient and amicable ends.

Not so, the strange case of Australia's Men at Work, whose breakout 1981 smash "Down Under" brought fame and adulation, for a brief period at least. Nearly three decades later, after the glory had faded, Larrikin Music, questionable rights holder to Marion Sin-

clair's 1932 children's song "Kookaburra Sits in the Old Gum Tree," was tipped off by a television game show that the flute interlude in the Men at Work song bore a slight resemblance to *their* song. They sued for 60 percent of the royalties from "Down Under" (they'd owned the rights to "Kookaburra" only since 1990, it should be noted), dragged the fight into court, and eventually won a 5 percent share of moneys collected since 2002, after flautist Greg Ham testified that he'd likely "subconsciously adapted" the tune while trying to give "Down Under" an Australian feel.

After the verdict, singer Colin Hay said, "It is indeed true, that Greg Ham unconsciously referenced two bars of Kookaburra . . . during live shows after he joined the band in 1979, and it did end up in the Men at Work recording. [But] it was inadvertent, naive, unconscious, and by the time Men at Work recorded the song, it had become unrecognizable. I believe what has won today is opportunistic greed, and what has suffered is creative musical endeavor."

What else suffered was Greg Ham, who, according to friends, "took it hard" and "was never the same" and who took his own life two years after the verdict. He left no note, but those close to him blame the ruling and its effect on Ham's perception of his legacy.

POWER STATION

There are many more musical examples, of course. I suspect that if you dig deep enough, you can find musical borrowings (conscious and subconscious) in nearly every popular song (and lots of unpopular songs, too! Ba-dum *crash*). For me, the paragon of musical ingenuity (I say this with deference to so many other bands who are, in their own ways, sui generis) is Rush, and not just because I like them, but because they're mutably assimilative (assimilatively mutable?). They change and grow, absorbing and learning with each album. Gore Vidal said of his friend Tennessee Williams that "he doesn't grow; he continues," but Rush is the opposite of that.

My favorite example of a too-traceable influence on Rush comes in the middle of their 1978 fever-dream instrumental "La Villa Strangiato," a song that begins by confounding expectations with a Spanish-guitar run before sprinting and sauntering through nine minutes and twelve movements of varying depth and speed and meter. If you've never heard it before, well, you've probably heard at least part of it. "Monsters!" a guitar-driven jaunt, calls to mind nothing less than Saturday-morning cartoons. This is because its melody was subconsciously borrowed from Raymond Scott's 1937 "Powerhouse," which has been licensed for use in all kinds of cartoons, from *Bugs Bunny* to *The Simpsons*, and has so engrained itself in the public consciousness that when you hear it, you involuntarily crack a smile and revert to childhood. It is a mark of Rush's integrity that when they discovered what they'd done, some years after the statute of limitations was up, they arranged with Scott to make a "penance" payment.

In any case, in a cutthroat world, they should probably receive payment for musical ideas that they've given away to other acts, such as the buildup arpeggio in "Xanadu" (whose lyrical subject matter comes straight from Coleridge), which is mother of "Sweet Child o' Mine" by Guns N' Roses, or the closing three-chord movement in "The Necromancer," used to great effect by Judas Priest in "Living after Midnight" and by Cake in "Short Skirt/Long Jacket" (an unlikely place, perhaps, but musical cross-pollination scoffs at generic boundaries [John Frusciante claimed no influence from Tom Petty on his guitar part in (the long-ago-mentioned) "Dani California," but he *did* credit Wu-Tang Clan, which, he said, when processed through him became something Lynyrd-Skynyrdish]). But in the end, all things probably even out. Within hours of Rush's new single release, listeners were pointing out how the bridge section of "Caravan" sounded just like the bridge from the *A-Team* theme song. And it does.

THE LAST PARAGRAPH

With this, the last paragraph, I have surpassed thirty thousand words, a silly number of signs to string together under a single heading but a worthy goal nonetheless, as it is approximately the length of Montaigne's longest essays. Is this, then, the preposterous yet logically inevitable result of my trajectory toward longer and longer essays? No? Yes? Maybe? I have risked losing the few readers I have, simply for the sake of arbitrariness, yet it was more than this. It was the way the thoughts accreted and would not dissipate, the way Nicholson Baker took off on "lumber" with a completist's passion, the way there is no end to thought. Thirty thousand hardly approaches infinity, though the approximation is apt in any case, in this time of brevity and compression — as all times — when attention spans are shortening, as they've always been doing. The notion is a good one, that whatever we may convince ourselves, we will never know it all, and no matter our cries of originality, we are ever repeating, singing back the melodies we heard somewhere before, whether we remember or not. As my still-favorite band — who reinvent themselves with each new record, absorbing musical influences from the blues to Spanish guitar to madrigal to jazz to reggae to rap, yet who remain defiantly themselves — once plastered in their recording studio as mock wisdom (the only kind of wisdom for me):

Individually, we are a ass;
But together we are a genius

POSTSCRIPT

This one brought me to deep laughter tinged with knowing tears: *Just* as I was finishing this essay, after working nearly *seven years* on it, I was browsing Cambridge University Press's collections when a selection of George Sampson's essays caught my attention because I'd never heard of George Sampson, and in its contents I found "On Playing the Sedulous Ape," which I recognized (as do you) from Robert Louis Stevenson's admission and humble self-assessment. So I tracked down the essay to read it, and — wouldn't you know it? — Sampson propounds essentially the same argument I've explored here, nearly one hundred years ago. Of course, his essay is certifiably *not* this essay, his melody is not my melody, but the idea is essentially the same. As André Gide knew well, "Everything has been said before, but since nobody listens we have to keep going back and beginning all over again."

Fixity

When the full tide of human life pours along to some festive shew, to some pageant of a day, Elia would stand on one side to look over an old book-stall, or stroll down some deserted pathway in search of a pensive inscription over a tottering door-way

WILLIAM HAZLITT, "Elia and Geoffrey Crayon"

This was my first day in England, ever, in my life. I had begun by taking a nap at Pat and Michele's apartment, to catch up on the sleep I'd missed on the plane from Utah. When I awoke, my friends were not yet home, so I took out a map, wrongly judged the distance from the Isle of Dogs to Greenwich, and set off on a walk to set my bearings.

It was through rows and rows of brown two-storeys; then a jaunt to the riverfront path; then underground, underwater, through the tunnel, amid all the bicycle riders standing on one pedal — the more ready to suddenly comply with the No Riding signs posted at even intervals, should the need arise — then up the tubular elevator (the riders who'd clicked past me were waiting patiently) to the gray dusk of Greenwich, a town that far exceeded my imaginings because, as I realized then, I had never quite imagined it. Its frequent invocations as the prime meridian, that from which all earthly space and time are set, appeared in my mind as abstractions only. And here it was, the place itself.

The landscape was pleasant enough, old and storied, pitched and thatched, and walked this way and that: cars seemed subservient, swerving round in paths left vacant only temporarily as people thronged and abated, moved to rhythms surging up and out from pavements and apartments. I was one of them; my feet caught "the pulse and the purposeful stride"; I glanced into shop windows, wondered at menus, felt a hunger only for experience, with which I was, truth be told, sated.

I hooked right, down a narrow alley toward the back of a church and into a graveyard garden. In any case, I was pleased to get beyond the hubbub to the peace amid the silent dead (their gravestones lined the outer walls, holding back the crumble, it seemed, with the roots of vines and trees). A pair of pedestrians shortcut past, in one gate and out the other, as I wandered, reaching for significance, reconstituting in my imagination some small semblance of the folk underfoot, the lives behind the graven names and dates and trite quotes of piousness and longing. One particularly well-preserved marker caught my attention:

BENEATH

this stone is deposited

the remains of *Sarah* wife of

Joshua Fountain who departed

this life October 28th 1790

in the confident hope of Gods mercy

and a glorious resurrection.

Aged 44 Years.

She was a most affectionate

endearing and obedient wife

a fond loving yet most prudent mother

a kind neighbour and firm friend

She was the mother of ten children

five of which are deceased

226 *Fixity*

two of which Joshua and Elizabeth

are buried near this stone

In respect to her memory and virtues

this stone is erected

by her disconsolate husband.

His passion is long gone, swept away with "the tide that smoothly bears human life to eternity." The children's stones are not easily discerned from the lot; I doubt they've been moved alongside their mother's, though why not? There may be some comfort in supposing their spots remain together, far from the slated walls, under a patch of grass or small tree; but what of the other three children, or, by now, the other eight?

Across the distance of centuries, it seems no longer to matter much. Joshua, senior, likely in his late forties when Sarah died, will have lived on, tended to his younger children until they married and drifted away. Perhaps he remarried. Perhaps his work brought him a measure of satisfaction. Perhaps he found a standard, unremarkable kind of joy in his grandchildren or sorrow in yet more children's deaths?

There are sorrows, it is true, so great, that to give them some of the ordinary vents is to run a hazard of being overthrown.

LEIGH HUNT, "Deaths of Little Children"

It is likely that even the great-great-great-great-great-great grandchildren of Joshua and Sarah Fountain know and care nothing about their disconsolate forebears' indelible pain. It is likely that given the steady erosion of soft stone, my poor rubbing of Sarah's inscription, set here in zeroes and ones in reproducible form, will outlast those letters chiseled by a hand well-practiced in the somber art of remembrance. One can hope.

But despite anyone's hope, they're all dead now: Joshua, Sarah, their ten children, five who preceded them, five who succeeded Sarah, according to the record; and we know of them only because Sarah's marker was made of stronger stuff or was engraved more deeply or was kept out of the elements by its fortuitous location or a loved one's care or the invigorating coffee and rashers that filled the belly of the worker charged with the relocation of headstones decades ago. The Fountains serve as stand-ins for all of them who suffered, died, and were buried in every little corner of the world not so long ago, which may make us feel small and insignificant, as so much of experience does, if we're paying attention. Or we may feel joy in living now, knowing that as there was a beginning, so shall there be an end, but not yet.

> In the meantime I am alive. I move about. I am worth twenty of thee. Know thy betters!
>
> CHARLES LAMB, "New Year's Eve"

Lamb emboldens me, living now — long after he, too, returned to the earth — but not too much. I think that our understanding of events depends almost wholly on the time from which we fix our reckoning. For Lamb, facetious in the face of them who went before, it was December 31, 1820, when he was forty-five years old, a bit melancholic about his prospects but full of life nonetheless. For most of my friends and neighbors after several tornadoes struck Athens, Ohio, recently, it was when the calm returned, when, in taking stock, they realized that despite the damage, not one life was lost. But for others, it was the day before, when their homes and school and stately trees stood still. Luck, as we would have it, succeeds or fails based on point of reference. For the young woman I know who survived a vicious car accident nearly intact, it was the moments after the collision, dizzy with the realization that it could have been much worse. For her brother, headed for months in hospital and years in therapy, it was the moments before the car stalled turning left in the path of oncoming traffic. The "miracle" would have been that the car kept going through the intersection, the truck never hitting it, which is to say that nobody would have known, as we never know the myriad ways we might have gone amiss.

228 *Fixity*

A week ago, my oldest daughter returned late to her school after a field trip. Her younger sister, who always waits for her so they can walk home together, was nowhere in sight. Adriana assumed that Sara had been picked up by their mother, so she headed home alone, but when she walked in the front door and Karina asked "Where's Sara?" they realized that Sara was missing. Karina called me at work, frantic, demanding that I call the school. "About what?" I asked, already aware that this was no time for a rejoinder about her habitual vagueness. When she explained, between huffs and sobs, some plumb bobbed to the pit of my groin. I called the school and then neighbors and friends, mobilizing a search while I sat hollow in an office surrounded by books. Nobody had seen her, she was not with her teacher, not in the hallways, not outside the school waiting, hadn't walked with the Andersons, wasn't shrieking joyously with the girls bouncing on the trampoline in their backyard. Adriana stayed at home to wait for Sara's return while Karina called the police from the school office, where she'd arrived in the meantime. Three-foot-six, regular build; brown hair, shoulder length; gray eyes that say *I love you, Daddy,* before the sound escapes her mouth. What had she been wearing?

. . . for nearly half an hour, though such measurements fail to contain . . .

Then Adriana called to tell me that Sara was home. She'd arrived with the Ross girls, taking the back way, nonchalant though wondering why Adi hadn't been there to walk home with her. This was forty-five minutes after school let out. I called Karina, who told the office staff, who called the police to cancel the incipient Amber Alert. When we pressed her for an explanation, Sara's chronology made some sense, but she couldn't quite account for all that time. So the absence continues to weigh, though the door of imaginings has been closed, or the boundless possibilities my mind conjectured have resolved to what really happened, which, of course, brings a heavy sigh of relief.

But I remain haunted: That she made it home safely because the bad guy didn't happen to cross her path that particular afternoon, in her moments of vulnerability. That she found friends who led her home but never thought to return to her teacher or to the office

Fixity 229

staff to call her mother or ask for help. That every day, someone's daughter doesn't come home from school or from her friend's house or from soccer practice, and that's it; she's gone forever. That the bad guy is all around us. You can find him lurking. The Internet reveals his last known residence. Every few months he strikes in public, makes the news. Just the other day, he grabbed a preschooler who'd gone off to look at the toy section. Her mother couldn't find her, asked for help, found her with him in a men's bathroom stall, he ran, incensed shoppers gave chase and took him down, held him until police arrived.

I have six children, ages twelve down to less than a year; Sara is in the middle. All are healthy, all are intelligent, beautiful, funny, active, inquisitive. All are well. I don't spend my life waiting for the other boot to fall, but neither do I exude the gratitude I should. Still, every now and then when I take stock, I think that I am simply lucky.

Certainly you don't need my progressive, detailed description of everything I saw in Greenwich, nor could I produce anything more than the remnants of memory, especially when my purpose has only been to lead you to the gated exitway from a small market, to consider the quote over the door, then to think on abominations and reality. So let us move quickly to the next scene in our outer narrative. The themes, too, will shift gears, but only slightly, and they will reunite eventually.

> Let me begin with whatever subject I please, for all subjects are linked with one another.
>
> MONTAIGNE, "On Some Verses of Virgil"

I'll compress the shoe leather into a Pythonesque sentence: More walking, more observing, more silence and unease amid the city's resonances. Buses creaking past, cars humming, radios retranslating invisible waves to reverberations bouncing off my tympanic membrane as one small voice in a chorus of citysound. Duck under an archway down a deserted pathway to an open alcove surrounded by walls and doors and windows and filled with merchants packing their wares in crates and boxes on hand trucks, dismantling tables and tarps in the shade of afternoon; look above the northern entrance to

A false balance is abomination to the Lord
But a just weight is his delight

I recognized this pensive inscription, though not in quite those words. Years ago, simply hoping to employ the word *divers* without the *e* (penchant for the archaic? delight in the ambiguous?), I had stumbled upon a proverb (20:10) that echoes its sentiment:

Divers weights, and divers measures, both of them are alike abomination to the Lord.

Dispensing with the abominable stuff, I borrowed it simply as an excuse of a title for a set of brief nonfictional vignettes: "Divers Weights and Divers Measures." I meant, simply, "lots of stuff" (in the spirit of Francis Bacon, whose best essay [perhaps his only *real* essay] is "Of Vicissitude of Things"). When my friend Desi tracked the phrase to her Bible and tried to fit an allusive meaning to my choice,

Fixity 231

I didn't stop her. A subversion of the mania for exactness? A critique of the tendency to endow God only with abstract ideal qualities? An affirmation of the essay's beauty as incomplete, unbalanced, real thinkingart? Sure. Sounded good to me.

But I remained troubled by the proverb until this startling moment as I stood confronted by its sister scripture (from Proverbs 11:1, as I later found out), surrounded by vendors in a square of space seemingly long used as a market. My mind then gathered in a surrogate vision of the past together with the weekly *ferias* I'd wandered in Montevideo, to realize that God and I both dislike inaccurate weights on the scale weighing out my tomatoes or ground beef, assuming that such inaccuracies are most likely to favor the seller. God and I both want your one-pound weight to weigh one pound. And throw in a little extra for good measure. (This phrase, which I've heard and used countless times, suddenly seems tied to exactly this type of exchange: a seller, to allay a buyer's fears of unjust weights, adds to the pile after weighing, "for good measure.") It's not that different weights are bad (you need, after all, a set of them to make the necessary combinations), but weights that differ from their advertised value — those are bad, just as the merchant's thumb on the scale is bad.

What a thought to have! And how appropriate to have it here, in Greenwich! We need to anchor ourselves in time and in space, to feel we belong somewhere, to embark on our daily excursions from a home or a bed, to sound off the meters or the minutes.

(The foxes have holes, and the birds of the air have nests; but the Son of man hath not where to lay his head.)

We desire fixity and foundation, some reference point to push off from, something solid to judge by, terra firma, beginnings and endings, compartments to contain experience to know when one thing's done and the next begun. When we weigh, we don't want tradition or common accord on the value of one kilogram; we don't want the added complication of measuring one liter of water and then weighing it; we want a platinum-iridium cylinder stored climate controlled at the Bureau International des Poids et Mesures in Sevres, France, plus forty replicas scattered throughout the world hidden in laboratories beneath double bell jars. Yet even this redundancy (with periodic checks) is not enough for those who care deeply about such standards. They resist the artifact dependency of this holdout (all our other measurements are now defined by fundamental concepts of nature, like the "meter," which is no longer a bar etched precisely; it is the distance light travels in $\frac{1}{299,792,458}$ of a second) and seek new methods of definition based on physics that defies my attempts at understanding.

If my mind could gain a firm footing, I would not make essays, I would make decisions.

MONTAIGNE, "Of Repentance"

In practice, though, ordinary life offers any number of candidates for semifixed reference points — hometowns and homesteads, families and societies, birthdays and sunrises — each appropriate to its launches. But the painfully introspective mind wanders beyond the limits imposed by circumstance to wonder what's beyond or before. And once the earth itself became only a ball of dirt and water floating invisibly tethered to a 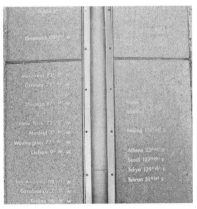 ball of gas, which itself roamed the arm of a vast configuration of swirlingly attracted elements expanding to the edges of everywhere . . . it's no wonder people sought some firm ground to still the swill of relativity.

Here I was in Greenwich, fundamental human reference point, prime meridian of the world, from which all points on the globe are measured, from whence all hours are calculated, divider of hemi-spheres, beginner of each day, each year, each millennium! A revelation on the nature of reference seems uncanny.

That day, I didn't actually visit the Royal Observatory, whose tran-sit circle telescope's eyepiece's crosshairs define the prime meridian, though I wish I had. So I have done some reading to learn the story I walked past that day in Greenwich:

It's easy to conceive of a time when time was measured only by its natural manifestations: sunrises and sunsets, buds and flowers, births and migrations, patterns of weather and temperature. Eventually, crude devices were devised to count off smaller increments: shadows on a dial, drops from a vessel, granules through an hourglass. Curi-ous astronomers could chart relative positions of celestial bodies to calculate more precisely the cycles of day and year. But for nearly all of human history, until the late 1800s, time was a local phenomenon, something to guide our waking and working and sleeping, but nothing to standardize across continents. Although the impulse to comprehend and to exert some control over time is universal (all human societies have developed calendars), even the development of mechanical clocks did nothing to make time universal.

Enter the railroads. While general local agreement on clock time was typically sufficient for human interaction on the village, town, or even city level, once the iron horse connected localities across vast distances, the position of the sun in the sky became less important than the position of the engine on the tracks. For reasons of safety, travel, and commerce, engineers had to know when the path would be clear, and locals had to know when their relatives or supplies would arrive and when they'd depart. And because the railroad crossed wide swaths of territory in a single day, because a trip of only forty-eight miles (in the contiguous United States) corresponded to a difference of about four minutes solar time, the station clock became official, that to which others must conform.

This same effect eased telegraph communications and simultaneous scientific measurements across the country, and today we'd find it difficult to imagine telling time locally by the sun's passage overhead (how would

234 *Fixity*

we know when to tune in for our favorite television shows?). The United Kingdom's rail companies organized to establish one common time zone for the whole island by 1855. In the United States, conformity lagged until 1883, with four time zones across three thousand east-west miles.

Speaking of lagging across time zones, this particular difficulty may be the most important reason for our dependence on Greenwich today. I say "our" fully recognizing that not everybody in the world charts their location or time from southeast London; not everybody even cares what time it "really" is beyond the movements of the sun. But most of us do schedule our lives at some hourly increment from Greenwich mean time, and this is why:

For centuries, at least as long as our species had been making long sea voyages, sailors sought some way to know their position on the globe. Beyond ascertaining some estimate of "how much longer," they needed an accurate means to determine where they were and where they were headed. The sun and stars could give a captain his distance from the equator, but until John Harrison solved the bedeviling "longitude problem" in 1759, no one and no thing could tell you your east-west location in the sea. Resigned not knowing had, during hundreds of years, led to ships run aground and supplies exhausted; thousands of deaths could be chalked up to that continual conundrum.

Why? Because ships had no odometer, no tachometer even (though sailors could briefly approximate speed by letting out knots), and they traveled with the wind and waves, not in straight lines. The fundamental problem, then, was that once a ship was out at sea, it had no fixed reference point. Theoretically, if you could know the time on board and the time back home, you could know your distance from home. Time on board could be measured by the positions of celestial bodies (the sun directly overhead at noon, for instance), and simple division determines that the earth rotates about 15 degrees an hour (360 degrees per twenty-four-hour day), so the calculations would be straightforward (if you're two hours earlier than your friends back home, you're 30 degrees west of them; if you know your latitude, you can also know how far you've gone). But there was no way to communicate the time between port and ship, and clocks in the eighteenth century were imprecise, needing regular resetting and relying on mechanics and pendulums that would fail in the humid, irregular rocking of a boat, so there was no way to know the time back home. Any clock you brought on board would quickly become inaccurate.

After a 1707 naval disaster in which four British ships sank just off the coast on their return from battle, Parliament offered a twenty thousand–pound prize to whoever could solve the longitude problem within half a degree, the winning method to be tested on a cross-Atlantic voyage. For decades, prize suitors came up with all sorts of "solutions," most of them bunkum. Serious scientific effort was expended on creating a set of astronomical charts to compare the positions of the moon and the stars, but this method ultimately proved too crude and too difficult to implement on a pitching ship. As none of the experts were successful, and plenty of crackpots were so vocal, the phrase "finding the longitude" came to mean a fruitless pursuit, like "squaring the circle."

It is only certain that there is nothing certain, and that nothing is more miserable or more proud than man.

PLINY THE ELDER, *Natural History*

236 *Fixity*

It is perhaps appropriate, then, that the solution to the longitude problem came not from the great, educated minds of the day (before his death in 1727, Isaac Newton chaired the Board of Longitude; he was certain that the answer lay in star charts) but from John Harrison, a humble joiner from Lincolnshire, far north of London. His experiments with mechanical clocks (counterbalancing pendulums, near-frictionless gears) took him almost forty years to perfect, and once his son had proven his work on a trip to Jamaica (after two months, Harrison's timepiece ran only 5.1 seconds slow), the board refused to give him the prize money until they tested the clock again and he provided them with plans detailed enough to duplicate. Bureaucracy, jealousy, and skepticism kept the reward tied up for over a decade. Ultimately, King George III intervened, and Harrison, now eighty years old (he would die at eighty-three), was publicly and monetarily recognized as conqueror of the great scientific problem of his century. With his hand-sized pocket watch, sailors suffering under all sorts of temperature, pressure, and attitude changes could know the time back in England, and thereby their location on the earth, with tremendous precision.

A hundred years later, after the British had con-firmed their naval and commercial superiority and the railroads had made a strong case for uniform times across every fifteen degrees of longitude (or so), delegates from twenty-five countries gathered in Washington DC, at the 1884 International Merid-ian Conference to determine 0 degrees longitude. Essentially, they went with what was most convenient. Although there were some other contenders, most maps (or most maps available to the delegates) of

that time already used Greenwich as the prime meridian, as did the United States' time zone system, so they made it official: time and space would be measured from the Royal Observatory. But their decision was also an affirmation of John Harrison's genius, an hom-age to the man who had finally allowed us to know where we stood.

What a frustration, then, that in yet another instance we prove that the more we know, the less we understand (as Don Henley put it) or

Fixity 237

"the more we know, the more we know we don't know," as Socrates may have said, with different pronouns, or as others have surely said in his wake. Forget about a few seconds' mechanical error after a trip across the ocean; we can't even define our days and years precisely. We can accommodate the earth's elliptical orbit and tilted axis of rotation (principally by ignoring the difference between clock time and solar time, but we *can* calculate their discrepancy); we can account for an extra quarter day every year by adding February 29 to our calendars every four years; we can even remove that leap day every hundred years to recalibrate to our planet's actual position in the solar system; beyond that, we can reinstate leap day on centuries divisible by four hundred to further refine our approximation of when we are. By this point, we've defined the year as 365.2425 days long (that's an additional five hours, forty-nine minutes, and twelve seconds), but we're still a few seconds off (the average vernal equinox year is 365.242374 days), which, over thousands of years, will mean that we get behind a day once again.

> We have no other way of computing time but by years. The world has been using this measure for many centuries; and yet it is a measure that we have still not succeeded in fixing, and such that we are every day in doubt.
>
> MONTAIGNE, "Of Cripples"

Of course, there are other calendars in use even today, and they've all had to contend (more or less successfully) with this incongruence between the planet's rotation and revolution. The only calendar I really know, the Gregorian, is a direct descendent of the Julian, revised during the Renaissance into its current form. Although Roman astronomers understood the need for a leap year, they did not account for the one-day slippage every century; and once the Roman Empire had given way to the Holy Roman Empire, Catholics found Easter falling away from the vernal equinox (the calculations for finding Easter were devised centuries ago by mystics and are frustratingly convoluted but can be shorthanded to the Sunday following the full moon following the vernal equinox; when I was younger, I was excited to find Easter on my birthday twice;

had I known how rare this really is [it will not happen again until 2062, when, if I make it, I will turn ninety-one] I think I would have savored the moments more fully). In recompense, Pope Gregory XIII decreed a ten-day jump from October 4 to 15 in 1582 (his papal bull, known by its opening words, "Inter gravissimas," declares this calendar rectification to be "among the most serious duties" of the pastoral office). Catholic countries made the change without much complaint, though other lands languished in their late seasons for years, even centuries longer.

'Tis now two or three years ago that they made the year ten days shorter in France. How many changes may we expect should follow this reformation! it was really moving heaven and earth at once. Yet nothing for all that stirs from its place: my neighbours still find their seasons of sowing and reaping, the opportunities of doing their business, the hurtful and propitious days, just at the same time where they had, time out of mind, assigned them; there was no more error perceived in our old use, than there is amendment found in the alteration; so great an uncertainty there is throughout; so gross, obscure, and obtuse is our perception.

MONTAIGNE, "Of Cripples"

Add to all this uncertainty interpolation: the earth is not static; its movements are not constant. Subtleties such as population density or vegetation growth can lead to small mass redistribution on a spheroid that's already bulged at the equator. Weather patterns and tidal action on a grand scale for us below induce a planetary wobble imperceptible to all but time itself, meaning that a year is never exactly a year. In comparison to our most accurate clocks, which now derive time not from solar observation, not from pendulum swings and gear tics, but from hyperfine measurements of cesium-133 oscillations ("The second is the duration of 9,192,631,770 periods of the radiation corresponding to the transition between the two hyperfine levels of the ground state of the caesium-133 atom," according to the Bureau International des Poids et Mesures), the earth's rotation brakes at an irregular rate, adding one second every few years lately, so that the International Earth Rotation and Reference Systems Service has seen fit to insert an additional "leap second" twenty-four times in my lifetime, most recently in 1998, 2005, and 2008. This is nothing we can control or worry about, except that it undermines our innate desire for a fixed reference point.

Nevertheless, we've got one in Greenwich. While this convention or agreement is relatively recent, our species has certainly always sought such sureties. For primitive humans, an understanding of the day was essential to survival. Get caught too far from home when night came and you might freeze or be eaten. With the development of agriculture, our ancestors needed to know when to sow and when to reap. Eventually, calendars became more than essential; they began to feed curiosity, or to cause it, such that our impulse to fix referents could find an outlet in ritual or playful abstraction. For example,

I gathered the creation of the world did fall out upon the 710 year of the Julian Period, by placing its beginning in autumn: but for as much as the first day of the world began with the evening of the first day of the week, I have observed that the Sunday, which in the year 710 aforesaid came nearest the Autumnal Æquinox, by astronomical tables (notwithstanding the stay of the sun in the dayes of Joshua, and the going back of it in the dayes of Ezekiah)

happened upon the 23 day of the Julian October; from thence concluded that from the evening preceding that first day of the Julian year, both the first day of the creation and the first motion of time are to be deduced.

For those keeping score at home, that's October 23, 4004 BC. The author is James Ussher, Anglican archbishop of Armagh, Ireland, whose 1650 calculations took into account not only Judeo-Christian but Egyptian, Roman, and other sources and who understood the astronomical slippage of the year, which was not corrected in his native Great Britain until more than a century after his death.

Which is all well and good, but what good is time if no one is there to observe its passing? To put it another way, if an immutable God existed "before" creating the world yet no mortal mind minded being and passing, then what estimate might we make of time after the fact? Perhaps it's best, then, to think of time beginning only when the first observer came on the scene. If so, then John Lightfoot's 1642 calculation may serve: "Man created by the Trinity about the third hour of the day, or nine of the clock in the morning."

This search for the originary point continues despite the obvious faults of such literal interpretation of religious texts. In fact, the prevailing scientific explanation for the origin of the universe was first proposed by another man of the cloth, Monseigneur Georges Lemaître, a Belgian priest and physicist who, in 1927, posited a "primeval atom" from which all matter and energy began. I refer, of course, to the big bang, which supports quite well the best observations we can make of our universe, which seems to be expanding ever faster and cooling, as if thrown out from a kind of cataclysmic explosion approximately 13.7 billion years ago, give or take a few hundred million years (we're not so arrogant as to think that we can pinpoint a precise date [yet], but we do think we can identify and describe six distinct "epochs" of physical law and particle formation within the first second after the fireworks began), on "a day without yesterday," according to Lemaître. In any case, that we by and large accept this theory as plausible, perhaps even true, represents a fine reversal of popular viewpoint. Many of

Lemaître's contemporaries refused to believe that the universe had a beginning, having been brought up on Newton and Maxwell and having been wowed by Einstein, whose work all posited an infinite, steady universe. Even into the 1960s the theory was derided and disbelieved. The "big bang" was Cambridge astronomer Fred Hoyle's attempt to discredit it through ridicule. And who knows what idea may eventually supersede this one, but we've once again come to a conception of time that begins with a moment of creation, though a bit earlier than supposed by clergy centuries before.

Of course, all such speculation is superfluous. Time began at 4:26 p.m. (EST) on a blustery twenty-sixth of March in the year of our Lord one thousand nine hundred seventy-one, which is to say that, small insecurities in timekeeping notwithstanding, and ineffable mysteries of conception and in-spiration left to their mystical realm, one sure beginning is the moment of one's birth, granting, always, that its accuracy depends on the observation of third parties.

Which is how you necessarily apprehend my essay, dear reader: by depending on my observations as I in turn depend on the observations of others, near and far, here and long gone. Back to England with us, then! I want to say "without knowing it," but that would be false, so *partly* knowing it, partly guiding my life by principles I have discovered through readings both surreptitious and intentional, I spent my afternoon wandering purposelessly. This was my purpose. When I felt penned in by the crowd of my pedestrian peers swept up in their various aims, I aparted myself to commune with the dead, who're also crowded together, but at peace, left rotting underfoot, calling out only in faded inscriptions left by their also-now-dead loved ones. These say, "Remember me," but even that small request is soon impossible or transforms to, "Imagine me." Were I not so scattered in my paradoxical quest (to find what's unremarkable in this novel place), I might have made more of an effort, but I was drawn mostly to thoughts of my own dead or my own death. Then, curious about what other quotidian wonders I might find, I discovered a market in flux watched over by an ancient inscription, a call to right action in transactions. Both, I determined, were appropriate to the environment. Both have left me thinking, even now, of rigid

242 *Fixity*

foundations and relative freedom, the way we flail against nothingness or take stock from temporary origins and movable objects.

Essays occupy the margins, explore liminal spaces, turn back upon themselves, deal with seemingly ordinary things, tolerate meanderings and incompletions, estrange the familiar.

CHRIS ARTHUR, "(En)trance"

Essays also weigh, though not so accurately as God would like, I'm afraid, nor so manically as the International Bureau of Weights and Measurements would require, though the comparison is valid and perhaps enlightening, as the verb *to essay* derives from the Latin (as it is dead, a lively root language in which to end our etymological searches) *exigere*, "to ascertain, to weigh."

For me, there's no better way to grapple with the vast incomprehensibility of the world than to essay, in written form, gathering thoughts and ideas of one's own and of others, studying histories and theories, remembering experiences and associating through a kind of thinking process rendered artistic. In the absence of any obtainable immovable foundation, or in the rejection of arbitrary artificial substitutes, a person might do worse than to posit an antisystem, a kind of subversion to the very notion of fixity, with orbiting ideas held together by their own gravity. The point of reference for the essayist is the self, and the essay's humble attempt at understanding or at being can't but be admired by any god I know.

I stood still in a Greenwich market, reading the words of the prophets overhead, pondering quantification and abomination, the immutability of God, the weight of thought. In the meantime, 111 degrees 52 minutes 24.1608 seconds west of me, my son Marcos, yet unnamed and unknown, awash in near senselessness, felt strange electric impulses animating his limbs. His mother stirred in her chair with the sharp jolt of an elbow to her belly. The jab reminds Karina of the great uncertainty that is life, her own and her children's, that even the simplest repeatable processes sometimes go wrong; routine fails to repeat. On the one hand: everybody you see, everybody you will *never* see, crowded in vast teeming

Fixity 243

cities sweating under the incessant sun when you're asleep, or trotting on a windblown prairie draped in a thick woolen poncho while you're reading a book at the beach, people arriving, people playing, people suffering, chasing girls through the schoolyard at recess, holding hands across a couch, tapping out a beat with the right foot, strumming and singing, people lying broken under buildings or unconscious in a hospital bed surrounded by family, people with one foot out the exit door or long reconstituted by the earth underfoot . . . everyone has passed through the gauntlet of birth, most of us unscathed. On the other hand: nearly a year and a half earlier, in the doctor's office, with shirt raised and pants scrunched below her grown belly, she hears only metallic static from the handheld sonic probe as Dr. Gordon shifts and presses, searching for the quick liquid rhythm that's lit up our imaginations before. That's strange, he says, and tries the other side. The machine offers only whimpered squawks, like a rubbed balloon. She squeezes my hand and looks over at me for affirmation or comfort. I whisper, "I'm sure it's fine." Dr. Gordon tells his assistant, "We're gonna hafta get a sonogram," tells Karina, wiping the gel from her taut skin, "We can't find a heartbeat, we want to make sure this baby's all right, we'll go next door for an ultrasound, okay?" Then, minutes later? hours? a lifetime? a ghostly still silhouette on the screen to the left, a nurse taking measurements, a doctor explaining between calm sighs that this sometimes happens we don't know why it's no fault of yours it's the body's natural mechanism to terminate what's gone wrong before it's begun, then days of sudden long tears and plans and questions about the great whys. Resettling in time from this reverie, Karina realizes with a start that had this lost child come to term, there would have been no time for this new person inside her now, so strikingly active and so near to advent; that the loss of one is the profit of another.

All this, or something like this (the mind does not speak our language; we write to translate it), in an instant no longer than the prod from inside my wife's womb, as she sits in a chair thinking on her faraway husband, as he stares above him toward a small epiphany over a tottering door-way. This was, as we calculate now, looking back, a scant two weeks before 9:34 p.m. (GMT-6), September 15, 2008 — Marcos's birth, again the great beginning of all time.